# ENDURING
# HARVESTS

"Barrie Kavasch has done the world of food lovers and cooks a tremendous favor. This volume provides a look at food in its total cultural, geographic and seasonal context! It has been a privilege to travel through the calendar year [with *Enduring Harvests*] and experience the richness of Indian Country."

> —*Janine Pease Pretty On Top, President, Little Big Horn College*

"*Enduring Harvests* is thoroughly enjoyable! It's more than a collection of recipes. In it, Barrie Kavasch reminds us how much foods and their preparations are living Indian traditions . . . ."

> —*Ron Welburn (Southeastern Cherokee), Associate Professor English Department,*
> *University of Massachusetts Chair, Five College American Indian Studies Committee*

"Exuberantly, but reverently, leads us through the most notable ceremonial feasts of America's indigenous peoples."

> —*Alberto C. Meloni, Executive Director, The Institute for American Indian Studies*

"*Enduring Harvests* presents a wonderful collection of edible wonders and living history. Surely the recipe for the book must have read: Mix one part narrative steeped in rich cultural traditions with equal parts of freshly gathered ingredients and time-tested directions. Serve with love and pride, share with friends and enjoy!"

> —*Theresa Hayward Bell (Mashantucket Pequot), Director*
> *Mashantucket Pequot Museum and Research Center*

"Barrie Kavasch's cookbook . . . is rooted deeply in the good earth of the people who made the food . . . . [Her] respect and passion for the Native world will remind everyone of just how Indian America is."

> —*Rayna Green, Director*
> *American Indian Program, National Museum of American History*
> Smithsonian Institution

"A tasteful, intelligent contribution to Native foodways . . . Excellent reading and great eating!"

> —*José Barreiro, Editor-in-Chief*
> Native Americas Journal, *Cornell University*

# ENDURING HARVESTS

E. BARRIE KAVASCH

NATIVE AMERICAN

FOODS AND

FESTIVALS FOR EVERY

SEASON

*Illustrations by Mitzi Rawls*

OLD SAYBROOK, CONNECTICUT

Cover and text designed by Laura Augustine
Illustrations by Mitzi Rawls

Library of Congress Cataloging-in-Publication Data
Kavasch, E. Barrie.
       Enduring harvests: native American foods and festivals for every season / E. Barrie Kavasch:
       illustrations by Mitzi Rawls. — 1st ed.
              p.  cm.
       Includes bibliographical references and index.
       ISBN 1-56440-737-3
       1. Indian cookery. 2. Indians of North America—Food. 3. Indians of North America—Rites
       and ceremonies. I. Title.
       TX 715.K205  1995
       641.59'297—dc20                    95-24857
                                       CIP

Manufactured in the United States of America
First Edition/First Printing

*To my dear family and all my relations*

*and the eclectic worlds of Native American cuisines*

*and the inspired cooks who create them*

*Mitakuye oyasin*

*("With all beings and all things we shall be as relatives")*

—Black Elk, Oglala Sioux Holyman

# CONTENTS

ENDURING
HARVESTS

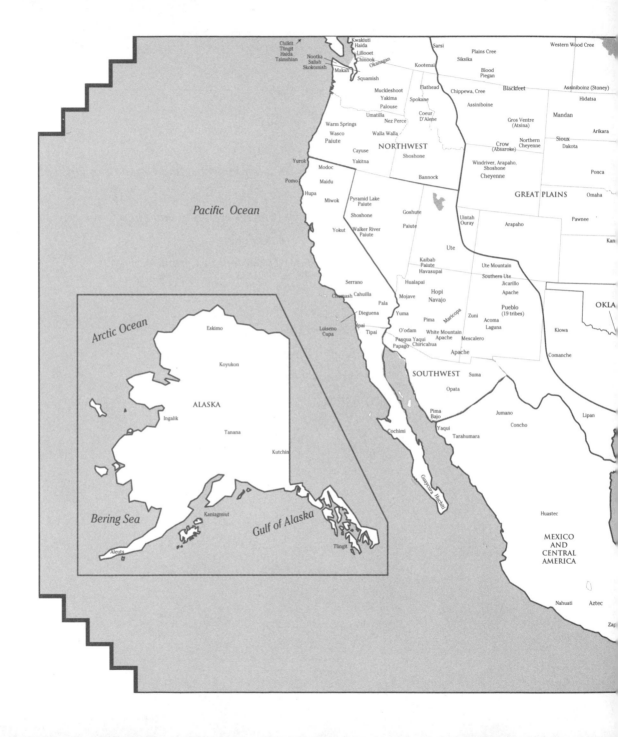

Chilkit
Tlingit
Haida
Tsimshian

Nootka
Salish
Skokomish

Makah

Kwakiutl
Haida

Lillooet
Chinook

Squamish

Okanagan

Sarsi

Plains Cree

Siksika

Western Wood Cree

Kootenai

Blood
Piegan

Blackfeet

Assiniboinz (Stoney)

Muckleshoot
Yakima
Palouse

Flathead

Spokane

Chippewa, Cree

Hidatsa

Umatilla

Coeur
D'Alene

Assiniboine

Mandan

Warm Springs

Nez Perce

Gros Ventre
(Atsina)

Arikara

Wasco
Paiute

Walla Walla

NORTHWEST

Crow
(Absaroke)

Northern
Cheyenne

Sioux
Dakota

Cayuse

Shoshone

Windriver, Arapaho,
Shoshone
Cheyenne

Ponca

Yurok

Yakitna

GREAT PLAINS

Omaha

Modoc

Bannock

Pomo

Maidu

Pacific  Ocean

Hupa

Miwok

Pyramid Lake
Paiute

Shoshone

Goshute

Uintah
Ouray

Arapaho

Pawnee

Yokut

Walker River
Paiute

Paiute

Ute

Kan

Serrano

Chemash

Cahuilla

Pala

Mojave

Kaibab
Paiute
Havasupai

Hualapai

Ute Mountain

Southern Ute

Jicarillo
Apache

Hopi
Navajo

Zuni

Pueblo
(19 tribes)

Acoma
Laguna

OKLA

Dieguena

Ipai

Yuma

Pima

Kiowa

Luiseno
Cupa

Tipai

O'odam

Apache

White Mountain
Apache

Mescalero

Pasqua Yaqui
Papago  Chiricahua

Comanche

Apache

SOUTHWEST

Suma

Opata

Lipan

Arctic Ocean

Eskimo

Pima
Bajo

Jumano

Koyukon

Cochimi

Yaqui

Concho

ALASKA

Tarahumara

Ingalik

Tanana

Kutchin

Bering Sea

Kaniagmiut

Gulf of Alaska

Guaycura  Huchiti

Huastec

MEXICO
AND
CENTRAL
AMERICA

Aleuts

Tlingit

Nahuati

Aztec

Zap

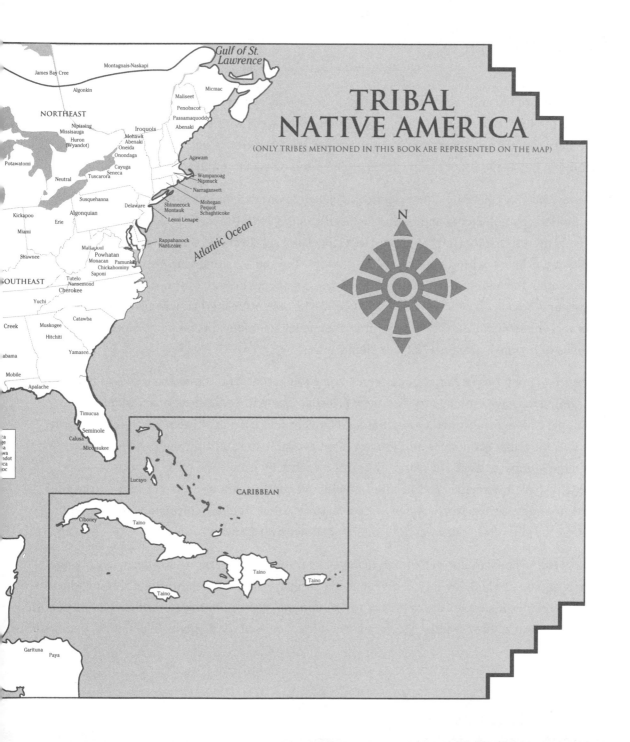

# TRIBAL
# NATIVE AMERICA
(ONLY TRIBES MENTIONED IN THIS BOOK ARE REPRESENTED ON THE MAP)

Gulf of St. Lawrence

Montagnais-Naskapi

James Bay Cree

Algonkin

Micmac

Maliseet

Penobscot

Passamaquoddy

NORTHEAST

Nipissing
Missisauga

Iroquois

Abenaki

Huron
(Wyandot)

Mohawk
Abenaki
Oneida

Potawatomi

Onondaga

Agawam

Cayuga
Seneca

Neutral

Tuscarora

Wampanoag
Nipmuck

Susquehanna

Narragansett

Kickapoo

Algonquian

Erie

Delaware

Mohegan
Pequot
Schaghticoke

Shinnecock
Montauk

Miami

Lenni Lenape

Shawnee

Rappahanock
Nanticoke

Atlantic Ocean

Mattaponi
Monacan

Powhatan

Pamunkey
Chickahominy

SOUTHEAST

Tutelo
Nansemond

Saponi

Cherokee

N

Yuchi

Catawba

Creek

Muskogee

Hitchiti

alabama

Yamasee

Mobile

Apalache

Timucua

Seminole

Calusa

Micosukee

Lucayo

CARIBBEAN

Ciboney

Taino

Taino

Taino

Taino

Taino

Garituna
Paya

# INTRODUCTION

Every aspect of life and death is celebrated, in some way, with food. For Native Americans this can take the form of a pinch of cornmeal offered to the wind with prayers for rain and renewal or an elaborate thanksgiving feast, complete with honey-smoked duck and stuffed pumpkin, or anything in between. All of these rituals are inspired by passion and respect for life.

*Enduring Harvests* celebrates the eclectic pageantry of our original Native cuisines with all of their modern complements and enthusiasms. Beginning with the harvest season in September, it proceeds month by month throughout the year, exploring Native American events and foods, people and prayers, within their changing seasonal flow and visiting various tribes and regional landmarks all through Indian Country. Following the success of my first book, *Native Harvests: Recipes and Botanicals of the American Indian,* which was published almost two decades ago, *Enduring Harvests* continues to expand the vital, delicious realms of Native cuisines through glimpses of regional, seasonal Native celebrations.

There are many types of Native American festival foods that lend themselves well to being prepared in massive amounts to feed huge crowds. There are countless other older, more traditional Native celebration foods that feed families and friends at home. Still others spring from specific tribal economies and are not often available in robust amounts sufficient to feed very large numbers. *Enduring Harvests* draws respectfully from each of these sources—and more—to share 150 recipes and profile 75 major events throughout Indian Country, from the Peruvian Andes, across North America, to the Arctic Circle, moving through Native moon times and seasons and often following the legendary "Powwow Highway."

Some of the recipes are for pan-Indian dishes, like frybread, chili, tacos, barbecues, guacamole, and rice medlies, which are enjoyed year-round at many different celebrations nationwide. I've included recipes for especially delicious regional forms of these Native favorites. Likewise, corn, squash, and beans, the essential Native American triad, enliven most events in countless variations.

On the other hand, many of these recipes, such as Maize Mushrooms and Calabacitas, Alligator Crawfish Jambalaya, Buzzard's Breath Four-Alarm Revenge Chili, Mount Saint Helens Salad with Volcanic Lava Dressing, and Raspberry Fool, are actually inspired by, rather than encountered at, specific events. Also, some events do not have a particular recipe to offer but are described here in order to take you deeper into the diverse, fascinating world of Native American traditions.

These wonderful recipes are continually changing and evolving, and they are rarely written down. The greatest cooks I have had the pleasure of working with are accomplished, instinctual gourmets. I never see them consult a recipe or exactly measure the many ingredients that are lovingly added as a dish progresses. Watching them is like witnessing an almost mesmerizing dance of cooking preparations, and this dance can unfold anywhere—around a winter campfire on Indian Island in Maine, at the Pawnee Senior Citizen Center Kitchen in Pawnee, Oklahoma, at a Pacific Coast campfire on the Makah Reservation in Neah Bay, Washington, or in an elegant modern kitchen penthouse in New York City, Boston, or Rome, Italy.

Capturing the salient details of these recipes—the specific ingredients, their proportions, and the particulars of preparation—and committing them to ink and paper has been a lifelong challenge for me, and I have been very careful to ensure that the instructions in this book are clear and accurate. One special note about herbs: Unless indicated otherwise, all herbs used in these recipes should be fresh. If you only have dried herbs on hand, you'll need to use only one third the amount given in the recipe, since dried herbs are much more concentrated in flavor.

Some of you may wish to attend the festivals described in these pages and enjoy the communal feasting and festivities yourselves. Most of them offer a generous array of foods to buy and try, and most Native festivals generously welcome visitors. If you'd like more details about when and where they are held, check the travel guides listed in the bibliography at the end of this book. Always call ahead to double-check schedules. Remember to show respect when attending any event in Indian Country. Ask permission to take photographs, if you're in doubt. Listen for etiquette cues from the master of ceremonies or director of the event. Above all, have a good spirit and warm heart, and feel welcome.

In these modern times we continue to be nurtured by a vast array of foods that have been developed from Native American origins and enlivened by centuries of cultural cross-fertilization. At the core of these preparations is respect for life and Native inventiveness—the keys to much of Native American thought and survival. *Enduring Harvests* helps remind us that for our ancestors food was at times an artful expression of respect, a nurturing cultural gift, a delicious way of offering prayers to the Creator.

# September

*September gathers the achievements of summer and presents the fall, emblazoned with changing colors and punctuated by seasonal shifts in animal and plant behaviors. Cooler weather heightens our creative energies as we celebrate the many harvests. Reflecting upon earlier Native American calendars, we feel the urgencies of gathering and celebrating foods.*

*September was the period of the Harvest Moon of the Narragansett and early Agawam Indians of southern New England (Rhode Island and Massachusetts); the Ripe Corn Moon of the Wampanoag Indians in Massachusetts; the Green Corn Moon of the Creek and Cherokee Indians of the Southeast and Oklahoma; and the Corn Harvest Moon of the Tewa Pueblo Indians of New Mexico. For the Micmac, September brought the Moose Calling Moon; for the Penobscot it brought the Moon of the Eels, the Rutting Caribou, and the Moose to their homelands of the Maine and Canadian maritime regions. For the Dakota Peoples of the Plains, this was the Moon When the Wild Rice Season Begins. For the Dogrib, Canadian Athapascans of the Lake Regions in the subarctic, it was the Moon When the Caribou Are Abundant in the Woods.*

*Each moon period, the twenty-eight days from new moon to new moon, marked tribal observations associated with their key survival needs. Food and nature held life in balance, and to ensure this continuation, people celebrated and gave thanks frequently.*

In September, as days grow progressively shorter and nights lengthen and cool, Native People gather their harvests and celebrate the gifts from Mother Earth. Drawing together periodically in festivals called powwows, they pay tribute to their friendships and culture through activities firmly based in tradition, ritual, and camaraderie. Through food, music, dance, and much more, contemporary powwows offer Native Peoples various pathways to their heritage.

Led by the sometimes serious, often hilarious observations of the powwow master of ceremonies, these colorful modern events offer diverse foods, arts, crafts, music, dancing competitions, and traditional storytelling. Although powwows take place throughout the year, more than fifty different tribes and Indian organizations gather annually on Labor Day weekend for one of the biggest American Indian festival periods. From the White Mountain Apache Tribal Fair and Rodeo in White River, Arizona, to the Cheyenne River Sioux Fair and Rodeo in Eagle Butte, South Dakota, to the Cherokee Nation Holiday and Powwow in Tahlequah, Oklahoma, to the Shinnecock Powwow in Southampton, New York—the memorable refrain "Everybody powwow!" rings out above the crowds.

One such event takes place in Southampton, New York. On Labor Day weekend thousands of people converge on the Shinnecock Reservation, as they have for almost fifty years, to join more than 350 tribal members and friends in celebrating their traditional ceremonies. Folks come from all across the continental United States, Canada, Alaska, Hawaii, Mexico, and Central and South America to camp and enjoy the beautiful South Fork of Long Island on this special weekend.

The Shinnecock, originally allies of the powerful Montauk Confederacy, are Algonquian Indians whose tribal name means "Those Who Live Where the Land Levels Out" or "People of the Flat Land." Today they share more than 500 acres fronting the south Atlantic Ocean where it laps the shore of Long Island, New York. Much of the reservation is rich tidal marshland, teeming with

2

shorebirds and coastal life. Their solar-assisted Oyster and Clam Project, started in 1984, is one of the most unique Native American tribal enterprises, with the potential to supply many Long Island and New York City restaurants.

The Shinnecock People historically were noted whalers and fishermen, knowledgeable in wild edible and medicinal plants and noted for their foods. Marguerite Smith, labor arbitration lawyer and former Shinnecock tribal counsel, lives on the reservation and reflects that her people have developed many of the delicious foods that continue to inspire our contemporary American cuisines. Also noted for their dancing, hospitality, and generosity, the Shinnecock People host a gathering with all four gifts in abundance as hallmarks of their festivity.

3

### Cleaning, or "Feeding," Clams

*Dig or purchase your live clams, if you can, a day before you need to prepare and cook them. Scrub each one well in cold water and place them in a large, deep bucket. Cover them to a depth of 6 or 8 inches with cold seawater or cold freshwater into which you have mixed 1/4 cup sea salt. Sprinkle 1/2 cup fine cornmeal over the surface of the water and blend it in briefly with your hands so that it filters down to the clams. Allow to rest in a cool dark place for several hours or overnight. This cornmeal bath "feeds" the clams, stimulating them (and other shellfish) to flush the fine sand and internal wastes out of their stomachs. They will taste sweeter and be less gritty when you eat them. Rinse them again in cold water before preparing them. Native American cooks also use this technique to help cleanse and purify other shellfish and turtles.*

# Shinnecock Quahog Pies

The Atlantic coastal waters of the northeastern United States offer a delicious variety of shell-fish, and one of the meatiest favorites is the hard-shelled clam, or quahog, whose heavy shells produced centuries of Native American wealth in "wampum beads." The smaller shells were used as spoons, ladles, and scrapers, and the largest shells made serving dishes. Lucky for us, they still do! Here we select the largest, clean, unbroken half-shells to use as timbales or ramekins for our pies.

**3 dozen large, fresh quahogs (scrubbed and cleaned)**

**3/4 cup corn oil or sunflower seed oil**

**2 medium onions, finely diced**

**5 scallions or wild onions, finely diced (both white and green parts)**

**2 tablespoons red sweet pepper, finely chopped**

**1 medium green pepper, finely diced**

**1 tablespoon fresh garlic, finely chopped**

**3 tablespoons fresh parsley, finely chopped**

**1 tablespoon fresh dill weed, finely chopped**

**1 teaspoon dried oregano**

**1 cup fine cornmeal**

**2 medium eggs, beaten**

**2 cups bread crumbs**

**salt and pepper to taste**

**fine paprika or diced parsley**

**lemon juice (optional)**

Carefully open quahogs by hand or steam them quickly in shallow hot water over medium-high heat for 5 minutes to open. Save broth or juice. Clean clams by rinsing quickly in warm water, then chop into medium chunks. Place clam pieces in a generous bowl and set aside.

Heat 1/2 cup of the oil in a medium-sized heavy skillet and quickly sauté over medium heat, the onions and peppers, turning and stirring constantly for 3 or 4 minutes. Next add the herbs, balance the seasonings to taste, and stir to thoroughly blend. Sprinkle the cornmeal over everything and stir it in, continuing the sautéing for another 5 minutes. Add the clams to this mixture, plus enough of the reserved clam broth to keep this composition barely moist. Cook an additional 5 minutes, stirring and balancing flavors.

Remove from heat and cool slightly. Pour this mixture into a large mixing bowl and add the beaten eggs and bread crumbs, mixing thoroughly and adding sufficient clam juice (or water) to keep the mixture workable and fairly moist.

Select 36 to 40 of the best quahog shells and oil them with your fingers or a paper towel dipped into the remaining 1/4 cup of oil.

Generously stuff the shells with the quahog pie ingredients, patting them off to a mounded, round top. Dust the tops with fine paprika or diced parsley and sprinkle a teaspoonful of fresh lemon juice (optional) over the tops of each little pie. Place stuffed clam shells in shallow baking dishes or pans and bake in 350° oven for about 20 minutes. If they have been frozen beforehand, add another 10 to 15 minutes to the baking time.

Cool briefly and serve on small plates of watercress with lemon slices or wedges. One quahog pie per person is a filling meal for most appetites, but big, hungry folks may consider these fine appetizers.

Narragansett, Pequot, and Wampanoag cooks vary this basic recipe, adding their own signature ingredients and/or varying or subtracting from this ingredient list. Spicy diced sausages, hot red peppers, or chopped cranberries or blueberries make delicious variations.

**Makes approximately 40 clam pies**

# SOUTH FORKS PAN-ROASTED OYSTERS

*This classic, old-time dish varies little from coast to coast, but the South Forks version is quintessential. Easy, elegant, and delicious, this makes a great appetizer or a fantastic main dish, depending upon the appetites of you and your guests. Plump eastern oysters* (Crassostrea virginica) *like the ones farmed at the Shinnecock Oyster Plant are irresistible winners in this dish. It is essential to use the freshest oysters possible.*

**2 tablespoons sunflower seed oil**

**4 tablespoons (1/2 stick) butter**

**6 cloves fresh garlic, diced**

**8 scallions (or wild onions), finely chopped, white and green parts**

**3 tablespoons fresh parsley, chopped**

**50 freshly shucked oysters (about 3 pints)**

**salt and pepper to taste**

Heat a large iron skillet over medium-high heat. Quickly drop in the assembled ingredients: oil and butter first, then herbs, and oysters last, stirring constantly or shaking the skillet to evenly cook and coat all ingredients, for about 5 minutes, until the oysters plump (releasing their liquor) and their edges just begin to curl. Lift the hot oysters into warmed individual serving bowls. Serve immediately with extra parsley, lemon wedges, and warm bread.

**Serves 6 to 8**

*The native Pacific oyster,* Ostrea lurida, *and the coon oyster,* Lopha frons, *of the southern mangrove swamps, are also choice edibles increasingly cultivated for discerning restaurant and gourmet markets. You may substitute either of these or use Atlantic bay scallops,* Argopecten irradians, *or Atlantic deep-sea scallops,* Placopecten magellanicus.

# SHINNECOCK CLAM AND BLUE POTATO CHOWDER

*Long before European settlers arrived on these shores with their iron kettles and dairy products, shellfish provided year-round, mineral-rich food reserves among Indian Peoples, as their huge pre-historic shell middens reassure us.*

*Varieties of clams were staple foods to many American Indian coastal tribes. Indeed, numerous Indian groups made seasonal migrations to the shore to harvest and enjoy the many diverse shell-fish, either raw, steamed, smoked, dried, or cooked in many unique ways.*

*Modern clam chowder recipes, including those of the Shinnecock, have evolved from diverse ancient origins and continue to improve. Ancient species such as the Atlantic surf clam,* Spisula solidissima, *the jackknife clam,* Ensis directus, *the razor clam,* Tagelus plebeius, *the soft-shelled clam,* Mya arenaria, *and the hard-shelled clam or quahog,* Mercenaria mercenaria, *are still delicious and sought-after gourmet treats.*

*This recipe is inspired by Long Island Shinnecock traditions updated with a unique ingredient: a small Peruvian blue potato that is just one of hundreds of special potatoes originally cultivated thousands of years ago in the highland Andes of South America. Various small, new potatoes may be substituted if you are unable to find the Peruvian blues.*

*Chowders are typically described as thick shellfish, vegetable, or meat soups, enriched with select, seasonal vegetables and salt pork, with a broth that is developed with either milk, tomatoes, or clear stock. According to many chowder fans, this soul-satisfying concoction tastes better the second day, as the varied flavors mingle and develop!*

**8 quarts quahog clams (in the shell, fresh), or 2 pints shucked, fresh clams**

**2 medium onions, quartered**

**1 teaspoon whole peppercorns**

**8 stalks of celery, coarsely cut**

**enough water to cover the clams**

**salt to taste**

All freshly dug clams can be sandy and should be processed in a light, cold cornmeal bath. See "Cleaning or Feeding, Clams" on page 3.

After you have cleaned the clams, place all ingredients in a deep, heavy iron kettle and cover with water. Cover the pot with a lid, bring water to a boil, and steam the clams over medium heat for 10 minutes. Remove from heat, remove lid, and cool slightly.

Strain and reserve two gallons of the broth made from this process. Purée the onions, celery, and peppercorns, along with some of the reserved liquid, in a food processor. Add this mixture to the two gallons of reserved chowder stock and return mixture to the (cleaned) kettle. Coarsely chop the cooked clams and add them to this broth.

Then add:

**20 small blue potatoes, quartered**

**3 cups fresh cooking tomatoes, quartered**

**3 fresh bay leaves (6 fresh bayberry leaves may be substituted)**

**2 green sweet bell peppers, cleaned and coarsely chopped**

**2 red sweet bell peppers, cleaned and coarsely chopped**

**1 cup fresh parsley, finely chopped**

**1 cup fresh chives, scallions, or wild onions, finely chopped**

**1/2 cup fresh dill weed, finely chopped**

**salt and pepper to taste**

Bring liquid back to a near-boil and steam all ingredients together, stirring occasionally, for 15 minutes. Continue to cook over medium heat until potatoes are tender but not soft. Serve hot.

**Serves 10**

## Powwows—Then and Now

*The roots of powwow are indeed ancient. One of the earliest documented and most enduring Algonquian words,* powwow *was interpreted by European translators in the early 1600s (from the proto-Algonquian/Narragansett language) to mean "a conjurer," a "medicine person," "sorcerer," "shaman," or "ceremonialist," or "someone who divines the future." Powwows were spiritual leaders and counselors who served to maintain the integrity and balance in Algonquian societies. Years of training and special abilities enhanced the powers of select individuals, who often walked the medicine pathways of herbalism and healing. Both men and women were powwows.*

*Powwow also came to designate special gathering places: rivers, ponds, hills, immense boulders, and special clearings where Indian People gathered, since earliest times, to celebrate important periods in their ceremonial cycles, to establish alliances, and to hold healing rituals. During Colonial times, powwows continued despite religious and legal persecution and repression. In some ways, modern powwows are reflections of these ancient sites and rites.*

*Trudie Lamb Richmond of the Schaghticoke Reservation in Kent, Connecticut, describes the contemporary powwow as "one of the most visible of American Indian cultural celebrations. It has a different meaning for participant and visitor. For Indian People today it is a time to come together, to join in the dancing, singing and visiting; renewing old friendships, making new ones. It is a time of spiritual and cultural strengthening . . . passing down traditional values to the younger generations, and offering a sense of oneness with others and with Mother Earth."*

*Modern powwows are also important commercial events, with profits helping to support the tribe, college, museum, or organization "hosting" the gathering as well as the vendors, drummers, dancers, artists, cooks, and storytellers who have traveled to the site. In fact, many Indian folks travel on the "Powwow Highway," carefully planning each stop on the circuit to earn their living through the commercial opportunities these festivals offer. Foods, artwork, and handicrafts are abundant at each powwow.*

9

The famous Four Corners Region is home of the Dineh *(The People),* also known as the Navajo, our largest tribe of more than 260,000 people. Larger than all of New England, the Navajo reservation covers 17.5 million acres and includes some of the most spectacular geographic landmarks and awe-inspiring scenery in North America. Embracing much of Arizona and New Mexico and parts of Utah and Colorado, Navajoland, Dine'bikeyah, draws more than 100,000 people each year to the Navajo Nation Fair, a five-day gala festival based in Window Rock, Arizona.

If you look at the landscape surrounding the festival grounds, you will feast upon the beauty of strikingly open, unbounded vistas of buttes and cliffs, angular mesas, and expansive plateaus that seem to dwarf the human inhabitants. Navajo creation stories explain these incredible geological formations as the petrified bodies of ancient monsters who inhabited the earth long before humans arrived here. The monsters were slain ages ago by Monster Slayer and Child Born of Water, the Sacred Navajo Hero Twins, during the Third/Yellow World. This made the land safe for the emergence of the "five-fingered people" who came into the present Fourth/Glittering World, Dine'bikeyah, more than 600 years ago.

You can feel that this beautiful land is filled with a rich pantheon of supernatural spirits, actively recalled in Navajo art, craftworks, chants, stories, festivals, ceremonies, and, some would also say, in their foods. Navajo ceremonies celebrate the sacredness of food. When a Navajo couple marries, the bride's grandmother gives the bride and groom a basket of cornmeal at the wedding, the couple exchange with each other a pinch of the cornmeal, receiving the strength and blessings of the spirit world through the corn.

# NAVAJO TACOS

*Navajo Tacos are the universal modern powwow food today. You are as likely to have Navajo Tacos at any and every eastern American Indian festival as you will be to have them at the Navajo Nation Fair. Actually, this contemporary classic is often just known as Indian Tacos and is a delicious, quick balance of the various food groups into a single-dish "fast food." Dressed with whichever usual accompaniments suit your fancy, the whole dish begins with frybread.*

## NAVAJO FRYBREAD

*There may be as many different recipes for this modern pan-Indian flatbread as there are Native cooks to make it. Endless regional and seasonal variations extend and enliven each recipe. Plains Indians like to tear it and dip it into their traditional wasnas and wojapis, sweetened wild plum or chokecherry sauces, to which jerked buffalo meat is sometimes added. Many eastern folks like the frybread topped with shredded salad and cheeses and wild mushroom sauces. Every variation is delicious, but try this version first.*

**3 cups sifted, unbleached flour**

**1/2 cup dry powdered milk**

**1 tablespoon baking powder**

**1/2 teaspoon salt**

**1 1/2 cups warm water or milk**

**2 quarts oil for deep frying**

Combine the first five ingredients in a large mixing bowl and knead until smooth and soft but not sticky. Depending upon altitude and humidity, you may need more or less water or flour, so balance accordingly. Be careful not to overwork the dough, or it can become tough and chewy. Brush a tablespoonful of oil over the finished dough and allow it to rest 20 minutes to 2 hours in a bowl covered with a damp cloth. When the dough has rested, heat the oil in a broad, deep frying pan or kettle to a low boil (375°). The magic is in frying the bread quickly! The less time it spends in the hot oil, the lighter in texture and lower in fat it will be. Pull off large egg-size balls of dough and quickly roll, pull, and pat them out into large plate-size rounds. They should be thin in the middle to about 1/4-inch thick at the edges. Carefully ease each piece into the hot, boiling oil, one at a time. Using a long-handled cook-ing fork or tongs, turn them once, allowing about 2 minutes per side. Drain and remove each piece to absorbent layers of brown paper or paper towels. Serve hot with honey, jelly, fine powdered sugar, or one of the other toppings suggested here.

**Makes about 24**

## NAVAJO GREEN CHILI STEW

*Many variations of traditional chili, in varying degrees of hotness, spring from imaginative cooks working with their seasonal gifts. This version makes an interesting springboard to others and is a great filling for Navajo Tacos. Adjust the seasonings to suit your tastes.*

**1/4 cup corn oil**

**3 slices of bacon**

**1 large onion, coarsely chopped**

**4 garlic cloves, diced**

**2 pounds lean ground beef or lamb**

**2 cups beef broth**

**2 cups stewing tomatoes, coarsely chopped**

**1 cup roasted, peeled green chili peppers, coarsely chopped**

**1 teaspoon fresh cilantro, diced**

**1 teaspoon dried oregano**

**1 teaspoon ground cumin**

**1 cup pinto, black turtle, or Anasazi beans, cooked (optional)**

**salt and pepper to taste**

**2 cups fresh, shredded lettuce and wild greens (if available)**

**1/2 cup shredded carrots**

**1/2 cup shredded or chopped onions**

**1 cup shredded cheddar cheese**

Heat the oil in a large heavy skillet; cook the bacon, onion, and garlic in the oil over medium heat for several minutes until the onion is just translucent. Draw these ingredients over to one side of the pan and add the ground beef or lamb, stirring and browning quickly. Add beef broth, tomatoes, peppers, herbs and seasonings, and beans, if desired.

Thoroughly stir these ingredients and simmer for 30 minutes. Balance and adjust flavors. Set aside or save overnight and rewarm. Blend greens, carrots, onions, and cheese in a medium bowl and chill until you are ready to serve the chili, spooned hot over these ingredients.

To assemble Navajo Tacos, top a warm piece of frybread with a generous handful of the chilled lettuce mixture. Spoon a generous serving of the Navajo Green Chili Stew on top. Some individuals may want additional shredded cheese and hot sauce on top of this. Selections of these condiments, and more, are usually provided, so that each person can dress his or her own tacos accordingly.

All of this is served with great good humor, which simply makes everything taste better!

**Makes about 24 tacos**

## *Powwow Protocol*

*If you are a visitor at a powwow or other Native American event, it is a good idea to observe some simple rules of protocol. Visitors are welcome to watch the competitions, and common courtesy suggests that guests be watchful and respectful and that they participate when invited. Dancers usually circle left while keeping time with the drum. In respect, women should wear or carry shawls in the dance circle. Visitors should not sit on the benches and chairs immediately encircling the dance area, as these are reserved for the dancers, drummers, and their families. It is polite to ask dancers and singers/drummers before taking their pictures and to listen to the directions of the powwow master of ceremonies.*

13

# Tulsa Native American Festival Early September

Native American Fall Homecomings and Winter Socials are usually blessed with countless regional dishes developed from long associations with those nutritious fruits of the vine—pumpkins, squashes, and gourds. Among the earliest plants cultivated in the Americas, going back more than 9,000 years and predating corn and beans, gourds are possibly the earliest, ancient ancestors of the later hybrids that are now used in recipes throughout the Native cultures. Pumpkin frybread, spicy pumpkin-raisin bread, pumpkin butter, pumpkin pie, pumpkin *empanaditas,* pumpkin fruit leather, pumpkin relish and chutney, roasted pumpkin seeds, and spicy pumpkin seed sauce are just some of the recipes that use this gloriously versatile fruit. Regional flair adds to the delight as we move around the continent from one powwow to another. The Tulsa Native American Festival is held annually every September and provides a perfect opportunity for sharing the autumn harvests.

14

## Oklahoma Pumpkin Frybread

*From the small, sweet, meaty Sugar Pumpkins, to the robust, squat, butterscotch-colored Cheese Pumpkins, to the huge, orange field pumpkins, these classic Native American vegetables signal the harvest with glowing generosity. Each hybrid has been developed for its special attributes. We choose the cooked, puréed, and slightly sweetened meat of the sugar pumpkin to make this delightful recipe, which was given to me by June Lee and her sister Hattie Daniels in Tulsa during the Native American Festival. These two creative Seminole cooks from Wewoka, Oklahoma, recall that this recipe was carried by their relatives from Florida, across the South, through their families' settlements in Texas, and on to them, being changed ever so slightly in each region by each family. Their creative inspirations nurture many tasty harvest foods.*

*We prepared and served this delicate frybread as a dessert during the ten-day festival celebrating American Indian artistic contributions in Rome, Italy. Elegant daily menus served in the museum restaurants at the Palazzo delle Esposizioni featured a broad array of American Indian festival and ceremonial foods. Of the dozens of choice selections offered, this one was a great favorite. Italian chefs arranged three little balls of Seminole Pumpkin Frybread on a dessert plate dusted with fine powdered sugar.*

*Most cultures have a fried-bread traditional food, and from Italy to Tibet to Patagonia, each is remarkably similar: basically wheat flour, water (or milk), baking powder, salt and oil or fat for frying. Spanish explorers first brought wheat flour to North America five hundred years ago, and now Native American frybread varies in composition, style, and subtle tastes from tribe to tribe and even within each tribe: from family to family. Savory versions are served with game, seafood, and other meats. Spicy herb variations are enjoyed with shredded salad toppings, cheese, salsa, and hot chili, as tacos. Sweet variations are delicious with honey, powdered sugar, or fruit sauces. Other variations include wild mushrooms and wild rice or roast cornmeal and chili peppers. Some may include healing herbs, seeds, and powdered roots.*

**3 cups unbleached flour**

**1 cup puréed pumpkin meat**

**1/2 cup honey, maple syrup, or granulated sugar**

**1/2 teaspoon salt (optional)**

**1/4 teaspoon ground cinnamon**

**2 teaspoons baking powder**

**1 cup warm water or milk (more if needed)**

**1 tablespoon sunflower seed oil**

Conbine first seven ingredients plus 1/2 tablespoons oil in a large mixing bowl. Mix thoroughly and knead until smooth, balancing the flour and moisture components as needed. lightly rub the smooth surface of the finished raw dough with the remaining oil. Cover the bowl with a damp towel, and allow to rest for 30 minutes to an hour or two, if desired. Heat sufficient oil or shortening in a heavy pot or skillet so that oil is about 3 inches deep and the pot is no more than half full. Heat on the stove to a medium-high temperature (about 375°).

With lightly floured hands, pinch off small golf-ball-size pieces of dough and gently flatten each piece in the palm of your hand until it forms a circle or triangle of 1/2-inch thickness, thinner (or with a hole) in the middle. you can also choose to roll each pinched piece of dough into a ball. Rest these pieces on lightly floured brown paper until ready to fry. The less you handle the dough, the lighter and more tender the finished breads will be.

Carefully ease each freshly shaped piece of dough into the hot oil, being careful not to splatter. Fry quickly, turning with long-handled tongs or a slotted spoon. Do not crowd dough pieces in the pot. Remove in 2 to 4 minutes and drain on brown paper or absorbent paper towels.

Remove while warm to a serving plate and dust lightly with powdered sugar. Serve warm. Enjoy!

**Makes 20 to 24 small frybreads**

# Spicy Roasted Pumpkin Seeds

*Every pumpkin cut open reveals a generous number of nutritious seeds. Pueblo artists sometimes dry them in the sun, then dye them vivid colors and string them into charming necklaces, which are often sold among other powwow wares. Seeds are symbolic of fertility and generosity, whether we wear them or eat them. Any kind of pumpkin or winter squash seeds can be substituted in this recipe, which is served at the Tulsa Festival and many other Native American festivals. A wonderful accent and condiment, they accompany most foods well. They are always served on our harvest table and are especially delicious mixed with raisins or currants, sunflower seeds, hazelnuts, and peanuts for a sweet and savory high-energy trail snack.*

**1 1/2 cups of seeds, more or less**

**2 tablespoons of sunflower seed oil or peanut oil**

**1/2 teaspoon salt**

**1/4 teaspoon finely ground black pepper**

**1/2 teaspoon chili powder**

**1/4 teaspoon ground cumin**

**1/2 teaspoon minced garlic**

Preheat the oven to 375°F. Scrape the seeds from a freshly cut pumpkin and separate them from their stringy pulp.

In a medium bowl, combine seeds and all the remaining ingredients, tossing and blending thoroughly. Spread out evenly on a foil-covered pan or cookie sheet and roast for 15 to 25 minutes, depending upon the size of the seeds. Seeds may pop and crackle as they toast. Roast until seeds are golden-brown and crisp. We enjoy them warm or cool, shell and all!

**Makes about 1 1/2 cups**

### *Roasting  Seeds,  Nuts,  and  Grains*

*Roasting certain ingredients just before you want to use them enhances flavors and fragrance. Think of the difference between eating raw peanuts and roasted peanuts, and you gain some idea of how roasting can improve rice, quinoa, cornmeal, whole wheat flour, and a broad selection of nuts and other grains.*

*To roast grains, start with a half cup spread in a clean, dry, hot cast-iron skillet, over medium-high heat. Roast for 3 to 10 minutes, depending upon the size and moisture content of the grain. Shake the skillet or stir with a wooden spoon to evenly roast and to keep the grains or seeds from burning. The moisture content of rice and some grains might cause them to pop much like popcorn. You can also spread the ingredients on a clean cookie sheet and toast them in the oven, especially for large amounts to go into a ceremonial or festival dish. Roast one ingredient at a time, as they each have such different personalities.*

Mashantucket Pequot Indians, The Fox People, of southeastern Connecticut, are giving new definition to the ancient feast of green corn, which is celebrated at seasonally specific times throughout North America. From their modern, well-developed, and federally recognized reservation on a tiny portion of their once-extensive ancestral homelands, the Mashantucket Pequot Indians are expanding their broad national and international reach with new economic style and originality. Mashantucket, meaning "much wooded land," describes the mixed hardwood forest, rolling hills, and rocky southern New England lowland soil of Ledyard. Mashantucket is also synonymous with the greatest tribal economic success story in North America, a remarkable feat of accomplishment for the Pequot, who are listed in some of our old history books as having been exterminated in the savage Pequot massacres of 1636–37. Centuries of genocide and forced assimilation endured, the Mashantucket Pequot are now shaping new horizons for their people.

Indian gaming enterprises have helped to return the Mashantucket Pequot to the status of economic leaders in southern New England, and their good fortune is continually being shared. Mid-September brings Indian People from all over the Americas to Ledyard for the three- to five-day Schemitzun: Feast of Green Corn and Dance. Thousands of colorful dancers, singers, drummers, vendors, and food people, representing more than 200 different Indian tribes, converge to enjoy and demonstrate all the traditional activities they each do best. The biggest purse of Indian prize money encourages some of the most spectacular drumming and dancing ever seen in North America. It is the biggest Green Corn Celebration ever, east of the Mississippi, in recorded history.

Indian corn as well as pumpkins, squashes, gourds, beans, sunflowers, and wild nuts and berries sustained ancestors of today's Native Peoples for well over a thousand years in the Northeast. Traditional celebrations evolved to pay respects and give thanks for recurring harvests, and these led to the Feast of Green Corn, which began with the earliest underripe "green corn" (what we now seek as "sweet corn"). Subsequent plantings of corn through the early growing season extended the availabilities of green corn and therefore its celebrations. Now, as you travel around North America, you may encounter Green Corn Festivals in various tribal regions from June through September. A diversity of delicious corn dishes as well as the delectable inventiveness of American Indian cuisines bless these events with new levels of gourmet excellence. At a recent Schemitzun in Hartford, buffalo burgers, Savory Venison Stew, Spiced Cajun Alligator Sausages, Blue Corn Tortillas with Salsa, Algonquian Three Sisters Rice, Smoky Mountain Salad, cranberry breads, maple butter, and strawberry drinks served many thousands of hungry celebrants, creating delicious memories.

### *New England Corn*

*Archaeological evidence shows us that the horticulture of corn and beans is well over a thousand years old in southern New England and much earlier in the southern regions. Roger Williams observed in 1643 ". . . when a field is to be broken up, [the Algonquians] have a very loving sociable speedy way to dispatch it: all the neighbors men and women forty, fiftie, a hundred &c joyne, and come in to help freely."*

*Algonquian women were the tribal members principally responsible for the gardens, and many of them became strong leaders called squawsachems. Roger Williams further recorded ". . . the women of the family will commonly raise two or three heaps of twelve, fifteen, or twentie bushells a heap . . . and if she have help of her children or friends, much more."*

# Salsa Cornbread

*The true gold of the Americas, corn endows us with an endless variety of tasty, nutritious preparations. This recipe is as good with game stews and chilis as it is with breakfast eggs, or it can be sliced cold and served with smoked trout, salmon, or catfish pâté. It is also wonderful grilled and topped with onions and caviar.*

**2 tablespoons melted butter**

**1/2 cup yellow cornmeal**

**3/4 cup all-purpose flour**

**1 1/2 teaspoons baking powder**

**1/2 teaspoon salt, and pepper to taste**

**1 tablespoon honey**

**3 eggs, beaten until light and foamy**

**1/2 cup milk or buttermilk**

**1/2 cup whole kernel corn**

**1 small onion, diced**

**1 clove garlic, diced**

**1 small jalapeño pepper, diced**

**1/2 cup chopped tomatoes**

**1/2 cup cheddar cheese, grated**

Generously coat an 8- or 9-inch cast-iron skillet with the butter and place it in oven while the oven preheats to 425°. Blending well, combine all of the remaining ingredients except for the cheese, which you should reserve to sprinkle over the top of the prepared batter.

When the butter has melted and the skillet is thoroughly heated, remove the hot skillet from the oven and carefully pour the batter into it, spreading it out evenly. Sprinkle the cheese over the batter. Return skillet to oven and bake for 20 to 30 minutes or until a knife inserted in the center comes out clean. Remove from oven and cool for 5 minutes. Serve warm, and enjoy!

**Serves 8 to 10**

# SAVORY VENISON STEW

*An amazing increase of deer populations in various regions, especially the Northeast, as well as the numerous successful ranching operations for deer and other game animals, helps to bring many more sophisticated game recipes to popular attention. This classic stew, served at the Feast of Green Corn, has numerous variations, depending upon the season.*

1/2 cup corn oil

1 1/2 pounds trimmed venison, cut into bite-size chunks

1 medium onion, coarsely chopped

3 large cloves garlic, finely diced

8 small red potatoes, quartered

3 celery stalks, diced

3 carrots, cut into 1/2-inch rounds

2 bay leaves

1 cup wild mushrooms, cut in bite-size pieces

1/4 teaspoon dried finely crumbled sage

1/4 teaspoon dried parsley, chopped

1/4 teaspoon coarse salt

ground pepper to taste

1/4 teaspoon hot sauce (such as Tabasco)

2 cups water or vegetable or meat stock

1 8-ounce jar prepared salsa, mild or according to taste

In a large cast-iron skillet or pot, heat oil over medium-high heat; add venison and quickly brown on all sides, stirring frequently. Add the onion, garlic, and potatoes, stirring well. Add remaining ingredients, blending and stirring well. Cover and cook for 30 minutes or until venison and potatoes are tender. Balance seasonings to taste. If seasonings are too hot, serve with sour cream. Enjoy!
**Serves 6 to 8**

# ALGONQUIAN THREE SISTERS RICE

*This special medley of flavors and tastes is inspired by Native gardens, where the three sisters—corn, squash, and beans—are a sacred triad, as compatible in the gardens and fields as they are in the meal. Like succotash, which has its roots in early Algonquian dialects and gardens, this classic combo is so nutritionally well-balanced that it can be a complete main course or a colorful side course. It is a staple at Schemitzun and other Northeastern gatherings.*

3 cups chicken stock or water

1 cup long grain brown rice or wild rice

pinch coarse salt to taste

1 medium yellow squash, cubed

1 medium zucchini squash, cubed

2 cups of baby lima beans

2 cups of whole-kernel corn

1 red bell pepper, roasted and cut into bite-sized strips

1 green bell pepper, roasted and cut into bite-sized strips

1/2 cup sunflower seed or corn oil

3 cloves garlic, finely diced

1 cup diced onion

1/2 cup chopped fresh parsley

1/2 cup chopped fresh scallions

1/4 teaspoon white pepper

1/4 teaspoon paprika

In a large, deep pot over medium heat, bring the chicken stock or water to a rolling boil. Sprinkle in the rice and a pinch of salt, then lower the heat. Cover and steam for 20 minutes. Gradually add the squash, lima beans, peppers, and corn; stir well. Cover and steam for an additional 20 minutes.

While this mixture cooks, warm the oil in a medium cast-iron skillet over medium heat. Add the garlic and onions, stirring briskly and cooking for about 5 minutes until garlic and onions are just glistening and translucent but not brown. Add the remaining seasonings, stir thoroughly and remove from the heat.

Stirring thoroughly, add these ingredients to the steaming rice and balance the seasonings and liquids. Steam for a final 5 minutes, covered. Fluff and serve.

**Serves 10 to 12**

# ANNUAL PINE NUT
# FESTIVAL

The Walker River Paiute Tribe hold their annual Pine Nut Festival on the third weekend in September in Schurz, Nevada. Their reservation embraces 324,000 acres of rugged, arid land in western Nevada, east of Lake Tahoe and north of Walker Lake. Their collective economy is based upon their agricultural enterprises. Like the Root Feast in spring and the Huckleberry Feast in summer, the times for these celebrations are set by the tribe's Elder Woman. Based upon close observations of the harvest cycles, these ceremonial events give thanks and celebrate the bounty of Mother Earth.

The Pine Nut Blessing, music, round-dancing, pageants, arts, crafts, and foods are compelling features of the festival, drawing many people to join in the celebrations. The pine nut, *Pinus edulis,* also called the pinyon, or piñon, and the single-leaf pinyon, *Pinus monophylla,* are found in the dry mesas, foothills, and canyons of the American Southwest, where they have long been sought after and collectively harvested. Their egg-shaped cones produce delicious 1/2-inch wingless nuts that have been delicious staples for many American Indian tribes. These rich, oily nuts are protein-packed and are enjoyed raw, roasted, parched, or boiled in many different Native recipes.

# Windwalker Pine Nut Cookies

*Highly prized from the Great Basin region to the Pueblos and throughout the Desert Southwest, rich pine nuts, or pinyons, are as delicious in salads as they are in breads, meat pies, and desserts. Ground into a mealy paste, pine nuts are made into fritters or used to thicken soups and drinks. This delightful recipe was brought east by a good friend in Poughkeepsie, New York, and is shared with much appreciation. These cookies are a light, easy dessert.*

**1 cup (2 sticks) butter at room temperature**

**2/3 cup brown sugar, firmly packed**

**2 eggs**

**1 cup stone-ground white cornmeal**

**1/2 cup all-purpose flour, sifted**

**1 cup shelled pine nuts (about 6 ounces)**

**dash of cinnamon**

**pinch of salt (optional)**

Preheat oven to 325°. Lightly grease 2 cookie sheets. Cream butter and sugar together until fluffy. Beat in eggs, one at a time. Add cornmeal alternately with the flour, stirring thoroughly. Mix in the pine nuts and seasonings and blend carefully.

Drop a generous tablespoonful of dough onto the cookie sheets, spacing 1 inch apart. These are spreading, generous cookies. Bake about 10 minutes, until edges are lightly brown. Cool for 5 minutes and serve warm, or cool completely and store in airtight containers.

**Makes about 20 cookies**

This day was proclaimed "Indian Day" in Connecticut. Other states have established the same tradition, and celebrations of the day usually include educational, informative activities that include the opportunity to share Native foods.

Indigenous people in North America have evolved an earth-centered respect for life, and the bounty of the land usually supplies all their needs. When it does not, the people search for greater understanding, and ceremonies, festivals, and prayers are offered to help nourish the ongoing cycles of life. For many of the ancient people, the land was their culture, and everything they did was carefully interwoven with the processes of the land. Much of this essential thinking continues to be reflected in contemporary Native work and festivities.

The national Native American Day is celebrated in many schools and libraries with tribal story-telling, drumming, and dancing. Sometimes popcorn, dried fruits, and pumpkin and sunflower seeds are served with cranberry juice and sassafras or goldenrod teas, reminding folks of earlier foods that have now become the basis of valuable economic enterprises.

The following two contemporary recipes use native foods in clever, innovative ways and are offered here in honor of the Native Peoples' respect for the gifts of the land. Both are likely to be served during Native American Day celebrations.

# Maize Mushrooms and Calabacitas

*In the blaze of fall colors you can usually find equally colorful, abundant wild mushrooms in fields and woods, in schoolyards, on village greens, and in gourmet and farm markets.*

*One of the most unique delicacies is the maize mushroom,* Ustilago maydis, *also known as the Mexican truffle, or corn smut. Although this soft gray-white fungus is actually a wind-borne parasite on ripening sweet corn kernels, it is sought after in its under-ripe stage as a delicious food. The early Mayan and Aztec Indians called it "Cuitlacoche" (weet-la-COO-chee) or "huitlacoche." The maize mushroom is now popular in the informed gourmet market, where it can sell for as much as $18 a pound. Ancient American Indian cultures from Peru and Mexico to the Great Lakes and the Northeast prize these plump blisters of "meat" in many Native dishes. Most common in markets and on menus in Mexico and our Southwest, they are wonderful prepared in the following way. The small squashes (or calabacitas, Spanish for "little squash") used in this dish are also best small and under-ripe.*

1 tablespoon butter

1 cup maize mushroom pieces

4 medium-small zucchini or chayote squash, cubed (about 4 cups)

1 medium onion, coarsely chopped

1 fresh jalapeño pepper, seeded and finely diced

2 cloves garlic, finely diced

1 cup sweet corn

1/4 cup tomato, diced

1/2 cup warm water or vegetable broth

salt and pepper to taste

1/2 cup American white cheddar or Jack cheese, grated

1/4 cup fresh epazote or cilantro, chopped

Melt butter in medium skillet and sauté mushrooms, squash, and onion over medium heat, stirring frequently. Add the remaining ingredients except for the cheese and the epazote or cilantro, which should be added during the last 2 to 5 minutes. Stir to blend ingredients together, then sprinkle the cheese over the top. Cover the skillet and lower heat slightly; continue to cook over medium-low heat for 10 minutes until cheese melts. Uncover and sprinkle the epazote or cilantro over the top for the final 5 minutes. Serve hot with chilled sour cream or yogurt.

**Serves about 8**

# JICAMA-SUNCHOKE SALAD WITH HONEY MUSTARD DRESSING

*These two nutritious tubers provide a delicious medley of spicy flavors. This salad is always better the second day, if you can possibly save any, and is often found at powwows and other Native gatherings. We serve this often at the Institute for American Indian Studies in Washington, Connecticut, where it is exceedingly popular.*

**1 (2-pound) jicama, peeled and julienned**

**2 cups unpeeled sunchokes, thinly sliced**

**1 1/2 cups red kidney or cranberry beans, cooked**

**1 large bunch fresh watercress, coarsely chopped**

**1 bunch fresh mustard greens, coarsely chopped**

**1 medium green bell pepper, cored and julienned**

**1 medium yellow bell pepper, cored and julienned**

**1 medium red bell pepper, cored and julienned**

**6 green onions, coarsely chopped**

Combine all the ingredients in a large wooden bowl. Toss well with Honey Mustard Dressing and allow to marinate at room temperature for at least an hour.

**Serves 6 to 10**

# HONEY MUSTARD DRESSING

1/2 cup cider vinegar

1/2 cup raw honey

1/2 cup Dijon-style mustard

3 cloves garlic, finely diced

1 cup sunflower seed oil

3 tablespoons fresh parsley, minced

1 1/2 tablespoon fresh dill weed, minced

1 tablespoon fresh cilantro, finely chopped

salt and pepper to taste

Combine all ingredients in a small bowl and whisk together. Add to the vegetables, tossing well.

**Makes about 1 1/2 cups**

## *Tuberous Twins*

*J*icama, Pachyrhizus erosus, *is a large slightly sweet tuber, usually enjoyed peeled and sliced raw for its cool crispness. Also known as Mexican potato, it has a mild texture similar to apples and a taste reminiscent of water chestnuts. It does not turn brown, and it readily absorbs strong companion flavors—both traits make it deliciously useful. This and wild jicama,* Calopogonium coeruleum, *are ancient Maya root crops that lend themselves well to many culinary uses today.*

*Jerusalem Artichokes,* Helianthus tuberosa, *also known as sunchokes, are perennial sunflowers grown for their delicious, nutritious tubers. The creamy-white, fist-size tuber, with thin skin and crisp, mild texture, is delicious both raw and cooked. Similar in taste to potato, water chestnut, and carrots, it is yet uniquely different. This is one of the oldest, most widespread plants cultivated prehistorically throughout much of North America, and it is still common along old roads and borders in the Northeast.*

# OCTOBER

Golden days with brilliant sunsets melting into deep purples and frosty nights awakening with crimson predawn skies signify the earth's seasonal shift toward winter. October focuses our energies on harvesting the wild and cultivated wealth of such Native foods as cranberries, grapes, hickory nuts, pine nuts, and other regional abundance. The fragrances of wood smoke from home fires and from the smoke-curing of fine foods fills the air. Lengthening cold nights encourage traditional storytelling, as countless tribal recollections are shared with the ever-new young audiences that gather to listen.

October brings the Harvest Moon of the Wampanoag Indians of Massachusetts, the Autumn Hazelnut Moon of the Penobscot Indians in Maine, and the Animal Fattening Moon of the Micmac of eastern Canada. Out across the Great Plains to the Northwest Coast rises the Moon In Which Leaves Fall of the Arikara, the Sioux, and the Tsimshian. For the Cheyenne, October ushers in the Water Freezes On The Edges Of Streams Moon. The Store Food In Caches Moon of the Ponca and the Fishery Moon of the Slavey also rise now. In the Southwest, this period is the Dry Grass Moon of the Pima Indians and the Big Wind Moon of the Zuni. From Oklahoma to the Southeast is the Little Chestnut Moon of the Creek and Cherokee Indians.

October's diverse generosities bless Native American gatherings all across the country.

ENDURING
HARVESTS

Austere beauty and fantastic wild plant life characterize the O'odham villages scattered across the northern reaches of the Sonoran Desert in southern Arizona. Cacti, creosote brush, and mesquite bushes stud the hot, arid plains that are broken by the isolated mountain ranges considered to be sacred guardians and protectors of The People. Embraced within their creation story and held in their collective memories and oral traditions is their belief in their emergence from this ground—from sacred places reverently distinguished as "emergence points."

Tohono O'odham, or "two villagers," are the Desert People or Thirsty People (also known as Papago, or Bean People) who inhabit these regions along with the Akimel O'odham, or River People (also known as Pima), and the Yaquis and Maricopas. The desert country of southern Arizona was the ancestral homeland of the ancient Hohokam, who built sophisticated villages and irrigated extensive crops on these same seared landscapes now inhabited by their descendants. The Hohokam, "The Vanished Ones," created their prehistoric villages and pithouses among earthen pyramids and two sunken ball courts, characteristics that seem to associate them closely with early Mesoamerican cultures. Between 100 B.C. and A.D. 1500, they coaxed the deserts into productivity by irrigating fields of corn, beans, squashes, tobacco, and cotton and then mysteriously vanished, leaving archaeological sites, artifacts, and, most important, descendants. Despite these links to the past, much remains unknown of their ceremonies and festivals. Today, those descendants embrace what they know of those earlier days.

Today, Ak Chin People consider themselves neither Pima nor Papago, but Ak Chin O'odham. Their rich agrarian society is also rich in its collective memory of O'odham history, culture, and celebrations melded with those of later influences. Distinctive O'odham ways are, for instance, charmingly interwoven with early Roman Catholic contacts begun when seventeenth-century missionaries assigned a saint to each Indian village for protection and guidance. An especially important day for the O'odham is the annual Saint Francis Church Feast and Dance honoring their patron saint, Francis of Assisi, who loved nature and animals. (The Feast of Saint Francis is, in fact, celebrated in locations throughout the Southwest.)

Early October calls together many people and more than 500 dancers to celebrate the feast at Ak Chin, "The River's Mouth," in Maricopa, Arizona, due south of Phoenix. Traditional dances fill the afternoon and evening, and generous amounts of harvest foods are served. Chili stews, frybread, flour tortillas, corn, beans, cactus fruits, and other local foods are abundantly present and shared with great enthusiasm.

It is important to know that the Ak Chin Reservation is another bright success story of modern Indian political determination to establish self-sufficiency. Leona Kakar, along with other Ak Chin leaders, spearheaded and won a twenty-year fight to regain necessary water rights for their people, enabling their farms to succeed and to triple in size. Ak Chin agriculture means planting desert-adapted varieties of corn, cowpeas, squashes, tepary beans, and melons in July and hoping for full harvests in October and November. Today much of this high desert country between the Gila and Salt River Valleys is also used successfully for farming cotton, wheat, and potatoes.

Many wild foods are also gathered—wild chilies, amaranth greens and other wild spinaches, prickly pear fruits and pads, mesquite, agave, cholla buds, saguaro fruits, acorns, and devil's claw, all of which are being eaten and studied with greater appreciation based on knowledge gained from modern dietary research. Farmers and nutritionists are working together to overcome the modern "tin-can" diet that may be responsible, in part, for O'odham Peoples' increasingly high incidence of diabetes and other nutrition-related diseases. The "new" diets rooted in these traditional foods point to healthier lives for the O'odham Peoples and others. Changing diets and increased exercise patterns are brightening O'odham futures and are well reflected in the O'odham harvest ceremonies.

The following recipes are inspired by O'odham foodways.

# Tepary Beans on Wild Spinach Fiesta Salad

*Tepary beans,* Phaseolus acutifolius, *known since 3000 B.C. in Mexico and the Desert Southwest, are fine, small white beans (with color and taste variations) that are easily processed into flour. They are widely available in health food stores and specialty markets or by mail order. I suggest you try a number of "wild spinaches" in this recipe; those from the* amaranth *and* chenopodium *families are especially tasty. Medleys of such wild greens are excellent in this presentation. Any favorite salad greens can be substituted, including whole, fresh spinach greens easily found in the produce section of the supermarket.*

*This recipe has a deep, inspired connection with the O'odham people and their early food wisdom celebrated during the Feast of Saint Francis.*

**9 cups trimmed, packed wild spinach leaves**
**1/4 cup sunflower seed oil**
**1/2 medium red onion, coarsely diced**
**3 wild onions, or scallions, coarsely diced**
**1/4 cup pine nuts, cholla buds, or amaranth seeds**
**1 red bell pepper, roasted, peeled, and diced**
**1 cup cooked tepary beans, drained**
**1/2 cup cider vinegar**
**1 tablespoon honey**
**salt and pepper to taste**

Place the washed, dried wild spinach leaves in a large salad bowl. Heat the oil in a small skillet and add both kinds of onions. Cook over medium heat, stirring until onions are just barely translucent. Remove with a slotted spoon and sprinkle over the greens in the bowl. Now briefly cook the pine nuts in the same skillet until golden, then stir in the red pepper. Quickly stir until just heated, then sprinkle over the greens.

Add the remaining ingredients to the skillet, stirring over medium-low heat to blend well.

When these ingredients are heated through, add them to the salad. Serve immediately.

**Serves 6 to 8**

# FEAST DAY BREAD PUFFS

*These quickly made puffs are in themselves celebrations of the harvest and of seasonal ingredients. Each time I make them, I'm reminded of the special feast days and festivals where I've been served them. Crusty on the outside, soft and tender inside, they are best when eaten immediately. Wonderful accompaniments to salads and main dishes, they can also be enjoyed alone, without distraction of toppings or with prickly pear cactus syrup or jelly.*

**2 cups all-purpose flour (or substitute 1/2 cup tepary bean flour
for 1/2 cup of all-purpose flour)
2 tablespoons baking powder
1/2 teaspoon salt
1 whole green onion, diced fine
1/2 cup cilantro, diced fine
1/4 teaspoon each of ground pepper, chili powder, thyme, and cumin
1 cup cold water or milk
2 teaspoons honey
oil for frying**

In a large deep bowl, mix together all dry and fresh ingredients. Make a well in the center, and add the cold water or milk and the honey.

Stir dough well until all ingredients are thoroughly blended. Dough should be sticky.

Heat about 1 inch of oil in a deep frying pan, until about 375° and just bubbling. Carefully drop dough by generous tablespoonfuls into the hot oil, two or three pieces at a time. Fry quickly, turning so that all surfaces become light golden-honey colored.

Drain on layers of clean brown paper or paper towels. Serve pronto. (These can be enhanced with a savory flair by adding 1/2 cup of cooked, diced chorizo sausage, or roasted, diced chilies.)

**Makes about 20**

# Opuntia Cactus Salad

*Prickly pear cactus,* Opuntia polyacantha, *is common in the Desert Southwest, especially in O'odham country, and it has long been one of the tribe's delicious dietary staples. Nopales, the pickled or cooked pads of these cacti, are delicious vegetables, as are the fruits, called "tunas" and "pears." These opuntia cacti are also the sole food source for the famous Cochineal beetle, famous for its use in making stunning red Aztec dyes. Opuntias have spread far and wide, both in the wild, in gardens, and in the gourmet marketplace—another case of valuable economic impact from a "wildling." They can be found fresh in markets from spring through fall. Canned pickled pads are also available (see Source Directory).*

*The flat, oval, prickly green pads somewhat resemble beavers' tails, which is another colloquial name for these plants. Some of the large green pads are nearly spineless, while others are quite spiny or prickly. Like sweet or hot peppers, they are greatly improved in texture and flavor by roasting, resting, and slipping off their skins, at the same time removing the spines.*

6 fresh opuntia pads, singed, skin roasted, and peeled

1 medium red onion, very thinly sliced

1/2 cup fresh cilantro, finely chopped

1/4 cup fresh lime or lemon juice or vinegar

1 tablespoon honey

1/2 teaspoon red chili powder

1/4 cup sunflower seed oil

watercress and wild spinach greens

Slice opuntia pads into thin julienne strips and drop into about 3 quarts of boiling water into which you have added 1 tablespoon vinegar or lemon juice and a dash of salt for each quart. Simmer for 5 minutes; drain. Place opuntia pads in a medium bowl and allow them to cool, then add to them the remaining ingredients except for the greens. Blend carefully. Chill, covered, or allow to rest for an hour. Toss the mixture again, then serve over the fresh greens.

**Serves 4 to 6**

Pueblo Indians are the cultural descendants of the Anasazi (a Navajo word meaning "Ancient Ones"), who built the dramatic prehistoric cliff dwellings still present in the Desert Southwest. When Coronado arrived in 1539 at the region now known as New Mexico, he found more than eighty-five permanent mud-brick settlements constructed by the Native People who inhabited the land along the Rio Grande and other nearby waterways. The Spaniards called these villages "pueblos" after their own villages. Today, nineteen pueblos cluster mostly along the Rio Grande between Albuquerque and Taos. Their people share this scenic ancient culture area as well as a common history, yet each group retains unique, autonomous units. Each pueblo has its own independent government and religious and civic leaders, and five distinct Native languages are spoken: Tewa, Tiwa, Towa, Keresan, and Zunian.

Pueblo People are also noted for their art, jewelry, weavings, pottery, basketry, carvings, and drums. The works of particular artists have become famous internationally: the black-on-black matte pottery of Maria Martinez from San Ildefonso Pueblo, the painted pottery of Lucy Lewis and her family of Acoma Pueblo, the clay storyteller dolls of Helen Cordero of Cochiti Pueblo, and the highly polished pottery jars of Margaret Tafoya and her family of Santa Clara Pueblo.

A visit to the villages of Pueblo Country is most dramatic on feast days and other days set aside for ceremonial dances. Every Pueblo village holds dances for its special feast day—the holiday commemorating the Catholic saint who is its patron. Other dances are also held at special times that can vary from village to village. Not all dances and events are open to the public.

Their ancient religion permeates all aspects of contemporary Pueblo life, but Pueblo festivals often combine traditional Indian rituals with select Christian pageantry. Pueblo ceremonies are very elaborate, and all dances are ceremonial events. Every dance is a prayer, not merely a performance. Prayers for rain, good crops, game animals, good health, and thanksgiving are danced with respectful pageantry, as are the prayers for a bountiful life. The annual cycle of dances

38

include the Eagle, Elk, Buffalo, and Deer dances, and the dignified Corn and Basket dances, which seek to promote fertility and abundance.

Nambe Pueblo, a Tewa pueblo of more than 19,000 acres just 22 miles north of Santa Fe, New Mexico, is the site of one of these feast day festivals. The traditional core of Nambe Pueblo is well maintained and has flourished here since A.D. 1300. Striking terrain of mountains, lakes, and waterfalls draw many visitors to this high-country location beautifully juxtaposed beneath the snow-capped peaks of the Sangre de Cristo Mountains.

As with the O'odham, early October brings many folks here for the honoring of Saint Francis of Assisi on his feast day. Storytelling, ritual arts, crafts, and foods highlight enduring traditions while embracing modern needs. Nambe is noted for its great trout fishing sites and its delicious Pueblo cuisine.

Laguna Pueblo, adjacent to Acoma and 46 miles west of Albuquerque, is also rich in natural resources and Native traditions, both of which are celebrated on feast days. Keres People settled six small villages along the Rio San Jose Valley in the 1600s, and, like other Indian villages converted to Catholicism, each community observes the feast day of its own patron saint. Mid-October brings celebrants to Paraje Village, strikingly offset by mesas and mountains, for the fiestas and dances that honor Saint Margaret. Here, too, ancient Pueblo foods are a great part of the blessings shared.

## Song of the Sky Loom

*O our Mother the Earth, O our Father the Sky,*
*Your children are we, and with tired backs*
*We bring you gifts you love.*
*Then weave for us a garment of brightness;*
*May the warp be the white light of morning,*
*May the weft be the red light of evening,*
*May the fringes be the falling rain,*

*May the border be the standing rainbow.*
*Thus weave for us a garment of brightness,*
*That we may walk fittingly where the birds sing,*
*That we may walk fittingly where grass is green,*
*O our Mother the Earth, O our Father the Sky.*

**—Tewa Indian Chant**

Typical Pueblo feast day foods might include a feast-day soup called posole, bean and corn salads, red chili stew, green chili sauce, frybread, Pueblo bread, watermelon and other melons, small fruit pies called *empanaditas,* Pueblo bread pudding, Feast Day cookies, and Pine Nut Cookies. Menus vary from Pueblo to Pueblo and with each season.

# PUEBLO POSOLE (FEAST DAY SOUP)

Posolli *is the Nahuatl term for an ancient Mayan corn drink first encountered and recorded by Francisco Hernandez de Cordoba in 1517 near the island of Cozumel. Like its similar cousin,* atolli, *this early ceremonial corn beverage has endured through considerable time and trading. Now called posole and atole when prepared in the form of a soup, these dishes continue to evolve from family to family and clan to clan. Commonly served on feast days, each posole has a unique personality. Some cooks like to roast the corn kernels in the drying process, some do not. Some like a sweeter posole with honey and chocolate, others prefer chilies and meat. This one is a meat-based recipe, hearty enough for a main dish. (See the Source Directory for where to obtain posole.)*

**3 cups posole (dried corn)**

**8 cups of water**

**1 ¹/₂ pounds lean beef or pork ribs, trimmed of all fat**

**4 red chilies, roasted and finely chopped**

**2 teaspoons salt**

**1 medium onion, coarsely chopped**

**2 cloves garlic, finely minced**

**2 tablespoons fresh epazote or oregano, chopped**

Cook posole in a large, heavy kettle, in 8 cups water, over medium heat, until kernels pop, about 30 to 45 minutes. Add the raw meat and roasted chilis and half of the salt, and continue to cook, covered, about 2 hours, until the meat is tender. Add remaining ingredients and simmer for 20 minutes. Serve hot.

**Serves 8**

*Epazote,* Chenopodium ambrosioides, *is an exceedingly common and complementary seasoning in Mexican cuisine. Sometimes called "lamb's quarters," "Mexican basil," or "Mexican oregano," this versatile green is enjoyed like spinach and is especially compatible with beans. As a digestive aid, epazote is believed to reduce gas and bloating.*

# Pueblo Festival Bean Salad

*Beans and peppers, like their "sister" corn, are ancient foods in the Native American world, and like much else, they continue to undergo cultivation, experimentation, and delicious transformations. Beans and corn are also very compatible protein complements, so you rarely find them far apart in Indian preparations. At every celebration they are staples, nurturing those who gather to share the harvests.*

**2 cups cooked pinto beans**

**2 cups cooked black turtle beans**

**2 cups cooked green beans**

**2 large onions, very thinly sliced**

**1 large green bell pepper, thinly sliced**

**1 large red bell pepper, thinly sliced**

**3 cloves garlic, finely diced**

**1/2 cup honey or sugar**

**1/2 cup cider vinegar**

**2 teaspoons red chili, finely ground**

**1 teaspoon salt**

**1/2 cup epazote or oregano, finely chopped**

**1/2 cup oil**

Combine first 6 ingredients in a large bowl. Combine all other ingredients except the oil in a smaller bowl; blend well. Stir the oil into the small bowl, blending thoroughly, then pour this dressing evenly over the bean mixture. Toss this salad to blend well. To mingle the flavors, cover and refrigerate for 2 hours or more before serving.

**Serves 8 to 10**

# Narragansett Harvest Festival
# and Ceremony of Thanksgiving     Late October

Ceremonies and feasting are common in the Indian Northeast, especially as family groups return to their traditional homelands at important ceremonial times throughout the year. Communal festivals and feasts reinforce the ties between people, clans, and communities. The noted Mohegan minister Samson Occum writing on the Montauk Indians of Long Island in 1809 observed that they "make great preparations for these dances, of wampum, beads, jewels, dishes, and clothing. Sometimes two or three families join in naming their children. They will call their neighbors together, very often send to other towns of Indians . . . they will begin their dance and to distribute their gifts."

The Narragansetts, "People of the Bay or Point," were also known as Bay Indians. Strong Algonquian leaders throughout early New England history, they lived in stockaded villages and were allies of the Wampanoags and Nipmucs, as well as early allies of the English. Today, about 3,000 federally recognized Narragansetts are centered on and around their 1,800-acre reservation in southern Rhode Island, due north of Block Island. Noted for various prehistoric and valuable historic sites, their land is also dotted with wildlife refuges, swamps, ponds, and streams through rolling lowlands of mixed hardwoods and evergreens.

Narragansett People associate the tall spruce trees throughout their verdant regions with the blood and souls of their ancestors. These enduring sentinels give cool reassurance that the old ways are guarded, ever-present, and strengthening. Princess Red Wing, noted storyteller, historian, and former editor of the newsletter *Narragansett Dawn,* recalled, in 1936, that occasionally a spruce tree had been known to fall upon someone planning harm to their environment.

This deep Native attachment to homelands is echoed through much of recorded history. Narragansett Samuel Rodman, writing in 1880, caught this essence when he said, "and, not withstanding the deprivations under which we labor, we are attached to our homes. It is the birthplace of our mothers. It is the last gift of our fathers; and there rest the bones of our ancestors . . . We do not wish to leave it."

Ella W.I. Sekatau, Narragansett Medicine Woman, artist, teacher, and ethnohistorian, remembers that during her youth, she and other Narragansett children enjoyed picking and chewing on the green needles of spruce, white pine, and fir trees during their walks to and from school in Rhode Island, and they delighted in the tart-sour tastes that their Elders had said was good for them. Now we know that these needles contain high levels of vitamin C, as well as trace minerals. Fabulous "wilderness teas" are also routinely made from small, select needle bundles and branch tips steeped in hot water. The circle of the People continues.

Traditions are important, enriching our daily lives as well our festivals and helping to weave us all together. The Narragansett Harvest Festival in October is a religious celebration that marks one of the Narragansetts' periodic cycles of giving thanks. Ella Sekatau recalls, "Traditionally the October Thanksgiving meal took place after the hunting parties had brought in fresh meat, and the fruit, vegetables, and fish were dried and stored for the winter. At all these festivals the Indians expressed thanksgiving to the Great Spirit and the Earth Mother." Every twenty-eight days or so, throughout the year, the Narragansetts have a Thanksgiving Harvest Festival, according to Ella, "as our people have been doing this for hundreds, perhaps thousands of years." The Narragansett also make feasts that they call *Nickommo,* Giveaway Festivals, where they give gifts of foods and goods, in order to maintain a web of mutual trust, equality, and shared responsibility.

Menus for these events can include turkey, venison, seal, duck, rabbit, raccoon, squashes, sweet potatoes, sunchokes, corn, beans, wild rice, cranberries, oysters, and much, much more. Narragansett women are talented in many ways, especially with their foods. Ella shares two of her classic recipes here.

# JOHNNYCAKES

*These delicious griddle cakes have evolved through centuries of creation. Regional and seasonal additions change their personalities even further. First known as ash cakes, they were wrapped in cornhusks or grape leaves and baked in ashes at the edges of campfires. In some regions they were called "journeycakes" because of their value as foods. They are also known regionally as hoecakes, yokegs, or nocakes. Ella's excellent variation below can be enjoyed as is or easily adapted. Depending upon season, ingredients, and menu, you might want to substitute 1 cup of clams or quahogs and their juice for the syrup and cream. These are also great with fresh fruits added, such as cranberries, blueberries, or strawberries. This is a versatile batter for the creative cook.*

**1 cup white stone-ground cornmeal**
**1/2 teaspoon salt**
**2 tablespoons maple syrup**
**1 cup boiling water**
**1/2 cup medium cream or half-and-half**
**corn oil or butter for frying**

Mix together the first three ingredients in a medium bowl. Add the boiling water, and blend well. Thin batter with cream, but make certain it is thick and not runny.

Drop batter by tablespoonfuls onto a medium-hot, well-greased griddle or skillet. Allow to fry for 6 minutes. Turn johnnycakes over and fry on other side for 5 minutes longer.

**Makes 8 to 10 large johnnycakes**

45

# Oyster-Stuffed Acorn Squash

*Inspired by Narragansett traditions, the recipe below takes its strength from the generosity of both bay and garden. Together they make a delicious main dish or elegant side dish, paying respect to the many unique Native American coastal harvest traditions. The various tastes of autumn are gathered together in this composition.*

**4 acorn or 2 butternut or 1 blue hubbard squash**
**2 tablespoons of corn oil**
**Oyster-Sunchoke Stuffing**

Clean outside of squash. Slice in half and trim to make level. Scoop out seeds (save for roasting). Rub or brush cut sections with oil, inside and out. Place in oiled baking dish, skin side down. Stuff generously so stuffing mounds up. Bake 30 to 35 minutes at 350°.

## OYSTER-SUNCHOKE STUFFING

*Two native ingredients—oysters and sunchokes—are paired here as great "surf 'n turf" comrades, uniquely balanced here with seasonal fruits. Try your own variations to explore new tastes.*

**1/4 cup light sunflower seed or corn oil**
**1 pound chorizo, venison sausage, or other sausage, diced**
**4 medium onions, diced**
**1 pound sunchokes, diced**
**2 batches johnnycakes, crumbled, or 5 cups corn bread, crumbled, or wild rice**
**1 cup cranberries, coarsely chopped**
**1 cup raisins**

**1 pint oysters with liquid**

**1/4 teaspoon each of sea salt, pepper, sage, dill, parsley**

Heat oil in a large heavy skillet over medium heat. Add sausage, then onions, and cook for about 5 to 8 minutes, stirring often to cook evenly. Add sunchokes, blending thoroughly, and cook for another 3 to 5 minutes. Add remaining ingredients, stirring and blending well. Remove from heat. Balance seasonings.

This will also stuff a large 18- to 20-pound turkey or three brace of pheasant. You can also serve it in a generous baking dish or use it to stuff choice acorn, butternut, or blue Hubbard squashes.

**Makes about 14 cups**

*This Narragansett Indian prayer of Thanksgiving eloquently interweaves the Narragansett worldview with appreciation of all living things. Its very timelessness speaks to us as it carries us forward into the future.*

*We walked here once, Grandfather.*
*These trees, ponds, these springs and streams,*
*and that big flat rock across the water over there.*
*We used to meet with you over there,*
*Remember, Grandfather? And we would*
*dream, dance, and sing, and*
*after a while, make offerings.*
*Then we would sing the traveling song*
*and would go our ways, and*
*sometimes we would see your signs*
*on the way to our lodges.*

*But something happened, Grandfather.*
*We lost our way somewhere, and*
*everything is going away.*
*The four-legged, the trees, springs, and streams,*
*even the big water, where the laughing*
*whitefish goes, and the big sky of many eagles*
*are saying good-bye.*
*Come back, Grandfather, come back!*

*Thank you, oh, Great Spirit, for all*
*the things that Mother Earth gives!*

47

# CRANBERRY DAY FESTIVAL     SECOND TUESDAY IN OCTOBER

One of the biggest economic success stories of the botanical Americas is our lowly cranberry, denizen of acid bogs and marshes. A small, creeping evergreen shrub of the heath family, cranberry, *Vaccinium macrocarpon,* has more than 100 known varieties, five of which have commercial value. The shrub's slender vines produce dense clusters of pink flowers in spring, and the ripe, shiny red cranberries are harvested after Labor Day and through October.

Algonquian medicine people knew the healing virtue of cranberries and used them for numerous internal and external treatments. Wampanoag and Lenni Lenape (Delaware) Indians called them *ibimi,* meaning "bitter or sour berries." Another eastern Algonquian term for them was *sassamanesh,* and the Algonquian Indians of Wisconsin called them *atoqua.* The Leni Lenape chief Pakimintzen served cranberries at tribal feasts to symbolize peace, and his name soon became synonymous with cranberry feasts. The early Native American high-energy food concentrate called pemmican was made by pounding cranberries into a mixture of dried, smoked game meat, animal fat, and seeds.

Contemporary cranberry growers have turned a formerly seasonal business into a thriving $750 million-plus, year-round industry in five states (Massachusetts, New Jersey, Wisconsin, Oregon, and Washington), where most of the world's supply of cranberries are grown on less than 30,000 acres. Another 4,000 acres are cultivated in British Columbia and in parts of Quebec, Nova Scotia, Ontario, and New Brunswick. Today, Americans consume 340 million pounds of cranberries each year.

For more than 100 years, the second Tuesday in October has been a tribal holiday for the Wampanoag Tribe of Gay Head, Aquinnah, on Martha's Vineyard. Wampanoag families gather to picnic and pick cranberries in the wild cranberry bogs near the colorful Gay Head Cliffs and Herring Creek.

The Wampanoag "People of the Dawn" are coastal Algonquians who were noted fishermen, whalers, hunter-gatherers, village farmers, and warriors. They fought for and formed strong alliances throughout the Colonial period when wars, diseases, and displacement seriously reduced their numbers. Federally recognized in 1987, the Gay Head Wampanoag Tribal Headquarters is now on Martha's Vineyard, and the Mashpee Wampanoag Tribal Headquarters is in Mashpee on Cape Cod. A traditional sense of enterprise and self-sufficiency shapes the Wampanoag future, and Cranberry Day is an important time of reflection, sharing, and appreciation of the annual harvests.

Very high in vitamin C, cranberries can be enjoyed raw, like tart candies, but they are most often included in recipes to add colorful nourishment to every course. What great value and diversity the Wampanoags have created in their cranberry dishes!

# Wampanoag Cape Cod Cranberry Pie

*Delicious, tart, colorful cranberries enliven so many seasonal foods. This is a Wampanoag fall harvest favorite, yet it is equally fabulous any time of the year.*

**3 cups fresh cranberries**

**2 tablespoons flour or fine cornmeal**

**1 cup sugar**

**1 cup maple syrup**

**1/4 teaspoon salt (optional)**

**1/2 cup boiling water**

**1 cup dark currants or raisins**

**3 tablespoons freshly grated orange peel and zest**

**2 tablespoons butter**

**pastry for a two-crust pie**

Combine the first 8 ingredients in a medium saucepan and cook over medium heat, stirring thoroughly while you bring the mixture to a boil. Lower the heat to simmer, cover, and cook until the cranberries start to pop, about 5 minutes. Remove from the heat, and stir in the butter. Set mixture aside to cool slightly.

Preheat oven to 425°. Use your favorite pastry recipe to make pie crust. Place bottom crust into 9-inch pie plate. Pour cranberry filling into the pie plate. Slice remaining dough into long, thin strips, and arrange a latticework of pastry strips on top of filling in a basket-weave manner. Crimp and flute the pastry edges.

Bake pie for 40 to 55 minutes until crust is just golden and juice is bubbling. Cool slightly on a wire rack. Serve hot or chilled, with your favorite topping.

**Makes one 9-inch pie**

# Autumn Bluefish Harvest Throughout October

Many native fishermen in the Northeast enjoy the seasonal "runs" of their favorite saltwater fish and shellfish. The Wampanoag, as well as the Shinnecock, Montauk, Mohegan, Pequot, and Narragansett, were also noted whalers, as immortalized by the characters of Tashtego and the Gay Head harpooners in Herman Melville's classic, *Moby Dick.* Fast-swimming predators with razor-sharp teeth, bluefish, *Pomatomus saltatrix,* travel the East Coast in great schools, following their choice prey—menhaden *(Brevoortia tyrannus).* The intensity of their feeding frenzies on these herring often bring them almost up onto the beaches of New England and its eastern islands in late summer and autumn. Blues are certainly great eating, and they are prized by anglers on sports fishing outings. Native fishermen also have long sought and prized this rich, oily fish, whose steaks and fillets are found at Native American festivals, powwows, socials, and gatherings throughout the East. Almost as many recipes and types of preparation exist for bluefish as exist Native cooks. Grilled, smoked, blackened Creole-style, pickled, smothered with wild mushrooms or with beans and rice, bluefish is served with imagination, always!

51

# GRILLED SMOKED BLUEFISH WITH CRANBERRY-DILL SAUCE

*Oily, rich bluefish needs the acidic companionship of fresh, tart cranberries to help balance flavoring and the earthy essence of pungent dill weed to aid digestion. When the blues are running off the Atlantic coast, this meaty fish can become a daily staple on your menu. Bluefish fillets are the most choice selections, and they are great simply broiled, baked, grilled, smoked, or panfried. Do not overcook blues.*

**3 pounds bluefish fillets, with skin on**
**freshly cracked peppercorns and sea salt to taste**
**1 large fresh lemon**

Stretch bluefish fillets out on a clean plank or platter. For maximum flavor, it is best not to wash the fillets; rather, pat them dry with thick paper towels. Season sparingly with the salt and pepper, then squeeze fresh lemon juice liberally over all.

Build a good fire in a barbecue grill or campfire pit. Place several large handfuls of apple wood chips or hickory bark chips in a large pan, spray generously with water. When the fire is just right and the coals are set, evenly spread the damp chips over the hot coals.

Lightly oil the grilling rack, and set it about 5 inches above the coals. Place the bluefish fillets, skin up, on the grill rack, and cover the grill, making sure it has open vents. Cook fillets for 10 to 20 minutes, estimating about 10 minutes cooking time per inch of thickness of fish at its thickest part. Remove to a hot platter when the meat begins to look opaque. Serve immediately with the following sauce and extra fresh or dried dill weed. Save an ounce or two of the well-cooked end pieces for the smoked fish pâté on page 54.

**Serves 8**

# CRANBERRY-DILL SAUCE

*This light sauce of unique complementary ingredients is a delicious aid to digestion and a wonderful companion to game and fish recipes. There seems to be a special alchemy here that does not overwhelm the unique flavors of the meat or fish upon which you use it.*

**1 cup fresh cranberries**

**1/4 cup red onion, coarsely chopped**

**1/2 cup green sweet pepper, coarsely chopped**

**1/4 cup maple syrup**

**1 teaspoon ginger, freshly grated or ground**

**pinch of sea salt to taste**

**2 tablespoons fresh or 1 1/2 tablespoons dried dill weed**

Combine all but the dill weed in a medium saucepan over medium-low heat. Cook, stirring to blend thoroughly, until cranberries begin to pop, about 10 to 15 minutes.

Add the dill weed, stir thoroughly, and remove from heat. Serve hot or cold. Flavors improve after this sauce sits for a day, covered and refrigerated. Great with grilled bluefish, venison, turkey, and much more.

Variations: A cup of this basic sauce can be added to diced green peppers and cilantro to make a salsa, or you can purée a cup of sauce, then cook it over medium heat until thick to make an excellent cranberry catsup. **Makes 2 cups**

# HICKORY-SMOKED BLUEFISH PÂTÉ

*This is a grand way to use and s-t-r-e-t-c-h small bits of a previously memorable meal, especially tidbits of smoked fish, pheasant or game, or smoked mushrooms. Many foods can be enhanced by "smoking." Simply add them to your grill or smoker while it is at work on a large preparation. Mushrooms, trimmed squash, or pumpkin pieces placed on the edges of a grill near fish or game pieces already being grilled or smoked are a delicious addition to any meal.*

**1 cup smoked trout, trimmed and flaked**
**1 tablespoon fresh lemon or lime juice**
**8 ounces cream cheese (or Neufchâtel), at room temperature**
**2 ounces butter, at room temperature**
**2 teaspoons grated horseradish**
**1 teaspoon fresh dill seed, crushed**
**1 teaspoon fresh dill weed, finely chopped**
**2 ounces scallions or wild onions, finely diced**
**salt and pepper to taste**

In a broad, medium bowl, using the tines of a sturdy work fork, mash the smoked trout. One by one, add each of the ingredients as listed, mashing and thoroughly blending together. Balance tastes and seasonings, but aim to store this for a day or two since it will taste better after the ingredients have mingled together.

Turn the mixture into a glass or pottery ramekin or serving bowl. Cover with tight-fitting plastic wrap or a lid. Refrigerate for 2 hours or overnight.

To serve, place the ramekin or serving dish of trout pâté on a large platter or in a shallow basket. Surround with mushroom chips and corn chips and trim with fresh watercress or cilantro. Place a small pâté knife beside the platter and invite your guests to share a "woods and stream" delight.
**Makes about 2 1/2 cups**

## October "Berries"

*In October, American barberry,* Berberis canadensis, *yields delicious red berries to be selectively harvested for use in juice, jams, jellies, and breads. Its small deciduous leaves can be collected now for kinnikinniks (smoking mixtures and incense), as can be select pieces of its outer roots, highly esteemed to reduce fevers and help check diarrhea.*

*Bayberry,* Myrica pensylvanica, *leaves (also deciduous and about to fall) are used extensively for seasonings, both fresh and dried. Quite similar to bay laurel, its relative of the Mediterranean region, bayberry leaf also provides bracing, restorative teas, and bayberry root bark can be poulticed to treat external inflammations. Though bayberry wax is toxic, it is useful in candles and other home products.*

*Bearberry,* Arctostaphylos uva-ursi, *is a diminutive, trailing, evergreen shrub, native to the Northeast and also ripe for harvesting in October. Bearberry has always been a sacred plant to many Eastern Woodland Indians, who prized these botanicals in ceremonial use and for foods, beverages, and medicines. Selected interior leaves and ripe, red berries are collected throughout fall and winter and used in cleansing, restorative teas, foods, and kinnikinniks.*

*The bearberry derivative known as "uva-ursi" has become a multimillion-dollar health food product valuable in treating kidney and bladder infections and complaints. Increasingly rare in much of its natural range due to overharvesting and other environmental pressures, bearberry is now on the protected species list in many eastern states. Numerous drug companies, especially European ones, cultivate this valuable herb, as they do many other Native American botanicals.*

Several generations ago the last Big House Ceremony ended, yet for many centuries including the twentieth, the Lenape (which means "the People") drew their people together in October for this annual twelve-night ceremony of renewal. Called the Delaware Indians by early Europeans, the Lenape were considered the "grandfather" tribe among many Eastern Indians, and they served to settle disputes and help keep the peace among rival tribes. Their original homelands were the regions that became New Jersey, southeastern New York, eastern Pennsylvania, Delaware, and parts of western Connecticut. Colonial settlement pressures, conflicts, and disease forced many Delaware to leave these homelands during several centuries of migration. As the tribe fragmented, the Christian Delaware were led west by Charles Journeycake. Many traditional Delaware also migrated west, and they actively continued to follow their Big House Religion.

Keepers of the Big House built their last log frame house in a remote location near the Caney River, west of Copan, Oklahoma The great lodge had its end doors opening east and west, and each doorpost was carved with the great Mesingw, or "Masked Being," the guardian spirit of the game animals. Twelve great Mesingw faces carved of hard burr oak adorned twelve vital positions within the Big House, especially its massive center post. Each face was painted half red and half black to symbolize duality, representing day and night, male and female, east and west, good and bad.

Ceremonial rites included cedar smudging for purification and a deer hunt before the sacred feast. People came to share their visions, pray, drum and dance, and sing the sacred songs. Families camped around the building, and this unique homecoming provided spiritual enlightenment to everyone attending. The last ceremony ended in 1924. Today's Delaware descendants live mainly in Oklahoma and in Ontario, Canada, though many remain in New Jersey and Pennsylvania. Many Delaware descendants continue to honor and follow their traditions, creatively working them into their modern lives.

October harvests and game hunts recall many earlier lifeways and continue to inspire nourishing foods from ancient origins. The autumn ruts of the white-tailed deer, *Odocoileus virginianus*, draw hunters into the meadows and woodlands today as they have for many centuries. The early deer trade among native tribes and settlers forged serious economic alliance and forced many conflicts during Colonial times. Today successful ranching opportunities have filled the increased demand for venison in the exploding gourmet and restaurant fields. Now abundant to the point of nuisance in some areas, sometimes, it seems, the deer supply is driving the demand.

# BLACK LAVA VENISON SOUP

*This spicy autumn medley blends, darkly, some common favorites: black turtle beans,* Phaseolus vulgaris, *var., venison, and black and purple peppers,* Capsicum annuum, *var. Delicious with hot frybread or corn bread and pumpkin butter and roasted pumpkin seeds, this soup may prove too hot for some palates. Serve a side dish of chilled sour cream or yogurt to cool things down.*

**1/2 cup corn oil**
**1 pound chorizo sausage, chopped into bite-size pieces**
**1 pound venison back roast, chopped into bite-size pieces**
**1 teaspoon salt, divided**
**2 medium onions, chopped**
**4 cloves garlic, roasted and chopped**
**1 tablespoon celery seeds**
**6 cups water**
**2 cups of black turtle beans, cooked**

2 cups tomatoes, cooked and chopped

2 bay leaves

any combination of the following:

1 small Negro or Ancho or pasilla pepper, roasted and chopped

2 medium Poblano or Mulato peppers, roasted and chopped

1 small jalapeño pepper, roasted and chopped

2 tablespoons ground cumin

1 tablespoon chili powder, roasted

1/2 tablespoon freshly ground pepper

2 tablespoons epazote or oregano, chopped

Heat the oil in a large skillet over medium-high flame, and add the chorizo, cooking and stirring quickly to sear in the juices. Spoon the chorizo over to one edge of the skillet, and add the venison bits, stirring and cooking quickly. Add half of the salt to the cooking meat, stir well, and spoon to one side. Add onions, garlic, and celery seeds. Cook thoroughly, stirring well. Cover and rest this while you prepare the next part.

In a deep soup pot, place the water, beans, tomatoes, and bay leaves, and cook over medium heat, moderating it to a slow, bubbling boil for 20 minutes, covered. Stir occasionally.

Add the hot meat mixture to the vegetable and bean pot, stirring thoroughly. Add all the remaining ingredients, blending carefully, and simmer for 15 minutes. Serve hot with additional hot sauce, cold sour cream, spicy popcorn, or favorite salsas and breads.

This soup is even better made in the morning and served in the evening, as the flavors mingle and develop a wonderful fragrance. The "hot lava" look of this soup is wonderfully enhanced by surrounding it with bright bowls of diced, colorful bell peppers, red onion, diced celery, and whole, fresh cranberries that can be used as garnishes.

**Serves about 10**

# Native Blue Crab Cakes

*Native crabs in Atlantic coastal waters have long provided mineral-rich foods for countless Indian tribes, who made coastal migrations for these fine periodic harvests. The blue crab,* Callinectes sapidus, *and the ghost crab,* Ocypode quadrata, *are choice for this recipe. Also, the eastern crayfish,* Cambarus bartonii, *denizen of clear freshwater streams year-round, is the finest inland alternative. Inspired from eastern Algonquian Indian foodways, this dish is especially appealing when accompanied with lots of spicy Chimichuri Sauce (page 60), a special gift from Central and South America.*

1/2 cup sunflower seed oil or peanut oil

1/2 cup onion, finely chopped

1/2 cup parsley, finely chopped

1/4 cup fine yellow cornmeal

6 cups flaked crabmeat (crayfish, clams, lobsters, or oysters may be substituted, if desired)

1/4 cup fresh lemon juice

1/2 teaspoon salt (optional)

1/2 teaspoon paprika

1/4 teaspoon white pepper

1/4 cup dill weed, finely chopped

1 cup celery, finely diced

1/2 cup red sweet pepper, roasted and finely chopped

1/4 cup scallions or wild onions finely diced (use greens and white parts)

1/2 cup chicken stock

6 eggs, well-beaten

1 cup corn oil, for frying

1 cup fine cornmeal

Heat the sunflower seed or peanut oil in a medium cast- iron skillet over medium heat, then quickly sauté the onion in the hot oil, stirring often. Add parsley and stir well. Add the 1/4 cup of yellow cornmeal, stirring continually and cooking for 5 minutes. Remove from heat and cool.

In a large bowl, combine the crabmeat, lemon juice, salt, paprika, white pepper, dill weed, celery, pepper, scallions, chicken stock, and eggs. Blend these ingredients thoroughly, cover, and chill for 3 hours.

Heat the corn oil in a large skillet over medium-high heat until hot. Shape the crabmeat mixture into 16 well-proportioned cakes about 3 inches in diameter and about 1 inch thick. Dust each side lightly with the remaining 1 cup of fine cornmeal, and ease the cakes one at a time, without crowding, into the hot oil. Quickly brown them on both sides, cooking for a total of about 15 minutes. Serve hot, garnished with additional green onions (scallions), watercress, dill, and lots of Chimichuri Sauce below.

**Makes 16 cakes**

# CHIMICHURI SAUCE

*I first encountered this spicy, delicious seasoning in San Pedro Sula, Honduras, where it accompanies many fine fish and poultry dishes. It is practically the national sauce of Argentina. Here in the United States, it resonates with its ancient Mediterranean and Hispanic origins while enhancing many of our dishes with its healthful, peppery flavor. Cilantro, the delicate, aromatic leaves of fresh coriander, provides its special essence, along with parsley and generous amounts of onion and garlic.*

**1/2 cup fresh cilantro, minced**
**1/2 cup fresh parsley, minced**

**1/2 cup onion, finely minced**

**1/2 cup roasted minced garlic**

**1 1/2 teaspoons oregano, finely minced**

**1 teaspoon ground cayenne pepper**

**1/2 teaspoon freshly cracked black peppercorns**

**1/2 teaspoon salt**

**1/4 cup balsamic vinegar**

**1/4 cup red wine vinegar**

**1/2 cup light olive oil, or more, to taste**

In a medium glass or ceramic bowl, combine all ingredients, blending thoroughly and adding additional olive oil, if needed. Taste the mixture and balance the seasonings, then cover and refrigerate for 2 hours or overnight. Serve cold or at room temperature. May be puréed for a finer sauce or prepared more coarsely for a salsa-like presentation. The additions of 1/2 cup roasted pine nuts and 1/2 cup grated Parmesan cheese brings this to the general nature of a cilantro pesto. This concoction should be peppery–spicy!

**Makes about 2 1/2 cups**

# November

*Frosty mornings edged with snow and ice expose bare wooded hillsides and mountains sculpted by time. The bones of the earth begin to show again. The ground freezes, thaws, and freezes again, and heaves with ice pockets and fat overwintering grubs. In the north, growing seasons are ending, except for the resilient wild onions and a few other rugged perennials. Favorable, golden days of Indian Summer allow brief respite, but the urgency of gathering additional harvests stretches our creative energies as we smoke, dry, cook, freeze, put by, and hunt for more food. Autumn constellations dance overhead through the lengthening nights. The time is ripe for storytelling.*

*This period is called White Frost on the Ground Moon of the Agawam, Wampanoag, Narragansett, and the Plains Cree; the Freezing River Moon of the Micmac and Penobscot of Maine and the Mandan and Hidatsa of the Great Plains; Moon When The Deer Shed Their Antlers of the Omaha; Beaver Moon of the Blackfoot; Little Beaver Moon of the Winnebago: Rain Moon of the Chumash: Taboo Moon of the Tsimshian; Gathering-In Moon of the Tewa Pueblo; Geese Fly Away Moon of the Kiowa; and Water Is Dark with Leaves Moon of the Creek.*

*This moon cycle marks many tribal observations and natural occurrences governing timeless traditions in an ever-changing world. These are days of remembering, cooking and celebrating, as we gather our families and friends together for thanksgiving.*

ENDURING
HARVESTS

One of Mexico's most important festivals since pre-Hispanic times, Los Días de Los Muertos (Days of the Dead) are occasions for drawing all levels of society together into shared experiences of death and rebirth. In celebrating death, the ancient Aztecs made continued life possible.

The Aztecs believed that when a person died the soul went to one of thirteen heavens or nine underworlds. *Mictlantec-uhtli,* the Aztec god of death, would be rejoicing, since death was not negative or frightening but simply a step to another stage of life in an eternal cycle. This ancient Aztec belief has evolved today into ceremonies full of nostalgia, gentleness, and loveliness. As their Aztec, Zapotec, or Mixtec ancestors had been accustomed to doing for centuries, contemporary Indians and Mexicans generously share their best offerings with their dead.

This festival is a distinctive blending of pre-Hispanic beliefs and practices with the Spanish Roman Catholic observation of All Saints' Day on November 1 and All Souls' Day on November 2. Though every city and Pueblo in Mexico celebrates, different regions have evolved their own unique customs and traditions, as the dead's annual homecoming takes on special flair and involves almost everybody.

Coincidental with the rituals of the ancient Aztec corn harvests, this is one of the happiest times of the Native American year and also one of the most prosperous times for the artisans who fashion the unique breads, candies, foods, and sculptures for this major festival. Urban stalls in the town plaza, or *zocalo,* and rural markets are filled with gaily decorated skulls and bones, miniature coffins and tombstones made of marzipan (a sugar-almond paste), amaranth seed skulls with peanut incisors, and *pan de los muertos* (bread of the dead), which are made only at this time of the year. Vendors also display enormous varieties of miniature skeletons of cardboard, wood, paper, and papier-mâché; some have tinfoil eyes and gold grins, some are serape-clad dancers, musicians, or gamblers in hilarious postures.

Mexican women clean their houses, make candles, purchase special sweet treats, and prepare quantities of tortillas, chicken, mole, verdolagas, atole, hot chocolate, and a special bread baked in shapes of twisted bones, round skulls, or little animals. Men and children create beautiful altars on which they place toys, candles, sweet foods, and favorite drinks for their departed loved ones. In Puebla, the fourth largest city in Mexico, tiny shops as well as private homes are lovingly adorned with decorations.

The special foods created for this festival serve many purposes. Families take time to honor and celebrate their dead, and also to mock death itself, and as they later share and eat the choice foods, they symbolically consume death. Together, the sweets and toys shaped like bones and skeletons serve to portray Death as an amusing, mischievous, and friendly figure.

At midnight, the people leave their homes carrying candles, precious food items, drinks, and sometimes musical instruments, as they make processions to the cemetery to arrange flowers and offerings on the graves of their dead, with whom they spend the long night. They know, when the candle flames flutter, that the souls, or alma (essence), are visiting, and eating the soul of the foods. Afterwards, as the new day dawns, the people return to their homes, after their night spent in communion and prayer, around their temporary altars in the cemetery, and enjoy the day resting, feasting, and reflecting.

Octavio Paz observes in his *Labyrinth of Solitude* that "Life extended into death, and vice versa. Death was not the natural end of life but one phase of a natural cycle. Life, death, and resurrection were stages of a cosmic process which repeated itself continuously." The distinction between life and death was not so absolute as it is to us today in our less mature society. Death has been a most popular subject in Mexican art for centuries, and this holiday is increasingly viewed as a reinforcement of cultural identity. Increasingly sophisticated museum exhibitions are devoted to this idea and to the festival, and almost all Mexican restaurants around the globe celebrate *Los Días de los Muertos* with the special breads and candies associated with the holiday.

# Pan de los Muertos (Bread of the Dead)

*In Oaxaca, the men of Teotitlán del Valle bake a certain kind of bread in great demand just at this time. Baking in constant shifts for three days to fill orders, they make considerable money for their families. In other parts of the country as well, bakers fashion this special bread to look like twisted bones, round skulls, or little animals* (animalitos) *glistening with white icing. These are placed on the beautiful* ofrendas *that are sanctuaries of the spirits and the places for rendezvous between the living and the dead.*

*Recipes differ from region to region, as do the shapes, flavors, and decorations, and* pan de los muertos *can be quite complicated to make. This is a basic version from which your imagination can take flight.*

1/2 cup water

1/2 cup milk

1/2 cup butter or light vegetable oil

1 teaspoon salt

1/2 cup sugar

1/2 cup honey

2 packages dry yeast

5 to 6 cups sifted flour, divided

1/2 teaspoon anise seed

1/2 teaspoon ground allspice

1 teaspoon freshly grated orange peel and zest

4 eggs, well-beaten and light

Heat the water, milk, and butter in a small pan over low heat, just enough to warm them well. Stir in the salt, sugar, and honey and blend well. Cool slightly to a moderate-warm temperature (comfortable to a finger-touch.) Remove from the heat.

Sprinkle the yeast over the top of this warm mixture, and stir it in gently. Set this to rest in a warm place for 15 minutes.

In a large bowl, combine 2 cups of the flour with the anise seed, allspice, and orange peel and zest. Add the warm liquid and beat well by hand or with a mixer. Add the beaten eggs and 1 more cup of flour; beat well. Using a wooden spoon, carefully blend in the remaining 2 to 3 cups of the flour, gradually adding the correct amount to make a soft dough.

Turn the dough out onto a lightly floured breadboard or other clean, lightly floured surface, knead for about 10 minutes. Place the kneaded dough into a greased bowl and cover with a damp towel; rest it in a warm place to rise for about 1 1/2 hours or until doubled in size.

Punch down the risen dough and pinch off varying amounts to begin making various shapes. Fashion several round loaves and place them, well spaced, on a lightly greased baking sheet. Roll and twist some small dough strips to be used as "bones" and festive symbols and designs on the round loaves. When the small designs are made, moisten them and press them as decorations onto the round loaves. Let these finished designs rise again for an hour. Preheat oven to 350°.

When breads have risen, place them on baking sheets in the oven and bake for 40 minutes.

Remove baked bread to cooling rack. You may wish to decorate the *pan de los muertos* with the simple icing on the next page.

**Makes about 6 loaves**

## PAN DE LOS MUERTOS BREAD ICING

**1/2 cup powdered sugar**

**1/2 teaspoon orange or vanilla extract**

**1 to 2 tablespoons milk or water**

**few drops of food coloring, if you like**

Beat all ingredients together until smooth, then drizzle or brush icing over the finished bread.

**Makes 1/2 cup**

### Zest

*The word "zest" certainly personifies the fine qualities that the colorful outer skins of oranges, lemons, limes, grapefruit, and tangerines add to foods. Using a hand grater, scrape only the colored outer portions of citrus skins, as the white inner membranes can be bitter.*

*Use zest sparingly, as the flavors can be intense. Citrus zest, in small quantities, along with small amounts of citrus juices, are excellent for people on restricted diets, adding delicate accents to foods that must be free of salt and vinegar.*

# ATOLE

*Atole, from the original Nahuatl word* atolli, *is a corn-based beverage or soup that has been documented as far back as the sixteenth-century records of the classic Mayan recipes written down by Spanish priests and observers, and it doubtlessly predates that century considerably. Ground much more finely than its cousin posole, atole is processed, like posole, by cooking in water with lime to soften the corn kernels. Called nixtamalization, this process tremendously enhances the nutritive value of corn as a food. Atole is then cooked as a soup, either with honey and cacao and sometimes with fruits or with epazote, beans, and chili. It can also be thinned with more water for a drink. Also, like posole, atole is often "rested" or fermented for two or three days until an agreeable sourness develops, making an even more digestible maize food very much like southern soffkee. In some regions, atole is also made with roasted maize, pine nuts, or seeds such as red amaranth, chia, or pumpkin. A great variety of "new" corn drinks available in health food stores today are based largely upon these ancient, valuable recipes. Atole and the following dish, Pollo en Mole Verde, are both served and enjoyed during Los Días de los Muertos.*

**5 cups warm water (4 cups for boiling)**

**1 cup fine yellow or blue cornmeal**

**1 teaspoon salt**

**pinch of chamisa (cooking ash)**

**1 tablespoon honey**

Dissolve the fine cornmeal in 1 cup of warm water. Bring 4 cups of water to a boil in a medium saucepan over medium-high heat. Gently add the wet cornmeal to the boiling water, stirring briskly as it thickens. Add the salt, chamisa, and honey and stir well, lowering the heat. Simmer for 5 minutes, stirring often.

Serve hot, warm, or cool. If you want a thinner drink, add additional water or milk. This fine corn drink is highly esteemed and is served at most festivals and celebrations, such as Los Días de los Muertos. It is also used as a curative drink for upset stomach.

**Makes about 6 cups**

# Pollo en Mole Verde
## (Chicken in Green Mole)

*Mole, from the Aztec* molli, *meaning combination or mixture, and* mote, *from the Inca word meaning boiled maize mixed and cooked with other foods, is a classic sauce/paste in Indian and Mexican foods. Some moles may have honey and chocolate as ingredients for holiday celebrations. As many different moles exist as there are cooks in Mexico, I would guess, and regional, seasonal ingredients dictate the development of these complex, flavorful sauces. Best eaten and enjoyed the day of preparation, the mole below tops a wonderful chicken mixture. There are seven distinct moles in the state of Oaxaca, each colored (and named) by particular chilies or herbs. This one is green.*

### CHICKEN BASE

**2 tablespoons corn oil**

**2 small onions, coarsely chopped**

**2 cloves garlic, coarsely chopped**

**1 large chicken, cut into serving pieces (about 4 pounds)**

**salt and pepper to taste**

**chicken broth or water to cover**

Heat oil in a medium pan over medium heat; when oil is hot, sauté the onion and garlic for 2 minutes, stirring quickly. Add the chicken and seasonings and cover with broth or water. Bring to a simmer and cover. Simmer for 25 minutes, until chicken is done but not falling apart or too soft. Set aside while you prepare the mole.

### GREEN MOLE

**1/2 cup raw hull-less pumpkin seeds**

**1/2 cup shelled sunflower seeds (raw)**

**1/2 cup sesame seeds**

3 whole allspice

3 peppercorns

3 whole cloves

4 tablespoons sunflower seed oil (lard is used in some areas)

5 Swiss chard leaves, chopped

1 large bunch cilantro, with stems, chopped

1 small bunch flat-leaf parsley, with stems, chopped

1 small bunch purslane plants, chopped

3 garlic cloves, chopped

2 green mild chilies, roasted, seeded, chopped

10 medium tomatillos, chopped

In another large, clean, hot frying pan, over medium heat, quickly roast the pumpkin seeds stirring and tossing constantly, shaking the pan so they do not burn, for about 3 minutes. Pour them into a large mortar and repeat this process with the sunflower and sesame seeds; add them also to the mortar. Grind the roasted seeds fairly fine, then put them into a small bowl and add 1/2 cup of the chicken broth from the cooked chicken; work this into a thick paste. Grind the whole allspice, the peppercorns, and the cloves and add them to this paste, mixing well.

Heat the sunflower seed oil in the large frying pan; add the paste and stir continually for about 5 minutes until it is golden.

Place the fresh chard, cilantro, parsley, and purslane, one bunch at a time, into a food processor, each with 1/2 cup of the chicken broth and purée. Add each of these mixtures, one batch at a time, to the seed paste in the frying pan, blending it well and continuing to cook it over medium heat. Scrape the bottom of the pan to prevent sticking or burning. Repeat this process until the four greens and the remaining raw or roasted ingredients are added to the paste. Cook for about 10 to 15 minutes until the sauce reduces and thickens.

Add the chicken pieces to the mole sauce and continue cooking for another 10 to 15 minutes, stirring occasionally. Serve hot with lots of corn tortillas, hot chocolate, and condiments.

**Serves 8 to 10**

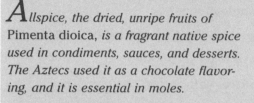

## Aztec Seasonings

*A*llspice, the dried, unripe fruits of Pimenta dioica, *is a fragrant native spice used in condiments, sauces, and desserts. The Aztecs used it as a chocolate flavoring, and it is essential in moles.*

*Aztec Sweet Herb,* Lippia dulcis, *is a small, intense member of the verbena family now being cultivated for its highly concentrated sweetness and its uses both in flavorings and medicines.*

*Aztec Heart Flower,* Magnolia mexicana, *called* yolloxochitl *in Nahuatl, has a fragrant edible flower that is likened to the taste of ripe melons and was used by the Aztecs to flavor chocolate drinks.*

*Yerba Buena,* Satureja douglasii, *is a savory little native mint that has been used for centuries to season foods; it* also relieves heartburn and indigestion.

*Another Aztec food gift, which continues to reach new economic potentials, is the edible freshwater algae,* Spirulina geitleri. *The Aztec dried fresh-gathered spirulina and used it as a condiment for such foods as toasted maize or tortillas.*

*Today we recognize this multimillion dollar health-food product for its pure energy gifts and easy digestibility. Many Native American dancers, drummers, and singers depend upon their spirulina supplements, which can be eaten in powder and tablet form, mixed into milkshakes, or purchased in premade granola or health bars. Not traditionally used in any particular festival dishes, spirulina is nevertheless a perfect food and ever more valuable to relieve the stresses of modern life.*

# Verdolagas

*Purslane,* Portulaca oleracea, *the common, creeping, native annual succulent is the magical essence of this delicious panfried main dish, variations of which you will find from the Southwest to the Northeast. Many folks still call purslane a weed (it does grow in most gardens uninvited), but it is now welcomed for its nutritional properties. We have served this dish at numerous late summer harvest festivals throughout the Southwest, including Los Días de los Muertos. Now that we realize it is high in omega-3 fatty acids and is a favorite healthful herb, it is all the more popular.*

1 tablespoon corn oil

1/2 pound lean pork, boned, cubed, and trimmed of all fat

1 medium onion, chopped

1 clove garlic, chopped

1 medium tomato, chopped

1/2 pound verdolagas (purslane) leaves and branches (stems)

1 medium red mild pepper, roasted and chopped

1/4 teaspoon thyme

1/2 teaspoon salt

pepper to taste

Heat the oil in a large skillet and brown the pork cubes, stirring to cook evenly. Add the onion, garlic, and tomato, one at a time, stirring well. Add the verdolagas and remaining seasonings; stir well, cover, and simmer for 15 to 20 minutes, shaking the pan occasionally and stirring once.

Serve hot, with condiments. Some folks like hot sauce, others like a light vinegar sprinkled over this steaming dish to enhance these great flavors.

**Serves 8 to 10**

After hundreds of years evolving traditions across the broad prairies where they lived in earth-lodges and were skilled farmers, the Pawnee were relocated to Oklahoma in 1876 from the eastern prairie regions of Nebraska. Today about 2,230 Pawnee live on 700-plus acres of tribal lands in north-central Oklahoma, about 50 miles west of Tulsa. Their Pawnee Agency, Tribal Headquarters, and Senior Citizens Center are located in beautiful old buildings of natural pink sandstone block; most were built before 1900 and are listed on the National Register of Historic Landmarks.

Noted artists and craftspeople, as well as leaders, teachers, nurses, dancers, and farmers, their civic sense and generosity are legendary. Famous for their prize-winning drummers and dancers, the Pawnee naturally draw big crowds when they host or attend events. Visitors may notice the Pawnee "Gold Star Mothers," who have lost a son or daughter in the service; only these special individuals may wear gold stars on their dance shawls.

74

Traditional Pawnee foods are served on special occasions like Veterans Day. Blue mush, corn with yellow squash (one of their oldest dishes), pork cubes with whole blue corn in a clear broth, frybread, ground roast pound meat with pecans, a corn and pork soup very much like posole may be among the dishes you can share. Bananas and strawberry shortcake are usually in great supply for desserts. Hours of creative, harmonious energies spent together in the big Pawnee tribal center kitchen mean that this food is prepared with much love and sense of community. It cannot help but be nourishing.

Seasonal fruits and vegetables lead the menu planning. Special preparations are made for Pawnee senior citizens and veterans, who are always served first after the prayers and special remembrances given on each occasion.

A special altar is prepared to one side of the food service tables, and great care and attention are devoted to its planning. Sacred plants of cedar and sweet grass are laid on a fine blanket beside four beautiful blue bowls, each filled with one of the important dried foods: whole kernel corn, cornmeal, squash, and beans. Pawnee baskets filled with colorful dried corn and gourds flank beautiful Pawnee dolls, beadwork, cornwork, jewelry, and more. Prayers amid such generous celebrations of life and loveliness are quite powerful! Giving thanks has great meaning at Pawnee.

# Pawnee Ground Roast Pound Meat with Pecans

*This recipe is inspired by the work of Velma Smith, her daughter June Hamilton, and members of the Pawnee Pocahontas Society. I watched them prepare this and other traditional foods in the huge community house kitchen at Pawnee. The beef replaces the buffalo meat formerly used in this dish. Native pecans,* Carya illinoensis, *complement the preparation, adding to its unique flavor and taste. Baked together in a moderate oven, this is quite a winner.*

**1 (5-pound) lean rump roast**

**salt and pepper to taste**

**1 cup warm water**

**2 pounds shelled pecan halves**

**1/2 cup sugar**

Preheat oven to 350°. Place the roast, lightly seasoned with salt and pepper, in a well-greased roasting pan and roast for 50 to 60 minutes until moderately well done. Remove roast and allow to stand and cool for 30 minutes. Lower the oven to 325°. Cut cooked roast into large chunks, and feed, one by one, through a hand-grinder. Coarsely grind the beef and spread it in another broad roasting pan. Place the first roasting pan over low heat and deglaze the pan juices with 1 cup of warm water, stirring and scraping all the meat residue from the pan sides and bottom to make a broth. Simmer for about 10 minutes while stirring. Pour the broth over the ground meat in the second roasting pan, then sprinkle the meat mixture with the pecan halves. Season overall with sugar, salt, and pepper. Place this pan in the 325° oven and roast for 20 to 25 minutes, stirring once to blend thoroughly. Serve hot and enjoy with other festival foods. This is especially delicious with hot corn and squash.

**Serves 10**

# Oklahoma Corn and Squash Pawnee

*This zesty vegetable side dish is a perfect complement to roast meat and frybread, and it makes a fine fiesta dish. This recipe is also inspired by the work of the talented cooks at Pawnee. A combination of seasonal, colorful peppers may be roasted and added for savory flavor and to turn up the heat, if desired.*

**4 tablespoons butter or corn oil**

**1 large yellow onion, chopped**

**2 medium yellow squash, cubed**

**1 red bell pepper, roasted, seeded, and chopped**

**4 cups whole kernel yellow sweet corn**

**1/2 cup parsley, chopped fine**

**salt and pepper to taste**

**1/2 cup water or chicken stock, if needed**

Warm butter or oil in a large frying pan over medium heat. Quickly sauté the onion for 3 to 5 minutes, stirring to cook evenly. Add the squash and chopped pepper, stirring to blend well, and cook for an additional 5 minutes. Stir occasionally to keep mixture from sticking. Add the corn, the remaining seasonings, and liquid, if needed. Blend thoroughly, lower heat, cover, and cook for 10 to 15 minutes, stirring once or twice. Serve hot and enjoy.

*Note:* Roasted and peeled peppers, are not only more flavorful but much more digestible.

**Serves 10**

## *Indian Veterans*

*Numerous Veterans Day gatherings to give thanks to the American Indian men and women who have served in the military are scheduled each year in November throughout the nation.*

*Military service continues to be a most compelling and honorable career for tens of thousands of Native Americans. Current census figures show that there are 160,000 living American Indian veterans. This represents about ten percent of all living Indians. Because of Indian prowess, pride, and willingness to train and serve in the military, service to one's country has a place of great respect in Native American life. Of the Native soldiers who have served in considerable numbers in both world wars in this century, many have been honored and decorated. Choctaw and Comanche Code Talkers were vital to the Allied success in Europe during World War II, as were the Navajo Code Talkers famous for their successful service in the Pacific. These special communications units worked behind enemy lines, communicating in codes in their Native languages on enemy military maneuvers, winning high praise and providing critical information to our military successes.*

At the Jemez and Tesuque pueblos in New Mexico, the November 12 dances and celebrations of San Diego's Feast Day reflect the fabulous interweaving of traditional religious spiritualities with particular inspirations from the Roman Catholic and Spanish traditions. These mingled traditions are mirrored in both the dances and the foods, which include many of the finest late-harvested vegetables and their complements.

Tesuque Pueblo, just 9 miles north of Santa Fe, is near Painted Cave and Bandelier National Monument. Its name is derived from the Tewa word *tecuge,* which means "Structure at a Narrow Place." Southernmost of the eight northern pueblos, Tesuque is the most conservative of the Tewa Pueblos, and most of their celebrations, such as their annual kachina dances in October, are closed to outsiders. While the San Diego's Feast Day Dances may be open to the public, it is always best to telephone tribal headquarters for details. Usually the Comanche or Animal Dance is performed in the Native cycle of traditions combined with a church service.

78

### Visiting Pueblo Country

*V*isitors are welcome throughout the year in Pueblo country and are encouraged to plan their trips around the many festivals and ceremonies that are open to the public. Call the Indian Pueblo Cultural Center at (505) 843–7270 in Albuquerque, New Mexico, for information and a calendar of events. This fine nonprofit organization has a museum, restaurant, and gift shop at its center and maintains an extensive schedule of Indian dances, festivals, and art exhibits well worth visiting.

Most Pueblos require a permit for the use of cameras or recorders or for sketching and painting on location. Others absolutely prohibit photography and recording at all times. Each Pueblo is home to many different families whose privacy and personal property must be respected. Please remember you are a visitor and show proper respect at all times. Abide by Pueblo laws and wishes.

The Tesuque Pueblo settlements were built near the banks of Rio Tesuque around A.D. 1250, and the tribal lands cover over 17,000 acres. Tesuque has had to struggle to keep enough land and water to support its way of life. Traditionally subsistence farmers, the Tesuque have increased their organic and market farming. As with many Native Americans, land claims, water rights, and economic development are central issues and concerns addressed by their political-religious systems.

Jemez is one of seven pueblos clustered at the base of the San Pedro and Jemez mountains, surrounded by high desert plains bordering the Jemez River. Reservation lands stretch over 89,000 acres, embracing diverse landscapes and sustaining the agriculture of corn and chilies, as well as some local forestry, gravel, sand, and geothermal industries.

Jemez Pueblo traditions say that their ancestors migrated to this beautiful Cañon de San Diego region from the Four Corners area in the late fourteenth century, following their emergence from the underworld at a place called the *Hua-vu-na-tota*. The principal village, Walatowa, meaning "This is the Place," is located in the southern end of the majestic Cañon de San Diego, about 55 miles northwest of Albuquerque and approximately 70 miles southwest of Santa Fe. Jemez Pueblo people are celebrated ceramicists, noted for their beautiful traditional polychrome pottery. They are also weavers of fine yucca baskets. Noted runners as well, they are champions in field and track competitions.

The Animal Dances at Tesuque Pueblo and the Corn Dances at Jemez Pueblo celebrate a giving of thanks in colorful, spiritual dimensions. The Pueblo festivals combine the traditional Native dances with Christian pageantry. The San Diego feast day celebrates the patron saint chosen for each village by Spanish missionaries almost 300 years ago.

For many Native Americans, dance is a language, full of mystery, prayer, natural observations, thanksgiving, special meanings of identity, and much more. As a form of prayer, dance balances the intricate interplay between individual beliefs and community worship. The Jemez and the Tesuque dance in thanksgiving for bountiful harvests and successful hunts, in hopes of curing diseases, and in celebration of the ongoing cycles of life. All of their beliefs are beautifully personified in their fine, colorful dance regalia and accoutrements, and in their pottery, weaving, carvings, jewelry, and foods.

# PUEBLO BLUE CORNMEAL MUSH

*This classic Native dish has been carried through countless centuries unchanged, except for the folks who fix it and the pots they cook it in. The fine or coarsely ground blue cornmeal, which is a major staple of Pueblo and Southwest Indian diets lends itself to numerous tribal recipes for every course. Reina Kohlmeyer of Jemez Pueblo shares this recipe using fine blue cornmeal. We enjoyed this hot delicious mush or soup with Reina and with Drew Lewis of Acoma Pueblo as they taught a fabulous, weeklong Pueblo pottery course. Reina suggests that this dish is fine steaming hot for breakfast (as cereal), for lunch (as soup), for dinner (as a vegetable side dish), or for dessert (as a pudding). It is delicious plain and needs no seasonings.*

*Many people believe that essential corn dishes like this one are healing medicinal foods.*

**3 cups boiling water**

**1 cup fine blue cornmeal**

**pinch of salt (optional)**

**1 tablespoon honey or molasses (optional)**

Bring the water to a boil in a medium saucepan and then reduce to medium heat. Slowly pour the blue cornmeal over the top of the boiling water. Add a pinch of salt and stir well until blended and just bubbling. Lower the heat and simmer for 20 to 30 minutes, stirring often, until the cornmeal is plumped and silky in texture. Stir in a tablespoon of honey or your favorite sweetener, if desired, and serve steaming hot.

**Makes 3 1/2 cups**

# Juniper-Sage Corn Sticks (or Muffins)

*Finely ground cornmeal is enhanced nutritionally by the addition of small amounts of cooking or culinary ash, which increases the mineral and protein complements available for the body to metabolize. Corn foods become healthier and tastier. Cooking ash is a subtle bluing agent in blue cornmeal preparations, especially the Hopi Blue Piki Bread. In this recipe we use juniper,* Juniperus communis, *and sagebrush,* Artemisia tridentata, *as flavoring agents.*

*Both sage and juniper are available at most markets and health food stores. Juniper is also our common Red Cedar growing throughout North America. If you have a resident or neighborhood cedar, you might want to snip off 3 or 4 inches of one branch tip and dry it. Toast or burn the juniper and sage, carefully, in a Pyrex baking dish or on a piece of aluminum foil beneath the broiler. Both the sage and juniper ashes can be omitted if you have difficulty obtaining them. Substitute ground juniper berries or a teaspoon of dried, ground sage.*

1 1/4 cups yellow cornmeal

1 cup all-purpose flour

2 teaspoons baking powder

1 teaspoon juniper ashes, sifted

1 teaspoon sage ashes, sifted

1 tablespoon honey or sugar

1/2 teaspoon salt

1 egg, beaten

3 tablespoons corn oil

1 cup milk

Preheat oven to 425°. Grease cast-iron corn-stick pans, muffin tins, or a 9-inch cast-iron skillet with oil or lard, butter, or bacon drippings. Place pans in the oven to heat. Place all of the dry ingredients in a large bowl.

Beat the wet ingredients into the dry ingredients with a few rapid strokes, blending thoroughly. Remove the heated pans from the oven and spoon the batter into the sizzling pans. Place in the oven and bake for 20 to 25 minutes. Serve hot.

**Makes about a dozen 3-inch muffins or 24 corn sticks**

# Pueblo Green Chili Paste

*Reina Kohlmeyer of Jemez Pueblo suggested this easy, natural version of her green chili paste. New Mexico produces more green chili varieties than any other state, challenging creative cooks to use them to good advantage. Reina prepares enough of this to freeze for future uses. This is excellent as a spread for corn tortillas or corn sticks; it can also be added to meats or vegetables for savory seasoning.*

**1 tablespoon corn oil**

**1 small onion, chopped**

**1 clove garlic, chopped**

**1 pound, about 16 fresh green chilies, roasted, peeled, seeded, and chopped**

**1 teaspoon salt**

**1 teaspoon pepper**

Heat the oil in a medium skillet; when it is hot, quickly cook onion and garlic, stirring and turning until they are translucent and limp, barely 5 minutes. Add the seeded, chopped chilies and seasonings and cook, stirring continually, for another 5 minutes.

Remove from heat and allow to cool. Purée the cooled mixture in a food processor until it is a thick paste. You can moderate the heat of this creation to suit your own tastes by using hotter or milder chili peppers.

**Makes about 3 cups**

Thanksgiving Day, the very American holiday celebrated the last Thursday of each November, conjures thoughts of "the first thanksgiving" in 1621 at Plymouth Colony in coastal Massachusetts, immortalized each year now at Plimoth Plantation. For several days 370 years ago, Indians and Pilgrims gathered to eat together and celebrate their survival, lofty ideals, and fall harvests. Together they shared long tables groaning with seasonal foods. Yet long before this encounter, most cultures had developed seasonal festivals of "giving thanks to the Creator" throughout the year, in the hopes of ensuring an ongoing cycle of bounty. Giving thanks is ancient in Christian and pre-Christian practices, as it has been among all Native American Peoples.

Throughout the seasonal year in the Northeast, Algonquian and Iroquoian People celebrated the periodic harvests, especially after gardening became important in many of their lifeways more than 1,600 years ago. Native People gave thanks at the midwinter ceremonies, the maple-sugaring times, the runs and spawning times of shad, sturgeon, salmon, alewives, and eels in early spring and again later in the natural cycles. The Strawberry Festivals, the Green Bean and the Green Corn Ceremonies, the Cranberry and the Blueberry Festivals, and the great seasonal hunts and harvests of other wild and cultivated foods were perennial points of thanksgiving, often involving rites of purification, prayers, sacrifices, and renewals that could last for days. Along with these more prominent celebrations in the native calendar year were the hunting of seasonal game and the harvesting, gathering, and smoking of abundant shellfish: clams, crabs, lobsters, scallops, oysters, mussels, and much more along our eastern, southern, and western coastal regions.

Today, as we gather to celebrate our modern Thanksgiving, it is important to remember that many of our ancestors celebrated thanksgiving all year long, in many ways, with many different foods, prayers, songs, and ideas. Regardless of what we eat during our contemporary Thanksgiving meals, some part of the tradition, if not most of it, was first celebrated by Native Americans.

The opulence of autumn harvests is demonstrated most often in modern America on Thanksgiving Day which was a purely regional holiday until George Washington's proclamation set Thursday, November 26, 1789, as the first national Thanksgiving holiday for our young nation. Subsequently, distractions with regional "growing pains" caused the holiday to fade from annual significance for most folks until Abraham Lincoln's proclamation in 1863, during the wrenching Civil War years, that the last Thursday in November be a national day of thanksgiving. Many Americans continue to view our Thanksgiving holiday as a time of prayer, healing, reflection, and celebration.

Throughout Native America this holiday is usually a private family event, drawing friends and relatives together from increasingly distant points. Bright dance socials and potluck suppers are held in various regions, and Thanksgiving Weekend annual powwows are celebrated from California to Utah to Arizona, and elsewhere. Native arts and craft shows embrace this weekend in Alberta and Calgary, Canada. The big Indian Market in Phoenix, Arizona, draws many thousands of people together. Wherever the gatherings, marvelous Native foods weave everyone together.

# Ferguson Scalloped Oysters Vera

*Although my Grandfather Estill lived in the fertile southern Appalachian farmlands of central Tennessee and probably never saw a coastal oyster bed, oysters were his favorite food, and this recipe was his favorite presentation of this treat. This dish became a sacred "soul food" along with certain others—like cornmeal-okra fritters, Grandma's biscuits, fried froglegs, and Hoppin' John— that were revered in our family's culinary lexicon. This particular dish became the touchstone of our Thanksgiving, and year after year this dish is the one dish we never do without. Also, as oysters were always expensive in Tennessee, we had this only once a year.*

*This was always the first major dish passed around our Thanksgiving table, and everyone got just one tablespoonful. Having the place of honor, everything else always seemed secondary to oysters.*

**1/2 cup butter**

**1 cup crushed soda crackers or bread crumbs, divided**

**1 quart shucked fresh (or frozen) oysters and their liquor (liquid)**

**2 scallions, finely diced (green and white parts together)**

**1/4 cup parsley, minced**

**salt and pepper to taste**

**2 cups cream**

Preheat the oven to 350°. Lightly dust a well-buttered 8-inch square or round glass baking dish with 1/3 cup of the soda crackers. Carefully place the oysters on top of the crackers and sprinkle with the scallions, parsley, and salt and pepper. Dot with bits of the remaining butter and carefully pour the cream over all this. Top-dress with the rest of the soda cracker crumbs. Place this dish in the oven and bake for 40 to 50 minutes. Serve hot, with reverence!

**Serves 8**

# McLemore Grilled Venison Steaks with Wild Mushrooms

*My father and mother first took me mushrooming in the Ohio woodlands when I was 3 years old. Responsible wild mushroom gathering has been a passion since then, as have been the seasonal wild game hunts and game feasts. Skinning, cooling down, butchering, and boning large and small game has deepened my respect for these foods and their earthy processes. Tender steaks cut from the leg, about 1 inch thick so they may be quickly grilled on the outside and remain rare in the middle, are best.*

1/2 cup peanut oil

1 clove garlic, diced

1/4 cup red wine vinegar

1/4 teaspoon salt

1/4 teaspoon pepper

8 tender venison steaks

In a medium sauté pan, over medium heat, quickly sauté the garlic in hot oil for 3 minutes. Add all of the remaining ingredients except venison steaks and balance seasonings. Brush this warm "dressing" over the venison steaks, covering both sides, and immediately place steaks on hot grill about 6 inches above glowing charcoal. Sear quickly on one side for 5 minutes, then flip steaks over and grill 4 to 8 minutes on other side. Remove grilled steaks to a broad platter and cover to keep warm while you prepare their wild mushroom complement.

# MUSHROOM TOPPING

1/2 cup peanut oil

1 stick butter (1/4 pound)

2 large yellow onions, thinly sliced

4 garlic cloves, chopped

1 pound bear's head tooth mushrooms, chopped

8 whole peppercorns, coarsely ground

1 pound oyster mushrooms, chopped

1 teaspoon salt, or to taste

1/2 cup vegetable or chicken stock (more or less)

Heat the oil and butter in a large sauté pan over medium heat; when oil and butter are hot, sauté the onions and garlic, stirring continually, for 3 to 5 minutes. Add the bear's head tooth mushroom chunks and the cracked peppercorns; stir well for another 5 minutes. Now add the oyster mushroom pieces and remaining seasonings and blend well, simmering for another 5 minutes. Add chicken stock, if necessary, to develop a nice gravy (the amount of stock will depend on how "thirsty" the mushrooms are). Simmer just until the mushrooms seem tender.

Serve the hot grilled steaks with the wild mushrooms spooned over and around them. Garnish with fresh watercress, parsley branches, and trimmed scallions.

**Serves 8**

## Talking Turkey: Thanksgiving Menus Past and Present

*A*s we approach our prominent national holiday of thanksgiving, it is easy to continue our enthusiasm about food that originated in Mexico, Central America, and Latin America. These native cultures first domesticated the turkey, Meleagris gallopavo, *and the muscovy duck,* Cairina moschata, *and obtained the eggs and raised the chicks of other large fowl in the tropics. Archaeological evidence confirms that turkey was a major food in pre-Columbian Mayan rituals. The king of Spain, by 1511, was ordering that ten turkeys, five males and five females, be brought back on every ship returning from the New World. Successful breeding of the birds as a food source followed rapidly in Europe, as was the case in the Americas. Yet in 1561, magistrates in Italy voted to "exclude turkeys from banquets as being overly luxurious!" according to Sophie Coe in* America's First Cuisines, *published by the University of Texas Press in 1994. Coe also notes that even today highland Mayans in* Guatemala cook their whole turkeys in atole for special celebrations.

*Thanksgiving menus may also revolve around rich constellations of foods like raw oysters on the half shell, boiled lobster with fiery butter sauce, grilled shark steak with wild mushroom caviar, planked salmon fillet, hickory-smoked, with salmon caviar salsa, stuffed pumpkin filled with steaming brussels sprouts and chestnuts, Algonquian oyster stew, or honey-smoked duck and wild rice salad. Medleys of holiday sweet breads are accompanied with many delicious alternatives to butter: puréed fruits and nuts generously fill carefully carved-out pumpkins and select acorn and turk's turban squashes, which are arranged as centerpieces on evergreens. Our favorite spreads are pumpkin-maple butter, black bean-chili butter, cranberry-nut butter, and cilantro-pecan butter.*

*Thanksgiving has always set us free to explore evermore versatile realms of culinary artistry!*

# Smoked Blue Mussels and Green Onion Salad

*The blue mussel,* Mytilus edulis, *is one of four species common along Atlantic coastal waters, and it is excellent food in various preparations, especially smoked. Wild onion,* Allium drummondii, *is the most common and widespread of our four species of Alliums; sometimes called "onion grass," the mineral-rich greens are cut for use in countless foods and many medicines. Scallions or green onions are most easily substituted for the wild onions in this and other recipes.*

2 bunches watercress, coarsely cut

1 bunch cilantro, coarsely cut

1 small white onion, sliced very thin, as for rings

1 cup small yellow tomatoes, cut bite-size

1/2 cup pimentos (roasted, peeled sweet peppers), julienned

1 pint smoked blue mussels

1/2 cup wild onions (or green onions), chopped medium-fine

1/4 teaspoon sea salt (optional)

1/2 teaspoon black pepper, coarsely ground

1/2 cup sunflower seed oil

1/2 cup herb cider vinegar (rosemary is best)

In a broad, medium-size bowl, arrange the watercress and cilantro. Sprinkle the greens with consecutive layers of white onion rings, yellow tomatoes, pimentos, and smoked mussels. Place the chopped wild onions and the salt and pepper in a medium jar with the oil and vinegar; shake vigorously and allow to stand for 15 minutes. Shake vigorously again and pour over the salad, tossing well to intermingle these diverse flavors. Serve in a large salad bowl or arrange small servings in peeled, trimmed, hollowed-out jicamas rubbed with lemon or lime juice. These can be beautifully fashioned to look like alabaster bowls! Delicious!

**Serves 8**

# Spicy Pumpkin Raisin Bread

*Pumpkin,* Cucurbita pepo, *is one of the earliest domesticated vegetables developed by Native horticulturists in the Oaxaca region by 8750 B.C. and in the eastern United States region by 2700 B.C. During this history, varieties of pumpkins have been developed and experimented with in every conceivable recipe. Sweet or pickled, smoked or dried, baked or puréed, pumpkins continue to share their wealth. This holiday bread with its sweet maple-butter companion will brighten many gatherings.*

**1 1/2 cups fresh pumpkin, cooked and puréed, or canned solid-pack pumpkin purée**

**1/2 cup honey, maple syrup, or sugar**

**1/2 cup melted butter or corn oil**

**2 eggs, beaten slightly**

**1/2 cup milk**

**1/2 cup raisins or currants**

**1/2 cup butternuts or black walnuts, chopped**

**1 cup all-purpose flour**

**1/2 cup fine yellow cornmeal**

**1/2 cup rolled oats**

**1 teaspoon baking powder**

**1/2 teaspoon ground cinnamon**

**1/2 teaspoon ground allspice**

**1/4 teaspoon ground nutmeg**

**1/4 teaspoon ground ginger**

**1/4 teaspoon ground cloves**

**1/2 teaspoon salt**

Preheat oven to 350°.

Place the pumpkin purée in a medium-sized bowl and add the honey, melted butter, and beaten eggs, stirring well with each addition. Stir in the milk, then add the raisins or currants, and butternuts or black walnuts.

Measure the dry ingredients into a large bowl and make a big well in the center. Carefully pour in the blended wet ingredients, stirring carefully and blending well without overworking the batter.

Pour the batter into a well-greased 6 by 9-inch loaf pan or a greased 2-pound coffee can. Bake for 1 hour or until a toothpick or knife inserted in the center of the loaf comes out clean. Remove to cooling rack for 10 minutes, then slide a clean table-knife blade around the edges of the loaf to loosen it. Turn the steaming loaf onto a board or rack to cool completely. Serve hot or wrap up and serve days later for great flavor and fragrance.

**Makes 1 loaf**

## PUMPKIN MAPLE BUTTER

*There are two versions for this delicious classic. Roasting, rather than steaming or boiling, creates a slightly caramelized flavor in each case; the rest is pure alchemy inspired from very ancient sources.*

Deeply pierce the thick skin of a small sugar pumpkin several times, using the long tines of a carving fork. This prevents the pumpkin from exploding during baking. Roast the pumpkin beside a cooking fire or fireplace, turning occasionally, or set in a baking dish and bake for 30-plus minutes in a 375° oven. Cool slightly and cut open, saving seeds and stringy pulp for other uses. Scoop out the cooked pumpkin meat and purée in a food processor with 1/4 cup maple syrup and 1/2 teaspoon crushed black walnuts. Spoon this golden "butter" into carved, trimmed pumpkin gourds or small acorn squashes. Garnish with diced onions.

**Makes 2 to 3 cups**

# PUMPKIN SEED BUTTER (PEPITAS)

Roast the pumpkin's seeds and season them according to the suggestions on page 17. Purée seasoned seeds in a food mill, adding 1 to 2 teaspoons of sunflower seed oil to form a buttery spread.

Fresh, green hull-less pumpkin seeds, or pepitas, can also be ground in a mortar with just a drop or two of oil. Work this mixture into a fine pumpkin seed butter; add a tablespoon of maple syrup to sweeten.

**Makes 1 cup**

# Nullakatuk: An Eskimo Thanksgiving

Eskimos (whose name in the Algonquian language means "eaters of raw meat") call themselves "the real people" in their own dialects. The Aleut People, close relatives of the Eskimos, inhabit the Aleutian Archipelago stretching from Alaska to Siberia across the Bering Sea. For many thousands of years whales have been vital to their diets and lifeways, as a primary source of food, oil, clothing, and building and creative craft materials. When a whale occasionally washes up on shore or when returning hunters bring in a whale, they hoist gay banners from their umiaks (boats) to signal that it is time for Nullakatuk, or thanksgiving.

Temporary windbreaks are created on the beach so that everyone can work on processing this rich resource. While the cutting, cooking, and cleaning are accomplished, the people prepare for sports, feasting, and dancing—all vital in the whole process of giving thanks. Men and women dance separately in very distinct styles. Many dances represent hunting and whaling exploits and have been handed down from generation to generation. They often incorporate spectacular masks and dance accoutrements specifically created to honor the *inuas,* or spirits of various beings. Eskimo People believe that everything possesses its own *inua,* from the moon, to a whale, to a beach pebble. Special respect must be shown for, and thanks given to, these phenomena. The more beautiful a mask or rattle can be made, the happier the *inua* will be.

93

Special foods are also prepared for honoring the *inua.* Cranberries and other wild berry fruits are cooked or pounded into whale or seal oil, like a form of pemmican, or boiled with caribou, or cooked with dried fish.

Iceland moss lichen, Cetraria islandica, a diminutive, silvery-gray fruticose lichen, grows profusely over rocks and on soil from Iceland as far south as New Jersey and Pennsylvania, and it is a staple in the diet of northern people, as are caribou and reindeer. Eskimos gather this lichen year-round and boil it in water, then dry and pulverize it into flour to use in breads, ash cakes, and many other foods. Boiled in fruit juices, water, or milk, it makes an important jelly-like food that is medicinal and provides starch and minerals.

An Eskimo thanksgiving menu—which might include caribou roast, walrus stew, Arctic char, and salmon, along with Iceland moss, bannock, cranberry–Iceland moss jelly, raspberry or cranberry snow cream, and wild rose hip tea—is very different from a thanksgiving menu in southern New England, as each are again different from thanksgiving menus in Florida Seminole country or southern California. But many things are common to all of these celebrations, especially the universal giving of thanks.

# December

Stinging sleety rain mixes with snow as the gray predawn sky whitens into day. Bare twigs and branches are covered with thickening crusts of ice. Blanketing the earth, snow gives each landscape a new perspective, delineating different features from the ones noticed last month or just yesterday. Autumn is drawing close to winter in ever-shorter days of thin sun and lengthening shadows.

This period is celebrated as the White Ground Moon of the aboriginal Agawam, the Long Moon of the Narragansett and Wampanoag, the Great Winter Moon of the Micmac, the Old Moon of the Penobscot, the Little Long Day Moon of the Onondaga, and the Intervening Moon of the Tsimshian. Native People felt the natural changes.

Oglala Sioux Holyman Black Elk recalled that he was born in The Moon of the Popping Trees (late December), in The Winter When the Four Crows Were Killed (1863). In tribal North America, December was and is the Food Almost Gone Moon of the Haida, the Cold Makes the Trees Crack Moon of the Delaware (Lenape), the Big Bear Moon of the Sauk and Fox, the Big Winter Moon of the Seminole, and the Frozen Ground Moon of the Yuchi, to name only a few of the more than 500 Indian tribes.

Many Native American moon calendars read like descriptive nature journals, feeling and living each season's subtle changes and its effects on all life.

The Zuni, who call themselves *A:shiwi,* meaning "the flesh," are descendants of the ancient Mogollon Culture of pueblo farmers who originally inhabited seven villages, or pueblos, along the upper Zuni River in western New Mexico. The A:shiwi say their ancestors emerged from beneath the earth after four successive journeys through the underworlds, and their emergence into this middle world occurred at the sacred opening called the sipapu. They continued to wander and search for years before they settled on this dry plateau near *Halona Itwana,* "the Middle Anthill of the World," which is now called Corn Mountain and is the Zuni's sacred mesa. Their ancestors return to their villages each year in the form of clouds and spirit messengers, bringing the scarce blessing of rain to these gifted farmers, jewelers, weavers, and artists.

Zuni Pueblo is the largest of the nineteen pueblos in New Mexico. At Zuni, 7,633 tribal members live in terraced, multistoried pueblos on 430,000 acres of reservation lands. One of the most magnificent Indian celebrations is the stunning Zuni Shalako ceremony. Each year near the first of December the 10- to 12-foot-tall messenger-bird kachinas, the Shalakos, return from their sacred kachina village to visit the people of Zuni and bring their blessings. In late afternoon, muffled cries are heard on the brittle air, and the gathering crowds fall silent. The rhythmic jingles grow louder in the dusk, and finally the stately Shalakos stride into the village plaza. Immensely powerful, commanding, colorful figures, they are part human, part beast, part spirit, with wide eyes, buffalo horns, and ruffs of raven feathers stiff beneath their domed, beaked heads. Below their stunning masks of brilliant red, turquoise, and black, they are adorned with beautiful jewelry, rattles, ankle bells, and pine boughs. Among them are Sayatasha, the rain god of the north, Shulawitsi, the little fire god, and Yamukato, the frightful warrior, who brandishes green yucca leaves to alert anyone who might try to fall asleep during their all-night dance vigil—unlikely with the chanting, drumming, and clacking of the great Shalakos' beak.

The Shalako prayers address everything in the universe and honor all life. As the kachinas encircle the plaza, the masked singers chant, carrying the rhythmic sounds of drums, bells, and rattles. The kachinas gracefully bend their knees and begin their classic back-and-forth dance-trot, that we see in many variations throughout Pueblo Country, as they dance to awaken the earth and stir the clouds. This brings the rain back to this parched land, and life continues for the Zuni People.

# ZUNI CHILI IN CORN TORTILLA BOWLS WITH FIESTA VEGETABLES

*Corn is the staple of Pueblo diets, the principal focus of many Pueblo ceremonies, and a symbol of the essence of their bodies and life. Corn continues to be woven into Pueblo life, spiritually, artistically, and through the nurturing generosity of their farms and foods. This recipe celebrates the varied gifts of livestock and garden embraced by a bowl made of corn.*

**6 bacon slices, chopped**

**2 pounds boned pork shoulder, cut into 1-inch cubes**

**2 pounds lean lamb, coarsely ground**

2 large onions, chopped

6 cloves of garlic, chopped

3 jalapeño chilies, roasted, seeded, and chopped

2 Anaheim chilies, roasted, seeded, and chopped

9 tablespoons chili powder

1 tablespoon paprika

1 tablespoon dried oregano, crumbled fine

1 tablespoon fresh epazote, chopped fine

1 tablespoon ground cumin

1 teaspoon dried red pepper flakes

1 teaspoon freshly ground black pepper

1/4 teaspoon ground cayenne pepper

1/2 teaspoon sea salt, more or less, to taste

3 pounds fresh tomatoes, peeled and chopped

1 pound pinto beans, cooked

4 cups beef broth

4 cups water

3 tablespoon corn oil

In a large, deep kettle, cook bacon over medium heat turning occasionally, until just crisp. Do *not* drain. Increase heat to medium-high and add the pork and lamb to the bacon, stirring frequently to brown evenly, for about 10 minutes. Add the onions and garlic to this and blend well, stirring frequently for about 5 minutes. Add the chilies and the remaining seasonings and blend well.

Add the tomatoes, beans, broth, and water to the kettle and bring to a bubbling boil. Reduce heat and simmer for 45 minutes to an hour, stirring occasionally. (This base recipe can be prepared earlier in the day or a day ahead and rewarmed when you are ready to continue.)

Next, heat 3 tablespoons of corn oil in a heavy skillet over medium heat. Add:

**1 1/2 pounds chayote, julienned**

**1 pound yellow squash, julienned**

**2 Anaheim chilies, seeded and julienned**

**2 Poblano chilies, seeded and julienned**

Stir well and cook just until tender-crisp, only about 10 minutes. Keep warm.

Last, assemble separate dishes or bowls of the following ingredients:

**enough corn oil for deep frying**

**16 large corn tortillas (blue or yellow corn, or both)**

**2 cups refried beans, heated**

**2 cups cheddar cheese, shredded**

**2 cups fresh cilantro**

Heat the corn oil in a deep fryer to 350°.

Carefully place one corn tortilla at a time into a wire tortilla basket mold or large potato nest, with cover to hold in place, and immerse briefly in the hot oil until just barely golden, about 30 seconds. As you remove each tortilla bowl from the oil, allow excess oil to drip back into deep fryer, then invert finished bowl over absorbent brown paper or layers of paper towels so that it may drain further. Repeat until all bowls are done.

To assemble each dish, spread one table-spoonful of  hot refried beans in the center of each plate and carefully press a tortilla bowl onto it (to "glue it" in place). Sprinkle a table-spoon of the shredded cheese into the bottom of each empty tortilla bowl, then fill each one generously with hot, steaming chili. Sprinkle another tablespoonful of cheese on top of the hot chili. Surround each steaming tortilla bowl with several tablespoonfuls of the hot sautéed vegetables and garnish with the fresh cilantro. Serve and enjoy.

**Makes about 16 servings**

*(An earlier version of this recipe was first printed in* Bon Appétit *magazine, November 1987, in "Bon Appetit Cooking Class: A Harvest of American Indian Specialties" by Zack Hanle, featuring the work of Barrie Kavasch.)*

**Chayote**, Sechium edule, *is a very versatile Native American squash that originated in Central America and has been a delicious staple in Mexican, Native American, and Caribbean cuisines for centuries. Some of its other fascinating names are mirliton, christophine, and vegetable pear. Aggressive vines produce pale-green, pear-shaped fruits, with light green flesh* surrounding a central seed. The mild flavor of chayote reminds some folks of cucumber and complements many different ingredients well. In Honduras, where chayote are thought to have originated, they are halved, stuffed with a mixture of cheese and egg, and baked as a delicious traditional festival dish called* chancletas, *meaning "old slippers."*

# WATERMELON-GINGER-RASPBERRY SHERBET

*This is a very easy, quick sherbet that makes a deliciously smooth, creamy dessert. Because of its low sugar content, it is best processed and then served within 30 minutes. Mound generous scoops of this blushing ice onto tiny dessert plates and sprinkle with carob or chocolate bits to resemble watermelon seeds or the cloud shadows over the Sandia Mountains.*

**5 cups watermelon, seeded and cut into 1-inch chunks**

**1/2 cup frozen raspberries**

**1/4 cup candied ginger, diced**

**1/2 cup heavy cream or yogurt**

**1/2 cup miniature carob or chocolate chips**

**fresh or candied mint leaves for garnish (optional)**

Place the watermelon chunks and the frozen raspberries in a large plastic bag and freeze them together until solid. Just 5 minutes before you are ready to make the ice, remove them from the freezer and break into chunks.

Place the frozen fruits in a food processor with a metal blade and briefly purée to produce a shaved ice. Add the ginger and cream or yogurt to the food processor and blend until smooth. Pour this mixture into a metal bowl or tray and put in the freezer, covered, for no more than 30 minutes.

Remove from freezer and scoop into sherbet cups or dishes. Garnish with the carob or chocolate bits, additional fresh or frozen raspberries, and mint leaves. Enjoy!

**Serves 4 to 5**

# Maple Twig Cookie Curls

*Simplicity is the key to the prize-winning quality of this perfectly sweet treat. The simpler the better to accompany and enhance flashier dishes, these light curled cookies can also be filled with fruits, dessert creams, or light pudding sauces. They're great "hollow" and plain, too.*

**1/2 cup maple syrup or honey**

**1/4 cup butter**

**1/2 cup fine sifted flour**

**1 teaspoon fine pecan meal (grind pecan meats in a food processor or hand mill)**

**1/4 teaspoon salt**

Preheat oven to 360°. Place the first two ingredients in a small pan over medium-high heat. Bring to a hard boil for about 1 minute, stirring constantly. Remove from the heat and add the remaining ingredients, stirring until very creamy and well blended.

On a greased cookie sheet, drop the batter by tablespoonfuls, each about 3 inches apart. Bake for about 10 minutes, until the cookies get maple-colored edges. Remove and cool for 2 minutes. Working quickly, lift each warm cookie with a broad spatula and gently roll each one around the clean, smooth handle of a wooden spoon. Slip out the spoon handle and repeat this process with all the cookies. You can also try to roll funnel-shaped cookies if you want to fill them with larger pieces of fruits or nuts. Experiment with cones, curls, or flutes to suit your dessert designs. The slim, 3-inch hollow maple twig all by itself is best; in December and January, lightly dust it with sifted powdered sugar for a snowy twig or branch.

**Makes about 3 1/2 dozen**

## Brave New World

On December 4, 1619, it is recorded, thirty-eight English settlers came ashore at the James River, in what would become Virginia, and offered a prayer of thanksgiving to God. Grateful to get beyond their ship's provisions, they little suspected the brave new world of mysterious foods that lay before them. Native American foods have been saving and changing lives for centuries ever since.

# Blackfoot Indian Art Festival     Early December

Early December brings the annual rush of year-end activities in Indian America, from the Mashpee Wampanoag Winter Social and Potluck to the opening of a very special Blackfoot Indian Art Show in Fort MacLeod, Alberta, Canada, at the Head Smashed in Buffalo Jump Interpretive Center, a fascinating seven-story building.

Blackfoot tribal member Louisa Crow Shoe explains that the show, called Heritage through my Hands, brings a number of unique Blackfoot Indians and their artwork and foods together. Paintings, fine beadwork, quillwork, sculpture, and much more are accompanied by selections of native foods like buffalo pemmican, venison pemmican, frybreads and bannocks, and fine jams and jellies made from native berries. I enjoyed some of these pleasures a few years ago when I camped near St. Mary's Lake at Chewing Blackbones on the Blackfoot Indian Reservation in northern Montana. It was barely above freezing in our densely sheltered aspen grove. The chill wind blew across St. Mary's Lake, coyotes howled nearby, an owl called through morning fog. One of many Native campgrounds on reservations very worth investigating, Chewing Blackbones has been unforgettable for me. Memorable region, memorable people, memorable foods.

Bannock, buffalo jerky, and pemmican are three favorite Native foods, among many others, that are enjoyed by visitors at the Blackfoot Art Festival. These classic foods are encountered again and again as we move from one Native event to another throughout Indian country.

# CANADIAN CREE BANNOCK

*Bannock is a Gaelic-Scottish term describing the oval round flattish cake easily made and tradition-ally carried by hunters and travelers. Mikka Barkman Kelley, Canadian Cree artist of Sachigo Lake First Nations Reserve in Northern Ontario, shares her family's recipe for this delicious favorite bread.*

**3 cups flour**

**1/2 cup sugar**

**5 teaspoons baking powder**

**1 teaspoon salt**

**1/4 pound butter**

**1 1/4 cups milk**

Combine all dry ingredients in a large bowl. Cut in the butter and blend with a fork until mixture is in pea-sized balls. Slowly fold in milk to form a single ball of dough, blending well.

Preheat oven to 450°, warming a well-seasoned or greased 10-inch cast-iron frying pan in the oven as it preheats.

Remove hot frying pan and turn the dough into this pan. Flatten the dough and turn it once to lightly coat both sides with the grease from the pan.

Return pan to oven and bake for 15 to 20 minutes until golden brown. Serve hot on a lightly sugared or cornmealed plate. Break off pieces of warm bread with your hand, and enjoy it plain or with butter or your favorite jam.

**Serves 6 to 8**

# HICKORY-SMOKED BUFFALO JERKY

*The word* jerky *originated from the Quechua (Peruvian) word* charqui, *meaning "thin." Traditionally, most game meat was prepared for storage and travel by cutting it very thin and curing it through smoking and/or long, slow drying in the sun. With the availability of salt after the 1860s, which greatly speeds the process and seasons the product, most recipes now include the use of pickling, kosher, or sea salt. The salt brine actually allows the jerky to keep longer.*

**2 pounds lean buffalo, trimmed of all fat**

**3 tablespoons coarse sea salt**

**1/4 cup brown or maple sugar**

**1 teaspoon ground ginger**

**1/2 teaspoon garlic powder**

**1/2 teaspoon ground black pepper**

Cut buffalo meat into strips 4 to 6 inches long and as thin as possible—1/8-inch is best if you can do it. Combine and blend all remaining ingredients in a shallow plate. Press and roll each meat strip quickly in this spice mix and place on the rack of a smoker. Keep the temperature in the smoker around 90° for about 10–12 hours, or until jerky strips are well glazed and snap when bent.

I use a small three-tiered metal smoker, no bigger than a two-drawer file cabinet, outside on my open porch. Cool smoking, using wet or damp hickory bark, mesquite, apple or grape wood, or corn cobs adds great taste and smells great during the processing. I smoke many kinds of fish, some herbs, pasta, squash, shellfish, and corn this way. A long, slow oven set at 120° for 8 hours will also achieve a similar effect.

**Makes about 2 1/2 pounds**

# HIGH PLAINS PEMMICAN

*The word* pemmican *is derived from the Cree word* pime, *meaning "fat," and refers to an extremely valuable, resourceful trail food developed and used by Native Peoples throughout the Americas. To create this food, highly condensed preparations of lean, jerked, dried meat or fish are pounded into or mixed with fat or tallow and wild fruits and seeds to form a thick paste which is pressed and shaped into cakes, patties, or balls. Often packed into parfleches or carried in small buckskin bags, this practical, high-energy food is nutritious and has good keeping qualities. Pemmican was a staple food for many Native People, especially during long winter months and periods of poor hunting. A small pemmican patty could be dropped into boiling water to provide an agreeable stew or soup, with or without additional ingredients.*

*In past regional traditions, a broad range of native wild fruits and seeds were incorporated into fish, vegetable, or animal oils or fats, with or without meat. The tradition continues as modern meatless pemmicans composed entirely of vegetable, fruit, and grain components are balanced nutritionally to provide necessary minerals, vitamins, and carbohydrates. This recipe, however, is based on jerked meat.*

**3 cups shredded buffalo jerky, or other jerked game meat**

**1 cup Saskatoon berries, buffalo berries, or raisins**

**1 cup roasted sunflower seeds or other seeds**

**1/2 cup roasted yellow cornmeal (optional)**

**1/2 cup to 1 cup sunflower seed or corn oil**

In a large bowl combine all ingredients, mixing well with a wooden spoon or your hands so that the ingredients are well pressed together. With your hands, form this mixture into small cakes or patties or roll and pat into bars.

Arrange on plates to serve immediately, or wrap individually and refrigerate or freeze for future use on your next trail walk or camping trip.

**Makes 10 to 12 patties**

# Buffalo Berry Wojapi (Syrup)

*Buffalo berries,* Shepherdia argentea, *also known as* Miksinitisim, *which is Blackfoot for "bull berry," are the fleshy, tart red berries of a common shrub found all across the plains. Long used in many traditional foods and medicines, these berries are best when collected after early frosts have sweetened them. As with herbs, it is best to collect them early in the day after the morning dew has dried. If buffalo berries don't grow where you live, see the Source Directory to obtain them. Buffalo berry syrup or jam is wonderful served with bannock, frybread, game, or vegetables.*

**2 cups buffalo berries, tightly packed**

**1/2 cup water**

**1/2 cup honey**

**1/2 cup maple syrup or sugar**

Place all ingredients in a heavy, medium-size pot, pressing and crushing the berries into the bottom. Simmer over moderate heat, stirring occasionally, until berries are tender and liquid is reduced and thick. Remove and pour into sterilized jars for future use or a small bowl for immediate use.

This recipe can easily be spiced up with allspice, cinnamon, and brown sugar to make a fine "butter." Rose hips, raspberry, blackberry, elderberry, currant, gooseberry, chokecherry, strawberry, saskatoon berry, salmon berry, and bearberry substitutions all provide easy variations on this basic, traditional recipe.

**Makes 2 1/2 to 3 cups**

In the Pueblo culture, the center plaza of each village is "the Heart Place." All of the balancing forces of their Pueblo world come together here in the plaza, forming a spiritual essence that represents the Pueblo way of life. Some Pueblo people feel that these combined forces create a radiant spiritual heartbeat that pulses through all life and must be honored and celebrated periodically. Each pueblo's feast day in honor of its patron saint is an especially lovely, vital time. These events traditionally take place in the village plaza. Patron saint feast days are the most popular events for the general public to attend, with special Pueblo foods being prepared and served at them.

At Jemez Pueblo in Jemez, New Mexico, at the entrance of Jemez Canyon, the people prepare for the Our Lady of Guadalupe Feast Day with special regard. The foods, dances, music, and costumes are all part of the Pueblo prayers for the whole universe. This is an important occasion for acknowledging the importance of love, peace, fertility, and care of the land and all of life.

Pojoaque Pueblo celebrates the feast day of Our Lady of Guadalupe in many similar ways. Resettled in 1706 by five families returning to its site after its population was almost destroyed by smallpox and other troubles, this Tewa Pueblo is now a bright, modern success story exemplifying traditions, determination, and public enterprise. Its original name, *P'o-zuang-Ge,* means "drinking place," and preparations for the feast day celebrating Our Lady of Guadalupe include traditional Pueblo ceremonial winter foods like corn soups, chili stews, Pueblo breads, and a constellation of other personal and popular dishes and beverages.

# BAKED STUFFED PUMPKIN

*Sugar pumpkins are great as vegetables and desserts and can double as baking and serving dishes as well. This marvelous classic dish weaves all of these opportunities together into one. Long before pies, cakes, and puddings, there were pumpkins—and imagination! Winter feast days and other special gatherings at Jemez, Pojoaque, and other pueblos feature this dish, with many delicious variations.*

2 cups applesauce

1 cup dark raisins

1 cup currants

1/2 cup pine nuts, lightly roasted

1/2 cup yellow cornmeal, lightly roasted

1/2 cup honey

1/2 teaspoon allspice

1/2 teaspoon cinnamon

1 (5-pound) sugar pumpkin

1/2 cup apple cider

In a large pot, over medium heat, combine the applesauce, raisins, currants, pine nuts, cornmeal, honey, and spices. Simmer, stirring occasionally, for 5 minutes. Set aside.

Preheat oven to 350°. Carefully cut the top from the pumpkin, and trim and save it. Scoop the seeds and pulp out of the pumpkin cavity. Prick the pumpkin's inner cavity with the tines of a fork, then place the pumpkin in a deep baking dish. Add about an inch of water to the dish to surround the pumpkin. Pour the hot applesauce mixture into the pumpkin cavity. Pour the apple cider on top, letting some run over the sides to coat the pumpkin skin. Place the top back on the pumpkin—lightly. Place this whole creation in the oven and bake for 40 to 50 minutes, until a toothpick stuck into the side of the pumpkin meets little resistance and the pumpkin seems done.

Don't allow it to bake too long or it may start to collapse.

Serve hot as a sweet side dish or as the centerpiece for dessert. Carefully remove the top. Scoop out generous portions of the pudding-like filling and serve in dishes; you might want to enjoy it by itself or with vanilla, peach, or pumpkin ice cream or yogurt. Then, with a long-blade bread knife, slice and serve slim wedges of the baked pumpkin to be eaten out of its skin. The cider should have caramelized, leaving a delightful flavor and fragrance. This is one of the easiest, tastiest desserts, and many variations on this recipe show up around the country at Indian festivals and gatherings. Cranberries and blueberries are nice additions to the pudding filling in autumn. Meat and diced vegetables or just corn and beans can be the basis for the center stuffing on other occasions and in other seasons.

**Serves 8 to 10**

# Hopi Soyal Ceremony at Winter Solstice

Winter begins around December 22, when the sun is farthest south of the equator and appears to be standing still. The day with the shortest daylight day of the year is called the Winter Solstice, from the Latin *solstitium,* derived from *sol* (sun) and *sistere* (to stand still). Earlier peoples observed this natural phenomenon with concern, some fear, and even a sense of crisis, and measures were taken to encourage the sun to come back again. Agricultural people and others dependent upon the sun for their livelihood used prayers, rituals, and ceremonies to help speed the sun's return.

Native Americans have long used various structures such as earth mounds, wood and stone circles, and rock formations to chart the movements of the heavenly bodies. In the Southwest, the sun shines brightly most of the year, and keeping track of the places where the sun rises and sets is vital in planning the year's activities. This is especially true for the Pueblo farmers of New Mexico and Arizona, for whom corn has been their life sustainer for more than 2,000 years. A successful corn crop requires careful timing of planting, watering, and harvesting. After the winter solstice, as days begin to grow longer and the sun's light gradually intensifies, Pueblo planting preparations begin with ceremony.

In the Pueblo villages a Sun Priest, or Sun Watcher, observes the sun and helps to guide ceremonial times and agricultural needs. The Zuni Sun Priest sits in a stone sun shrine before dawn, facing east, observing seasonal changes by noting the shadows cast by the rising sun. He predicts the date and time of the winter solstice, called *Itiwanna,* when a new fire is lit to rekindle the sun's light. The Zuni say the Sun Father holds up red feathers to make daylight. The Hopi of Walpi village time their winter ceremonies by changes in the sun's position on the horizon as it sets over the mountains. The Tewa divide themselves into winter people and summer people, and each group is governed by a female corn spirit of a particular color of their corn. Traditionally, White Corn Maiden Near to Ice governed the winter people who hunted. Winter was a deeply spiritual time for many tribes, during which they would make pathways of

111

communication with the spirit world through ceremonies, prayers, special foods, and other offerings.

Hopi ceremonies are deeply intertwined with their everyday life. Their kachina ceremonies serve to maintain harmony in the world and satisfy the spirits of the people, as well as the animals, plants, rocks, and all living things within the whole of Creation. According to Hopi belief, kachinas are spirits that live in the sacred San Francisco peaks near Flagstaff and come to Hopiland only for the ceremonies.

For days in advance of the winter solstice ceremony, Hopi priests pray and prepare the kiva, a large, circular, semisubterranean spirit room. During this time they purify themselves and abstain from eating all meat, salt, and grease. The kiva floor is sprinkled with sacred cornmeal, herbs, and various earth elements and medicinal items. Flowers are placed on the kiva floor in patterns that symbolize the universe, surrounded by ears of corn, eagle feathers, and other holy objects. Soon the entire kiva becomes an altar. Bear Clan Priests bless the prayer feathers for the good of the people, then messengers carry them, along with cornhusk "boats" filled with sacred cornmeal, to every Hopi home.

The rituals are followed with careful attention to detail in order to purify the villages and call back the sun from its southward retreat. At the solstice, the entire village enters the kiva as the Soyal rites that alter the sun's path and renew the cycles of the seasons are accomplished. The Soyal kachina wears a cornhusk star and heavenly symbols on his elaborate headdress; heavenly symbols also adorn his body. As he dances among the people within the kiva, he draws the sun's energies, enabling it to journey back toward summer.

## Hopi Kachinas

*Kachina spirits inhabiting the sacred San Francisco Peaks come to live in the Hopi villages for more than six months of each year in order to perform the necessary ceremonies, dances, and initiations so vital to Hopi life. Kachina cults are possibly the oldest healing, horticultural, and environmental societies in the northern hemisphere. Hopi men and women belonging to the various kachina societies become the masked impersonators during vital ceremonial times, carrying out the necessary tasks and rituals. Carving kachina masks and dolls is one aspect of their responsibilities, and before ceremonies Hopi men are busy carving pieces of cottonwood root into the various kachina beings, adding arms and legs, beaks, ears, horns, rattles, mantles, and feathers, bits of turquoise, coral, and shells.*

*During many of the dances, the kachinas have small kachina-doll likenesses dangling from their fingers and wrists. Between dances, these dolls are presented to Hopi children as constant reminders of roles they will undertake. Hopi boys and girls are initiated into kachina cults between the ages of seven and ten, joining their relatives and neighbors participating in the ceremonies.*

*More than 300 spirits enrich the Hopi pantheon of kachinas, taking many unique forms—animals, birds, vegetables, demons, ogres, clowns—each vital to the whole spectrum of Hopi life. Some kachina dolls are masterpieces of artistic concepts and are displayed in some of the finest museums and private collections in the world.*

The Hopi, descendants of the Anasazi, have lived in the Southwest for more than 2,000 years, yet Hopi traditions say they are much more ancient than this, as their spirits first lived in Tokpela—a boundless space, a beautiful world. Hopi ancestors have evolved through three earlier worlds and life cycles before emerging into Fourth World, where Masaw, the Caretaker of the Earth, resides and helps to guide their life cycles. Countless generations of migrations in the four directions finally brought the Hopi's ancestors to their Center of the Earth, where they live today, in one of the most geographically spectacular regions in North America.

The Hopi old stone villages perch atop three fingerlike mesas protruding sharply from the arid Colorado Plateau, surrounded by their more modern villages and settlements below. Old Oraibi, the most ancient, was settled by the Hopi in A.D. 1150 and is one of the oldest continuously inhabited villages in the United States. Hopi mesa villages are situated in northeastern Arizona on their 1.5 million-acre reservation, completely surrounded by the gigantic Navajo Reservation. Three major mesas rising up to 7,200 feet above the desert—First Mesa, Second Mesa, and Third Mesa—are home to twelve Hopi villages and the majority of the 9,000-member Hopi tribe. Coal and oil deposits provide some income to the tribe, and Hopi artists are well known for their fine jewelry, polychrome pottery, beautiful basketry, and especially their carved kachina figures fashioned from cottonwood roots.

A scant 10 inches of precipitation each year focuses much of Hopi religious concern on rain and the growth of corn. Four colors of Hopi corn represent the four cardinal directions, and corn pollen
and sacred cornmeal are used in many rituals to purify and bless and represent the generous fruitfulness of Mother Earth.

Corn is the lifeblood of Hopi society and naturally accompanies all religious—and other— aspects of their lives.

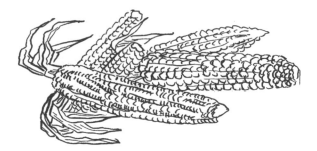

# Hopi Rabbit Stew

*Corn and game are important connecting links year-round, but they are especially necessary in winter. Blue corn is sacred to Hopi life and ceremonies and has a greater mineral content than other colors of corn. This recipe and the next link blue corn and rabbit to make a traditional-style Hopi meal.*

1/2 cup blue cornmeal

1/2 cup all-purpose flour

1 teaspoon paprika

1 teaspoon freshly ground black pepper

1 teaspoon salt

1 tablespoon epazote, finely minced

2 (3-pound) rabbits, cut into individual pieces

1/2 cup corn oil

2 large onions, diced

8 medium carrots, cut into 1/2-inch chunks

5 wild bayberry leaves, or 2 bay leaves

5 cups chicken or vegetable stock

salt and pepper to taste

Combine, in a shallow dish, the first 6 ingredients. Add the rabbit pieces, turning well to coat. Heat the oil in a large skillet over medium-high heat. Carefully add rabbit pieces to the heated skillet, being careful not to crowd. Quickly fry, turning often, for about 15 to 20 minutes. Next, add the onions and carrots, cooking briefly, and stirring well. Add the bayberry or bay leaves. Blend in well. Add the chicken or vegetable stock; stir until well blended. Add salt and pepper to taste. Stir well and scrape the skillet to incorporate any browned or caramelized bits into a light gravy. Bring to a boil. Stir well. Reduce heat, cover, and simmer for about 45 minutes to an hour.

**Serves 10 to 12**

# Blue Corn Marbles

*These delicious little dumplings are beautiful accents in various soups and stews or in their own broth. A small amount of cooking ash added to the cornmeal releases more nutrients, boosts flavor, and enhances the blue color. Ash is made easily by burning small amounts of Chamise (or Greasewood),* Adenostoma fasciculatem, *or Utah Juniper,* Juniperus osteosperma, *or Common Juniper,* J. communis. *Cooking ash is an important component in Hopi corn recipes. Baking powder may be used as a substitute.*

**1/2 cup blue cornmeal**

**1/4 cup all-purpose flour**

**1 tablespoon cooking ash or baking powder**

**1/2 teaspoon sugar**

**1/4 teaspoon salt**

**1 egg, beaten**

**1 tablespoon corn oil or melted butter**

**1/4 cup milk**

**1 tablespoon thyme, crushed**

Blend all ingredients together well in a medium-sized bowl and allow to stand for 30 minutes. Using a well-oiled teaspoon, shape the cornmeal mixture into marble-size balls and place on a plate sprinkled with fine blue cornmeal. When they are all made, stir the stew in which you plan to cook them and carefully add the blue corn marbles, fitting them in around the pieces of meat and vegetables. Cover. Raise heat to a lively simmer for 15 minutes.

Ladle hot stew and dumplings into generous bowls. Top with diced green onions, chopped peppers, parsley, and peaches.

**Makes about 3 dozen**

# CHRISTMASTIME IN PUEBLO COUNTRY

Traditional Christmas holidays are celebrated throughout Indian Country by Christians and non-Christians alike and are often enthusiastically interwoven with rich, traditional American Indian ceremonies and foods. Throughout the Pueblo Southwest and eastward to quiet New England village greens, folks now line roads and pathways with glowing luminarias and farolitos, inspired by cherished Southwestern traditions. Some folks decorate living or fresh-cut evergreen trees. Many others trim spare white birch saplings or aspens and alders with tiny gourds, cornhusk ornaments and dolls, brightly painted bread dough ornaments, and imaginative little dream-catchers, lovingly reinterpreting Christmas traditions anew.

Throughout the pueblos in New Mexico, brilliant dances and festivals of lights are scheduled to ever-increasing audiences. Taos Pueblo hosts dancers, warmed by bonfires, for Vespers, and for the Procession of Virgin Mary on December 24. The Spanish dance drama "Los Matachines" is at San Juan and Picuris pueblos as well as at San Ildefonso Pueblo. Acoma Pueblo hosts the Basket, Buffalo, Deer, Harvest, Rainbow, and Turtle Dances. The entire Acoma Pueblo is lit with luminarias, beginning at the scenic viewpoint and continuing as far as "Sky City." Various dances take place after midnight Mass at Laguna, San Felipe, Santa Ana, Jemez, and Zia pueblos. Christmas Day festivals are held at San Estevan del Rey Mission at Acoma Pueblo and Jemez Pueblo. Several days later the Children's Dance is hosted at Picuris Pueblo, and Holy Innocents Day is celebrated at Santa Clara Pueblo. Imagine the great energies and prayers here!

# SNOWY VANILLA PECAN CRESCENTS

*The generosity and sweetness of Pueblo foods at Christmastime is embodied in this recipe. Pecan,* Carya illinoensis, *from the Algonquian word* paccan *or* pacane, *is a tree native to the rich, well-drained bottomlands of the Ohio and Mississippi River valleys. The fine, delicious nuts of this tall, slim tree are valued by many people. Pecans are widely farmed in the south for their prodigious nut crops and fine-grained wood. Vanilla beans are the aromatic fermented seed pods of several wild South American orchids, principally* Vanilla planifolia. *The name derives from the Spanish word* vainilla, *meaning "little sheath" and referring to the appearance of the ripe bean pods. Together, these plants have an enormous economic and culinary impact around the world and are widely used in Indian festival foods and beverages. These cookies celebrate the gifts of both species.*

**1 cup powdered sugar, divided**

**2 sticks butter, or margarine, softened**

**1/4 teaspoon salt (optional)**

**2 teaspoons vanilla extract**

**1 1/2 cups all-purpose flour**

**1 1/4 cups rolled oats**

**1/2 cup pecans, finely chopped**

Preheat oven to 325°. In a large bowl, cream half of the sugar into the butter, then add the salt and vanilla extract, blending well. Next add the flour, oats, and nuts, and blend thoroughly. Place dough by the tablespoonful on ungreased cookie sheet. Shape into crescents. Bake for 15 minutes or until bottoms are light honey-golden. Remove to wire rack and sift remaining powdered sugar generously over warm crescents.

**Makes 36 to 40 cookies**

# SPICY HOT CHOCOLATE

*Another gift from Mexico and Central America is chocolate,* Theobroma cacao, *from the Aztec* xocolatl *(*xoco, *meaning "bitter," and* atl, *meaning "water"). Cacao can be traced back to the second millennium before Christ, to early Olmec, which was the ancient mother culture of Mesoamerica, predating the Maya. The Aztec Indians considered chocolate the food of the gods, and they introduced Spanish explorers to this noble wealth. Cacao seeds come from large, fleshy beans with thick husks that grow attached to their tree trunks. In some regions of Mesoamerica, cacao beans are still gathered, husked, and spread in the sun to dry, as they were prehistorically. Then they are fermented and roasted to develop their distinctive, familiar flavor. Try this hot chocolate variation, which uses native allspice and vanilla for added richness and diversity of flavor.*

Brew your favorite conventional hot chocolate and whip into it a dash of native, powdered allspice and a dash of vanilla extract. Whip it until frothy and serve it hot in heavy mugs to enjoy with Snowy Vanilla Pecan Crescent cookies.

# MICCOSUKEE ARTS FESTIVAL
# AND THE SEMINOLE FAIR

The week after Christmas, the Miccosukee Indian Cultural Center and Indian Village in Miami, Florida, host their big annual Miccosukee Indian Arts Festival, bringing together artists and crafters to exhibit their works in this much-anticipated event. Indian dancers, drummers, and singers gather here from all across the United States, Canada, Mexico, Central America, and South America. Traditional foods, alligator wrestling, and airboat rides are just some of the sparks for tourism, along with the trademark needlework, patchwork clothing and accessories, fine baskets, and carvings of the native artisans.

The fourth weekend in December also brings the annual Seminole Indian Fair in Hollywood, Florida, with many of these same colorful offerings. Understandably, thousands of Native Americans head south for this week of high festivities and networking with friends.

The Seminole and Miccosukee tribes occupy four federal reservations in south Florida. The Miccosukee Indian Reservation and the Big Cypress Seminole Reservation are in the Everglades. The Brighton Seminole Reservation is near Lake Okeechobee, and the small Hollywood Reservation is just north of Miami. Two additional state reservations are the Dania and the Immokalee.

Seminole is from the Creek Indian word meaning "separatists" or "runaways." Originally part of the great Creek Confederacy, the Seminole and Miccosukee Indians broke away during the periods of settlement and relocation to regroup themselves as *Ikaniuksalgi,* meaning "peninsula people." Many originally came from the lower Creek towns on the Chattahoochee River about 1775, and their folks fought fiercely for their lands in central Florida, where they could be free to live in their traditional manner. They continue to define themselves with warmth and style.

# ALLIGATOR SAUTÉ

*You are as likely to encounter this delicious native meat at the Miccosukee Indian Arts Festival and Seminole Fair as you are at increasingly diverse Native festivals throughout North America. Versatile, tasty alligator,* Alligator mississipiensis, *has been making a formidable comeback and commands new respect and admiration. Skilled Seminole and Miccosukee alligator wrestlers have long understood the strength of these awesome creatures. Now they and others enjoy the culinary strengths of alligator meat at Native festivals and powwows throughout the country. This revived cuisine gives new meaning to the term "wild foods."*

**3 tablespoons butter or hazelnut oil**

**2 mild Anaheim peppers, roasted and diced**

**2 medium onions, coarsely diced**

**3 cloves garlic, finely diced**

**2 pounds of alligator tail meat, cubed**

**1/2 cup (more or less) hot water or stock**

**1 tablespoon apple cider vinegar**

**4 scallions, coarsely diced**

**salt and pepper to taste**

Heat butter or oil in a large skillet over medium heat. Quickly sauté the peppers, onion, and garlic for about 2 minutes. Add the alligator meat and some of the hot water or stock. Stir frequently until the meat begins to look opaque (about 15 minutes). Add the vinegar, scallions, and final seasonings. Balance to suit your taste. Add additional liquid as needed. Serve hot over steamed brown rice, wild rice, or quinoa.

**Serves 4 to 6**

# The Ghost Dance Religion

*W*ovoka, a Paiute medicine man whose father was a noted mystic, experienced a powerful vision during a solar eclipse in 1889. This vision gave birth to the Ghost Dance Religion. "God told me to come back and tell my people they must be good and love one another, and not fight, or steal, or lie. He gave me this dance to give to my people." Wovoka was a prophet who foresaw a changing and better world for the demoralized, besieged western tribes. The Ghost Dance Religion he founded spread far and fast, yet was fearfully misunderstood and, sadly, precipitated the bloodiest ending of the Indian Wars at Wounded Knee in South Dakota in late December of 1890. Every year December 29 is marked with prayers of mourning, and in remembrance "spirit plates" of food are set at Indian tables throughout North America.

The Spirit Plate can be any small plate selected to hold a tiny bit of each food served at a gathering. It is blessed with prayers and set near the center of the table, on an altar, or in some other special location, where it is sometimes blessed with sacred herbs or tobacco. Wendell Deer with Horns, who is a Lakota Pipe-Carrier from the Cheyenne River Sioux Reservation in Eagle Butte, South Dakota, says that each food "has its own spirit form and nourishment. Although you might not see anything disappear from this spirit plate, the good spirits eat the energy of the food. It nourishes them, along with the prayers, and they know that they are remembered and celebrated." Wendell believes that it is important to do this at major meals and special gatherings, as it "is a sacred ritual thanksgiving to the 'ghost grapevine.'"

# January

Snowy mornings reveal numerous fresh deer tracks across the old meadows, and scent still hangs heavy in the hedgerows where the deer milled around and nested during the storm. Their myriad tracks seem to show they were dancing—with the rutting times past now, they are gathering and yarding up for different urgencies.

This month was known as the Whirling Wind Moon Of Midwinter of the Agawam and Narragansett, the Moon When The Sun Has The Strength To Thaw of the Wampanoag, the Hard Times Moon or Moon That Provides Little Food Grudgingly of the Penobscot, the Frost Fish (Tom Cod) Moon of the Micmac.

Farther south, this was the Cold Meal Moon of the Natchez and the Melting Snow Moon of the Navajo. Across the Great Plains this period was the Moon Of Strong Cold for the Sioux, Snow Drifts on the Lodge Moon of the Omaha, and Hoop And Stick Game Moon of the Cheyenne. And, up along the Northwest Coast, this was the Spring Salmon Moon of the Tsimshian.

The myriad lifeways of American Indian peoples are resonant with the seasonal shifts of the natural world. Winter foods, activities, gatherings, and celebrations are shaped by these seasonal shifts. Songs, dances, prayers, artistic accoutrements, and regalia are created and worked on during the winter months.

# PUEBLO NEW YEAR'S DAY DANCES JANUARY 1

Following the delicious crush of Christmas celebrations at the pueblos, the New Year is blessed and welcomed with much pageantry and enthusiasm. As Stephen Trimble says in his beautiful new book *The People: Indians of the American Southwest:* "Precise rituals prescribe proper living. There are no words in Pueblo languages for 'religion.' When speaking to outsiders, the People call sacred rituals 'Indian doings.' They learn more and more about their meaning the longer they live. . . ." We certainly see this in their celebrations and festivals.

New Year's Day dances and celebrations take place at most of the pueblos on January 1, but it is always best to check for times and particulars with each pueblo tribal office.

Taos Indian Pueblo is noted for their men's traditional animal dance, the Turtle Dance, performed in the afternoon. Corn dances and Matachines dances fill the afternoon at the Jemez Pueblo plaza, in hopes that all living things may be fruitful and multiply. These and other annual rounds of dances seek to ensure plentiful rain and crops, and at this particular time, an ample supply of game, as well as the continued healthy increase of humans. Accompanying these artistic rituals is a rich diversity of Pueblo winter foods to nurture families and guests.

124

### *Corn Dance at the Pueblos*

*At the Corn Dance, ancient chants and drumbeats imitating thunder accompany the dancers. Pueblo men and women dancers carry ears of ripe corn wrapped in evergreen branches in their hands. Some men carry large gourd rattles filled with seeds and small stones. As these rattles shake in unison, the sounds are like falling rain. The corn dance is a glorious moving prayer for plentiful rain, ample corn growth, and a bountiful harvest.*

*The Pueblo dance from sunrise to sunset in their finest clothes, beautiful jewelry and beadwork, and decorative turkey feathers and prayer plumes. The dancers' soft-leather moccasins gently pat and massage the earth of the plaza, awakening Mother Earth, reassuring her and reminding her of their reverence toward the balance of life and their need for their principal life sustainer—corn.*

# PUEBLO SQUASH BREAD

*Squash and their close cousins, pumpkins and gourds, in the great cucurbit family are believed to be among the earliest plants cultivated by prehistoric peoples in the Western Hemisphere well over 8,000 years ago. Carried along prehistoric footpaths and trade routes, these early cultigens were dispersed throughout the Americas thousands of years ago. Many of these plants were cultivated by the Pueblo peoples, who were very good farmers. Pueblo ancestors developed and hybridized many of our summer and winter squashes.*

*Native festivals and celebrations are nurtured by the Three Sisters—corn, beans, and squash— always feeding folks in deliciously different ways, like this.*

**1 cup grated zucchini squash**

**2 eggs, beaten until light and fluffy**

**1/4 cup honey or maple syrup**

**2 tablespoon sugar**

**1/2 cup corn oil**

**2 cups all-purpose flour**

**1/4 cup fine yellow cornmeal**

**2 teaspoons baking powder**

**1/2 teaspoon baking soda**

**1/2 teaspoon salt**

**1/2 teaspoon allspice, finely ground**

**1 tablespoon orange zest, finely grated**

**1 cup currants**

**1/2 cup black walnuts, or pecans, chopped**

Preheat oven to 325°. Grate zucchini and drain in a sieve or colander. In a large bowl, combine the eggs, honey, sugar, and oil, beating well together. Add the dry ingredients one at a time, beating well into the wet ingredients. Add zucchini, orange zest, currants, and nuts. Mix until everything is well blended. If too dry, add a small amount of water or milk.

Pour bread batter into a well-greased loaf pan. Bake in the center of the oven for 45 to 55 minutes until the loaf is golden and a knife inserted into its center comes out clean. Remove from oven and cool the pan on a wire rack for 5 to 10 minutes. Loosen the edges of the loaf with a bread or dinner knife and turn it out to cool completely on wire rack. Wrap securely and refrigerate until ready to serve. This bread has excellent keeping qualities and is even better when it is a day or two old, as its flavors mingle well. Slice generously and serve with condiments such as Spicy Pumpkin Seed Butter (page 92), Red Bean–Herb Butter (page 154), or Spicy Roast Sweet Potato Butter (page 127).

**Makes 1 loaf**

# SPICY ROAST SWEET POTATO BUTTER

*Among the most soothing of root vegetables are sweet potatoes. "A batata well cured and well prepared is just like fine marzipan," said Fernandez de Oviedo, who first took cured sweet potatoes to Spain in the 1500s. Sweet potatoes, Ipomoea batatas, sometimes confused with yams, were probably domesticated in western South America about 2800 B.C.—possibly earlier.*

*The thick, elongated roots of this delicious staple can vary from yellow and dry to dark orange and moist. There is even an old-fashioned white kind, borne from the ancient fields and hearths of the Quechua People.*

*Wherever you can get them, if you do not grow them, select fresh, firm specimens. During my childhood summers in Tennessee on my grandparents' farm, I would enjoy one whole baked or roasted potato as a meal in itself. I still enjoy them this way, and in my treasured lexicon of "spiritual" foods, this is a special "soul food."*

**2 large sweet potatoes, pricked once or twice with fork**

**1 medium tart apple, pricked with fork**

**1/4 teaspoon allspice, finely ground**

**1/4 teaspoon salt**

**1 teaspoon honey**

**black pepper to taste**

Preheat oven to 450° or light up an outside grill. If you are using an oven, place sweet potatoes in a large baking dish or on a baking sheet and bake for 20 minutes. Then place the apple in the oven with the partially cooked potatoes. Continue baking for an additional 30 minutes or until sweet potatoes and apple are soft.

Cool slightly. Peel sweet potatoes and apple, if desired, and process in a food processor with the remaining ingredients. Serve in bright ramekins or in carved-out fresh winter squash "bowls." This is excellent warm or chilled, in place of conventional butters or margarines.

**Makes about 5 cups**

# Three Kings' Day Festival and Dance January 6

Governor's Day, honoring the incoming governors and officers of various pueblos, is often combined with the celebration of the Three Kings and the Feast of Epiphany at Indian pueblos in New Mexico. Along with the Buffalo, Deer, Eagle, and Elk dances held at most pueblos, a colorful intermingling of compatible traditions is celebrated in festival foods for this feast time.

The Feast of the Epiphany commemorates the night the Three Wise Men brought gifts to the Christ Child in Bethlehem. Twelfth Night mirrors early Christian traditions during the Middle Ages when the Christmas season lasted twelve days, reflecting its roots in the earlier pagan Saturnalia. Pueblo Indian artistry overlays these traditions with Pueblo pageantry, meanings, and celebrations all beautifully interwoven.

Celebrations of the coming of the Three Kings are annual events at the pueblos at Pojoaque, Sandia, Picuris, Laguna, and Isleta. Elaborate food preparations are integral to each celebration, and Pueblo hospitality and generosity are the touchstones of these memorable, energetic events. Dancers, families, gathered friends, and many visitors must all be feasted.

128

# Little Indian Fruit Pies

*Spanish influences and contemporary tastes for sweetness merge to make these memorable little fruit pies, called* empanaditas *or* paselitos. *These are served at many Pueblo feast days, special gatherings, and especially at holidays. This basic recipe may be varied seasonally. Pumpkin or apple pie pockets are wonderful in winter; strawberry or peach pockets are summer delights. Raisins, currants, or combinations of wild fruits and nuts make these tasty on every occasion.*

## FRUIT FILLING

**1/2 cup honey**

**1/2 cup raisins or currants**

**1 cup cooked pumpkin, puréed**

**1 tablespoon water**

**1/2 teaspoon allspice, finely ground**

**pinch of salt (optional)**

Combine all ingredients in a small saucepan, stirring well with each addition. Cook over medium heat until mixture simmers. Reduce heat to low and cook for 5 minutes, stirring often. Set aside.

## PASTRY

**1 1/2 cups all-purpose flour**

**1 teaspoon baking powder**

**1/4 teaspoon salt**

**1/2 teaspoon sugar**

**1/2 teaspoon cinnamon**

**5 tablespoons chilled lard or butter**

**4 tablespoons ice water**

In a medium mixing bowl, combine the dry ingredients. Cut in the chilled lard or butter until the mixture resembles fine meal. Carefully add the ice water, a tablespoonful at a time, mixing the dough well until it is easy to roll. You may not need all of the water. Cut dough in half; wrap each half securely with plastic wrap. Place both pieces in the refrigerator to chill for 30 minutes.

# FINISHING TOUCHES

**1 egg, well beaten, with**

**1 tablespoon milk or water**

**1/2 cup sugar**

**pinch of sugar (optional)**

Preheat oven to 400°. Roll out half of the chilled dough on a lightly floured surface to a thickness of 1/2-inch to 1/4-inch. Cut 3-inch circles with a floured biscuit cutter or the rim of a glass. Put 1 generous teaspoonful of reserved fruit filling on half of each circle. Dip your finger into the tablespoonful of milk or water and run this wetness just around the edge of each circle. Fold circle of dough in half, carefully pinching and crimping the edges together like a half-moon. Press edges gently with a spoon or fork; prick the tops to vent. Repeat the process with the second half of the dough. Place each pie pocket about 1 inch apart on an ungreased pastry sheet. Brush their tops with the beaten egg, and lightly sprinkle with a pinch of sugar (optional). Bake in center of oven for 15 minutes until just lightly golden. Carefully remove to cool on a rack or sugared plate. If desired, lightly dust with sifted powdered sugar to make "snowy" paselitos.

**Makes 15 to 20 little pie pockets**

# Spicy Sunseed Popcorn Mix

*Popcorn is one of the most popular maize varieties. Easy to grow and easy to prepare, it has a fragrance that is undeniably classic. Pottery popcorn pots and large gold and silver peanuts have been found at some prehistoric South American Indian sites. These valuable objects suggest that these native vegetables were very important to the ancestors of today's Indians. For maximum nutrition, we now know to eat these two foods together. In this dish, this dynamic duo is the perfect snack to accompany Three Kings' Day celebrations.*

**1 cup shelled peanuts**

**1/2 cup shelled pecans, broken into quarters**

**1 cup sunflower seeds**

**1/2 cup pumpkin seeds, shelled**

**1/2 cup maple syrup, honey, or molasses**

**1/2 cup raisins**

**1 cup popcorn, any color**

**pinch of salt and pepper to taste (optional)**

Combine the peanuts, pecans, sunflower seeds, and pumpkin seeds in a shallow baking pan. Bake in the oven at 320° for 20 minutes. Heat the maple syrup and raisins in a small saucepan over low heat for 5 minutes, stirring. Set aside.

Pop the corn in a hot-air popper, allowing it to settle in a large, broad bowl. Remove roasted nuts and seeds from the oven and add to the hot maple mixture. Blend well and drizzle over the hot popcorn, mixing well. Season to taste. Serve warm.

This mixture can also be shaped into balls or bars for individual servings.

**Makes 6 to 8 cups**

# Iroquois Midwinter Ceremonies

Throughout Indian America, ceremonies are as unique as the people who plan them, and many come from ancient origins filled with inventive and powerful wisdoms. Among traditional Iroquois People the longest and most important event of the ceremonial year is the Midwinter Ceremony.

The Iroquois nations once extended from the Atlantic seaboard to the Mississippi River, and from southern Canada to the Carolinas. Today most Iroquois live on reservations and trust lands in New York, Wisconsin, and Canada. The famous warriors, hunters-gatherers, statesmen, and farmers noted throughout hundreds of years of early history continue to evolve while holding closely to the rich tribal traditions of such groups as the Seneca, the Oneida, the Onondaga, the Cayuga, the Tuscarora, and the Mohawk. Political pressures and internal conflicts consume considerable attention, yet the Haudenosaunee, as the Iroquois call themselves, continue to endure and to develop their many talents.

With the great spread of Iroquois People today around the country, it is harder to set the time of the Midwinter Ceremonies, and often the dates have to coincide with the chiefs' and peoples' schedules. Traditionally Midwinter begins on the fifth day after the new moon of January, and for the Iroquois this most special ceremony marks the end of one ritual year and the beginning of the new year.

Held when the Pleiades are directly overhead at dusk and after the first new moon (the thirteenth moon) after the Winter Solstice, the theme of the Midwinter ceremony is renewal, while the intent "is to give thanks to all natural and supernatural beings in this world," according to David Richmond, Snipe Clan Mohawk at Akwesasne.

# The Pleiades

*A*mong the forty-one constellations visible from the northern hemisphere, many hold valued points of honor in Native ceremonies, beliefs, and storytelling. The conspicuous cluster of seven bright stars in the constellation Taurus is called the Pleiades. Though easily visible, they are actually more than 400 light-years away from Earth. A key winter constellation in Iroquois traditions, the Pleiades have also been the focus of legends among other cultures. Each year the Seven Star Dancers circle the Sky World, and when they dance directly over the world of the Iroquois People in the crisp January nights of greatest darkness, during the new-moon, they remind the Iroquois that it is time to clean and prepare the lodges and longhouses for the Midwinter Ceremonies.

Lasting a week to ten days, the Midwinter Ceremonies begin each day with a thanksgiving address and the ritual burning of tobacco with prayers. The eighteen ceremonies are performed entirely in their Native language, and no outsiders are permitted to photograph, sketch, take notes, or visit the longhouse during this time.

Midwinter also marks the Iroquois New Year, and many take it as their birthday time. Naming ceremonies for newborn children, curing ceremonies, confessions, and thanksgiving for the False Faces and Medicine Societies also take place now. The Feast for the Dead is held at this time, and food and tobacco are offered to them so that their souls will be at rest.

Dreams and visions are valuable, essential forces throughout these ceremonies, as they often foretell illness and detail curing practices. Old dreams are renewed during the Midwinter Ceremonies, sustaining the intimate connections between the people and their whole worldview, or cosmology.

133

# IROQUOIS THREE SISTERS SOUP

*Traditional Iroquois recipes have been handed down for centuries from mother to daughter and son, subtly changing and always adding to our food concepts. These talented gardeners and hunters have hundreds of different recipes for corn alone. Iroquois succotash, Ogonsaganonda, is a favorite ceremonial dish inspired by generations of gardeners and great cooks. It celebrates the gifts of corn, squash, and beans, known to the Iroquois as the "Three Sisters." This recipe is developed from a number of Iroquois preparations working to balance the "Three Sisters" and their nutritional complements.*

**5 tablespoons butter or corn oil**

**2 medium onions, diced**

**1 medium green bell pepper, diced**

**1 medium red bell pepper, diced**

**3 cups whole kernel white corn**

**1 cup cut green beans**

**1 cup lima beans**

**1 cup red kidney beans, cooked**

**1 zucchini squash, cubed**

**6 cups chicken or beef stock, or water**

**2 bay leaves**

**1 teaspoon thyme**

**1/2 teaspoon paprika**

**1/2 teaspoon salt**

**1/2 teaspoon black pepper**

**1/2 teaspoon cumin**

In a large soup pot, over medium heat, melt the butter or oil and sauté the onion and peppers, stirring well for just 5 minutes. Carefully add each of the remaining ingredients, stirring well. Bring to a boil, then lower heat so that soup simmers actively while you prepare the dumplings recipe on page 135. Soup may simmer for at least 15 minutes.

**Serves 8**

# RED BEAN–CORN DUMPLINGS

*The late Irene Richmond, Snipe Clan Mohawk at Akwesasne, showed me how to prepare these favorite dumplings. I always think of her when I make this. She was a legendary cook in Hogansburg, New York, and her legacy lives on in her four children and many grandchildren and great-grandchildren.*

**1 cup fine yellow cornmeal**

**1/4 cup all-purpose flour, sifted**

**1 teaspoon baking powder**

**1/2 teaspoon salt**

**1/4 teaspoon black pepper**

**1/2 cup red kidney beans, cooked**

**2 eggs, well beaten with 1/2 cup milk**

**1 tablespoon corn oil or melted butter**

**3 tablespoons hot broth from the accompanying soup**

In a medium bowl, assemble all ingredients and mix well to form a batter. Drop this batter in generous tablespoonfuls, one at a time, into the simmering soup. Cover the pot securely. Continue to simmer for 15 to 20 minutes, then serve at once, ladling the dumplings and soup into big bowls. Garnish with diced green onions, if desired.

**Makes about 8 dumplings**

---

### A Winter's Tale

*An old Iroquois legend tells how the Frost Spirit goes about pounding the great maple, ash, and hickory trees with a huge club in the icy winter woods, as he has since long ago. During the long winter evenings in late December and January, when the people gather around warm fires to listen to the stories, they can still hear the occasional "pop" and "boom" echoing from the Frost Spirit's club as he races through the frozen hardwood forests. Perhaps you have heard it, too?*

---

# Strawberry Pan Cake

*Longhouse ceremonies as well as family gatherings are sweetened with many different desserts, and a favorite ingredient is the strawberry—a sacred herb and food in Iroquois life. This recipe for a strawberry cake is inspired by various Iroquois friends.*

1 stick butter, or margarine (1/2 cup)

1 cup sugar

1/2 cup maple syrup

4 eggs, beaten

1 teaspoon vanilla extract

2 cups all-purpose flour

1/2 cup fine cornmeal

2 teaspoons baking powder

1/2 teaspoon ground allspice

2 cups fresh or frozen strawberries, sliced, in juice

powdered sugar to sift over finished cake (optional)

Preheat oven to 350°.

In a large mixing bowl, cream together the butter, sugar, and maple syrup. Beat in the eggs until light and fluffy. Add the extract, then gradually stir in the next four dry ingredients. When well blended, turn this batter into a lightly greased or oiled oblong 13x9-inch cake pan.

Spoon the sliced strawberries into the batter at regular intervals, evenly, in about 14 to 16 spots. Bake for 45 minutes until light golden and test knife comes out clean. Cool slightly on wire rack. Cut into 14 to 16 servings and spoon onto plates. You may want to dust powdered sugar lightly over this and add a generous spoonful of strawberry or vanilla ice cream.

**Serves 14 to 16**

# Evening Firelight Dances and
# San Ildefonso Pueblo Feast Day

Late January is one of the best times to visit San Ildefonso Pueblo. Embracing more than 26,000 acres northwest of Santa Fe, in the shadow of Black Mesa in the heart of the Santa Fe National Forest, San Ildefonso is a member of the Eight Northern Indian Pueblos Council, working hard to maintain and preserve tribal culture and to improve economic conditions.

In January, their Vespers and Evening Firelight Dances include the Comanche, Deer, and Buffalo dances, many of which have been performed for hundreds of years much as you see them performed today. In these dances Pueblo Indians honor their Mother of Game and thank her for leading buffalo, deer, elk, mountain goats, and rabbits to worthy hunters. The significance of animals to Indian cultures goes far beyond hunting, ceremonies, foods, and material welfare to the tribes. Many creatures command respect for their spirit gifts, beauty, and physical agilities, and some animals play valuable roles in Native curing rites and treating certain illness.

Buffalo dancers are among the most striking performers, with their blackened faces beneath immense buffalo-horned headdresses. The Buffalo Dancers carry traditional gourd rattles in one hand and bows and arrows in the other hand, as they symbolically and stylistically imitate the revered buffalo.

# PUEBLO GREEN CHILI STEW

*This recipe is based on a traditional preparation of Ruth Obenstine's, of Santa Ana Pueblo, whose legendary cooking talents are well appreciated. Winter feast days are blessed with varieties of hot stews and soups and the wonderful Pueblo breads that accompany them. Fabulous traditional cooks, like Ruth, continue to share the radiant foods of festival times, eagerly sought-after at other times also throughout the year.*

1/4 cup corn oil

2 large yellow onions, chopped

5 cloves garlic, chopped

2 pounds lean beef stew meat, cubed

2 tablespoons chili powder

1 pound fresh stewing tomatoes, blanched and chopped, or 1 large can
stewed tomatoes, chopped

3 pounds fresh Anaheim green chilies, roasted and thinly sliced

1 small Serrano or jalapeño chili, roasted, diced fine

salt and pepper to taste

1 cup water, more or less

2 large bay leaves

1/4 cup epazote or Mexican oregano, finely chopped

Heat oil in a large kettle over medium-high heat. Sear onions, garlic, beef, and chili powder quickly in the hot oil, stirring well to keep ingredients from burning or sticking. Add tomatoes, chilies, and salt and pepper, stirring well. Add enough water to cover ingredients and fill kettle more than half full. Add remaining ingredients; stir well. Balance tastes. Simmer, stirring occasionally, for 45 minutes to an hour. Ruth says that for seasonal variations you can add diced, boiled potatoes or squash chunks. This is also great spooned generously over large, hot, sliced baked potatoes; top both with grated cheese or sour cream.

**Serves 8**

# FEBRUARY

*The vermilion predawn rim of the horizon flushes with sunrise, pulling up the eastern sky and barely warming the winter world. The slightest breeze through old winter oak leaves makes a sound like spring rain—a sweet dichotomy as I crunch by in deep snow, amazed at their music. Coyote skat marks the meadow path, saying much about the coyote's ample winter diet of deer and raccoon. The bald eagles are congregating near the broken ice on the lake, and the fishing is good.*

*In the Northwest, this is the Bald Eagle Moon of the Koyukon and Olachen Is Eaten Moon of the Tsimshian. Moving east, this is the Hard Time To Build A Fire Moon of the Nez Perce, the Snow Blinds Moon of the Teton Sioux, the Little Bud Moon of the Kiowa, the Fish-Running Moon of the Winnebago, and the Moon When The Geese Come Home of the Omaha. In the Southwest, this is the Moon Of The Cedar Dust Wind of the Tewa Pueblo.*

*Among the tribes in the Northeast, this is the Crusts Of Ice On The Snow Moon of the Penobscot, the Sun Is Very Strong Moon of the Micmac, the Moon When Ice In The River Is Gone of the Wampanoag, and the Moon Of Thawing, When The Spruce Tips Fall of the Narragansett. Crisp and brittle days of February have a different pace and flavor in every region. Native urgencies in deep winter signal unique celebrations, even when times are difficult. Sharing festival foods and celebrating survival warms many folks.*

Large stands of immense cedar, hemlock, spruce, and fir trees stretch along the rugged coastal region from northern California through southeastern Alaska in the lush land of mist and rain. Precipitous coastal mountains rise up from the ocean shore in most places, as warm Pacific winds drop their moisture on this varied, temperate rain forest that is the homeland of the Northwest Coast Indian culture. Chilkat, Tlingit, Gitksan, Haida, Tsimshian, Bella Coola, Kwakiutl, Nootka, Makah, Quinault, Chinook, and so many more are often called the Totem Pole People, although in truth only the wealthy, respected families were able to own totem poles. Totem poles are the tallest wood carvings in the world, the tallest being about 60 feet high. They are usually fashioned dramatically from native Western Red Cedar, *Thuja plicata,* or Giant Arborvitae, which has also been used extensively in clothing, basketry, mat-making, and foods.

In the Kwakiutl winter ceremonies, the faces, furs, feathers, and totems of the commanding "supernaturals" remind the people of unpredictable forces residing in their forests, seas, and skies. It is time to acknowledge, appease, and reaffirm their identity as Kwakiutl, and everything in their natural world seems transformed to convey this importance. Ritually dressed in strips of cedar bark, ceremonial performers wear an amazing range of ornately carved spirit masks, created to evoke the multitude of "supernaturals"— from ghosts, grizzlies, wolves, seals, ravens, and killer whales to wasps, bees, and owls. Some of the chiefs are splendidly wrapped in water-resistant Chilkat blankets woven of mountain goat hair and fine cedar-bark fiber twine. The dramatic dances, or *tseka,* pantomimed during the Winter Ceremonies were among the most spectacular in the Kwakiutl pantheon, reassuring their ongoing, day-to-day covenant with the supernatural world overlaying all of life. The Kwakiutl people believed that it was their duty to maintain their ancestral links with the spirit world. In a far distant time, before the Kwakiutl fully emerged, this world was ruled by animals with fantastic powers. Those supernatural beings conferred some of their powers on ancestral humans, who became the forebears of Kwakiutl hereditary clans.

## Raven Created the World

*Raven put the sun, the moon, and the stars into the sky, the salmon into the rivers, and the fish into the sea, and gave the People of the Great Land fire and water and diverse foods to eat, according to the legends of Alaska's coastal Natives. Full of supernatural powers, Raven could turn himself into anything, and he loved to trick and tease.*

*The Raven is one of the main crests of the Tlingit and Haida of southeastern Alaska. Tribal leaders and shamans often wear distinctive Raven masks during elaborate ceremonies performed to bless the hunt, drive away evil spirits, or illustrate important lessons.*

Today many imaginatively masked dancers attend the most important Hamatsa Dance, which is performed by a society whose members claim power from the Cannibal Spirit at the North End of the World. Long periods of training and withdrawal from normal society are demanded for the Hamatsa Society initiates, whose notoriety is often heightened with magical effects, ghostly calls, and wild behavior. Of the many highly stylized masks and dancers, one of the most contrary is the huge-nosed, black and red Fool Dancer, who serves as a messenger and also enforces protocol by loudly threatening members of the audience and even throwing stones at them.

The winter ceremonies included feasting, of course, and the feasting songs drew families and communities together. During the course of many days, foods were prepared to fill the elaborately carved feast dishes many of which are now in museum collections. Favorite feast foods were salmon, salal berries, high-bush cranberries, huckleberries, and blackberries in eulachon grease, crabapples, and soapberries whipped into a froth like whipped cream. Today, as in centuries before, many additional foods and seasonal resources are fished, hunted, and gathered from these lush environments. Contemporary winter foods and feasts reflect more of our modern commodities along the Northwest Coast.

Salmon was the most esteemed and versatile food of the Northwest Coast tribes, much as the buffalo was to the Plains Indians and deer and beaver were to Northeast Woodland Indians. The king or chinook salmon, *Oncorhynchus tshawytscha,* is the largest of the five native species of

Pacific Coast salmon that make annual "runs" up inland waterways to spawn. Coho, sockeye, dog, and humpback salmon are the four other species. According to Kwakiutl traditions, salmon were considered supernatural beings who lived in their own villages beneath the sea and had their own rites and ceremonies; some of these rites were passed on to Kwakiutl ancestors. The salmon caught during seasonal migrations needed to receive ritual respect before being eaten or stored. Each Northwest Coast tribe has its own traditions, ceremonies, prayers, and preparations for honoring the salmon, directed through legends given to them by the salmon people long ago. Accordingly, it is important to place the bones of the first salmon caught and eaten back in the river where it was caught, so that its soul may return to its village and inform the supernaturals that the people still remember.

## The Night Goddess

*The Northern Lights have spawned many colorful legends, but it is actually intense solar storms that provide the energies for this unusual display of vivid colors and ghostly forms. Charged electrons and protons released through sunspot activity strike gas particles in the earth's upper atmosphere. The force with which the gas particles are struck determines the color of the Northern Lights. Moving bands of red, purple, green, and blue extend from 40 to several hundred miles above the earth, where the Earth's gravity usually pulls them magnetically to the northern- and southernmost latitudes. The aurora borealis was first named by Galileo in 1619 for the Roman goddess Aurora. Those of us who have been lucky to witness this celebrated show of light have been dazzled by its supernatural qualities.*

# BAKED SALMON STUFFED WITH CORNBREAD AND CRANBERRIES

*Countless traditional and modern recipes served salmon planked, smoked, grilled, and jerked—indeed the versatilities of this impressive fish are limited only by the imagination and now by declining fish populations. Salmon is a key food served during the Winter Dance, and the many ways it was prepared underscored the importance of the host families. This is just one modern reflection on early Northwest Coast hospitality and generosity.*

*Eulachon, or candlefish,* Thaleichthys pacificus, *are abundant smelts that look like small salmon and are highly prized by Northwest Coast Indians. Their rich oil, used in this recipe, is a primary feast food used alone and with many favorite foods. Northwest tribes created beautiful wooden buckets and feast bowls specifically to hold eulachon oil, and the small, dried fish were also used as torches.*

2 tablespoons eulachon oil or corn oil

3 medium onions, diced

3 cloves garlic, diced

1 cup cranberries, cut in half

1 cup fine yellow cornmeal

1 1/2 cups water or vegetable stock

juice of 1 fresh orange

1 tablespoon orange zest

1 large (5-pound) salmon, gutted and cleaned

salt and pepper to taste

Heat 1 tablespoon of oil in a medium pan over medium heat. Add the onions and garlic and quickly sauté. Add the cranberries, cornmeal, water, and juice of 1 orange, plus 1 tablespoon of orange zest, stirring well, for several minutes to blend.

Rub the salmon inside and outside with the remaining tablespoon of oil. Lay it in a baking pan. Carefully stuff the fish, spooning in the warm cornmeal-cranberry mixture. Lightly season and bake for 40 minutes in a preheated 350° oven, or until the salmon turns pink and flakes easily. Serve with plenty of crisp fresh watercress and dill.

**Serves 8**

### Kwakiutl prayer offered before the first salmon feast:

*O Supernatural Ones! O Swimmers!*
*I thank you that you are willing to come to us.*
*Protect us from danger*
*that nothing evil may happen to us*
*when we eat you.*

# Buckskin Bread with Caviar

*This easy "quick bread" widely enjoyed by many Northwest Coast People is a great surface on which to present wild berry jams and syrups or the fresh raw or marinated roe and milt of favorite fish. Its soft texture resembles fine buckskin, and its flavor is enhanced by adding regional fresh or dried berries or mushrooms to the batter.*

**2 cups flour**

**1 teaspoon powdered kelp or sea salt**

**1 teaspoon baking powder**

**1/2 cup salmonberries or currants, dried**

**1 1/4 cups water**

**1 teaspoon eulachon oil or corn oil**

Preheat oven to 400°. Combine the first 5 ingredients in a medium bowl and blend well. Spread the eulachon oil in a 9-inch castiron skillet, and turn the batter into it, patting it out evenly. Bake dough for 30 to 35 minutes until honey-golden on top. Let pan cool on a rack for 5 minutes, then turn out the bread. Cool further or serve immediately with favorite condiments.

**Makes 1 loaf**

*K*elp, also known as Tangleweed, Laminaria digitata, *and* Sugarwrack, Laminaria *saccharina, is a common seaweed found along Pacific Coast beaches and a versatile food of many Northwest Coast tribes. Long used to wrap and encase foods to be boiled or broiled, it uniquely flavors and seasons many dishes. We continue to use kelp with special campfire and barbecued foods. The dried, powdered blades of kelp are a mineral-rich salt substitute in raw and cooked foods, and the fresh or reconstituted blades (leaves) are delicious vegetable foods.*

# Northwest Coast Caviar

*Caviar is salted fish roe (eggs), and many believe the finest kind is sturgeon roe. The protected endangered species called Pacific green sturgeon,* Acipenser medirostris, *is a slow-swimming bottom fish that can produce up to five million eggs each season. Its roe and milt (creamy male sperm) as well as that of numerous other game fish have long been esteemed seasonal feast foods. The Pacific herring,* Clupea harengus pallasi, *a relative of shad, alewives, sardines, and menhaden, is a favorite, as are the roe and milt of other game fish, especially the species of salmon. Fresh roe (often called hard roe) and the milt (called soft roe) are enjoyed raw, marinated-raw, parboiled, baked, or fried, and are always handled delicately and used when very fresh, as this vital food resource spoils easily. Brief cooking over low heat is best. The fine roe sac, or membrane, needs to be pricked several times with a needle to prevent it from bursting and spewing the tiny eggs.*

**2 cups fresh salmon roe (and milt)**

**1/2 cup eulachon oil or corn oil**

**1/2 cup cider vinegar or other favorite vinegar**

**1/2 cup hot water or fish broth**

**2 teaspoons powdered kelp or sea salt**

**1 teaspoon pepper**

Remove a fresh sac or two of roe from freshly caught salmon; carefully slit each sac to express the fine, little eggs. Place the roe and milt in a glass bowl.

Combine the remaining ingredients in a small saucepan. Stir well and heat this mixture until it boils.

Remove from heat. Pour mixture carefully over the roe. Stir just until blended. Cover and refrigerate. Serve cold with crackers or breads. This can also be marinated for seviche or escabeche (do not add lime juice) and keeps several days.

**Makes about 2 1/2 cups**

Across the north-central United States, early February is a time for Native American social and spiritual focus. A growing number of winter socials and intertribal gatherings throughout the country celebrate the Midwinter and the renewal of life marking the advancing New Year. Community feasts are held now for dancers, singers, drummers, elders, and visitors. Regional and tribal culinary specialties draw folks together in evermore resourceful ways.

At the Founders Day Powwow at Sinte Gleska College in Rosebud, South Dakota, drumming, singing, and dancing, as well as food, head the menu. The Honor Our Ancestors Traditional Powwow at the Negaunee Community Center, in Negaunee, Michigan, and the Annual Council of Indian Students Traditional Winter Powwow, at Bemidji State University in Bemidji, Minnesota, also offer opportunities to celebrate tribal traditions and share favorite winter foods. Some of the same modern powwow chow is found again and again at many of these events, along with the regional traditional soups, stews, and classic chilies. Foods of Ojibwa and Sioux origins dominate many festival menus.

147

# Sioux Plum Raisin Cakes

*Abundant wild fruits and nuts grow throughout this country and are the ancestors of many fine cultivated varieties. Eighteen species of wild plums and cherries are valuable members of the rose family, many forming large thickets that check erosion and shelter wildlife. This dark, moist fruit cake/bread was inspired by wild plums collected while staying on the Cheyenne River Sioux Reservation in Eagle Butte, South Dakota. Fire cherry, black cherry, and chokecherry also work well in this recipe.*

**1 cup dark raisins, cherries, or currants**

**1 cup boiling water**

1 (16-ounce) can  purple plums, drained and pitted

1 cup toasted hazelnuts, chopped

1/2 cup butter, melted, or corn oil

4 cups sifted all-purpose flour

3 teaspoons baking soda

1 1/2 teaspoons salt

1 1/2 teaspoons ground allspice

1 teaspoon ground cloves

1 cup honey

1/2 cup maple syrup

Preheat oven to 350°. Place the raisins, cherries, or currants in a small glass bowl.  Cover them with 1 cup boiling water; soak them until plump for about 30 minutes. Lightly oil 24 or more muffin cups. Mash the plums in a large mixing bowl. Add all the remaining ingredients to the plums and mix well. Add the soaked raisins (or other fruit) and their liquid. Blend all together well. Carefully measure by tablespoonfuls, filling each muffin cup halfway. Bake 25 to 30 minutes, until a toothpick inserted in the center of a muffin comes out clean. Cool for 10 minutes on a wire rack, then loosen sides, and turn out cakes. Serve warm with flavored honey or the companion butter in the next recipe.

**Makes 24 cakes (muffins)**

# RASPBERRY-PLUM BUTTER

*Tart-sweet fruit butters are delightful no-fat replacements for conventional dairy products and borrow from the ancient time-honored practices of using and appreciating wild resources. This version was inspired by wild raspberries I collected on the Muckleshoot Indian Reservation in Washington state before heading to Glacier National Park. Blackberries, close cousins of the raspberry, can also be used in this recipe.*

**1 cup fresh red raspberries**

**1 cup fresh wild plums, or canned purple plums, pitted**

**1 cup water or apple juice (or favorite fruit juice)**

**1/2 cup honey**

**1/4 cup fresh lemon juice**

Combine all ingredients in a medium saucepan over medium heat. Cook, stirring to blend well, for 15 minutes, mashing fruits with the back of the spoon. Cool slightly and purée in a blender or food processor. Serve hot or cold spooned over individual plum cakes or in a generous bowl beside them.

**Makes 2 1/2 cups**

# CANDELARIA DAY CELEBRATION AND DANCES

Dances at the Picuris and San Felipe pueblos in New Mexico celebrate Candelaria Day and the beauty of winter. Picuris, once one of the largest northern pueblo communities, was settled in the 1200s. Nestled in the wooded foothills of the Sangre de Cristo Mountains in north-central New Mexico, it shows some Plains Indian influences. Its Hidden Valley Restaurant serves Indian foods to growing numbers of visitors year-round. Although the people of the San Felipe Pueblo are extremely protective of their traditional customs, they are noted for the beautiful Candelaria Day ceremonial dances to which visitors are welcomed.

Also called Candlemas Day, Candelaria Day is the ecclesiastical festival honoring the presentation of the infant Jesus in the temple. Candles are paraded and blessed with much pageantry at these two northern pueblos, and the following recipe is inspired from traditional foods served on this day.

## Corn—The Real Gold of the Americas

First grown by Indians in the regions that are now central Mexico more than 7,000 years ago, corn was developed from selective breeding of a wild grass. During the following millennia, hybridization and trading of corn spread along pre-Columbian trade routes through much of the Americas.

European explorers detailed vast fields of Indian corn, each field growing different varieties and different colors of corn—yellow, red, blue, black, flesh-colored, and speckled corn—each with its own purpose and unique properties. Certain colors had religious and ceremonial importance; some could be eaten only on special occasions.

All plant parts were known to have uses in foods and medicines as well as utilitarian and ceremonial applications. Games, dolls, masks, and musical instruments were also fashioned from various parts of the plants.

Corn is still a major part of the modern American diet. The list of corn products is long and diverse. Corn chips, corn flake cereal, popcorn, corn on the cob, corn grits, corn puddings, corn crackers, cornbread, and more fill our pantries. Corn syrup sweetens and flavors many of our beverages, ice creams, puddings, baby foods, and candies. Cornstarch, corn oil margarines, and corn glucose and dextrose products are staples in food preparation.

# SPICY CORN-PEPPER SALSA

*Celebrating the gifts of Pueblo horticulture as well as the gift of natural color, this condiment reflects the diversity of Indian corn in all its delicious generosity. Taken around the world to feed every culture, corn comes back to us still in countless international cuisines. This recipe keeps corn closely connected to its Indian origins.*

1/2 cup sunflower seed or corn oil

2 medium green bell peppers, finely chopped

2 medium red bell peppers, finely chopped

1 small jalapeño pepper, very finely diced

3 medium onions, finely chopped

4 cups freshly cut whole-kernel yellow corn

1 1/2 cups apple cider vinegar, or more, to taste

1/2 cup fine cornmeal

1/2 cup honey or maple syrup (each has a unique taste)

1/2 teaspoon salt, or more to taste

1/2 teaspoon freshly cracked black pepper

1 teaspoon celery seeds

1 teaspoon mustard seeds

Heat oil in a large skillet and sauté the three peppers and the onion over medium heat for 5 to 10 minutes, until vegetables are just glistening and translucent. Add the corn, stirring thoroughly. Lower heat to simmer, and add last 7 ingredients. Stir well after each addition. Continue to simmer and stir occasionally, adjusting tastes, for approximately 30 minutes. Cool and serve, or cover and refrigerate for several days to develop fuller flavors. Use as a relish to accompany many different foods

**Makes about 10 cups**

# Hopi Powamu Ceremony and Bean Dance

The Hopi Powamu Ceremony is a ritual fertility ceremony to ask for plentiful crops. This sixteen-day-long collection of rites beginning on the new moon in February spiritually prepares the Hopi and their arid lands for the coming planting season. Beans are ceremonially blessed and planted in moist sand in boxes nurtured in the hothouselike warmth of the semisubterranean kiva, the sacred ceremonial chamber from which much of Hopi spiritual life radiates. Ceremonies to secure favorable planting conditions are powerful village events, necessary to ensure that the seeds will sprout and thrive with the warming weather. The seeds that had been brought into the kiva during the winter solstice are now blessed with the potentials for new life and fertile growth.

*Talavai,* or Early Morning Kachinas, usually appear in pairs to sing from the rooftops, waking the people by ringing the bells they carry with their sacred spruce boughs. The Talavai lead the other kachinas in their singing and dancing, often accompanied by Nataska, the Black Ogre, who is one of the disciplinary kachinas appearing early in the kachina ceremonial cycle. The ogres have fearsome attributes: large, bulging eyes, long, alligator-like snapping snouts; bizarre, jagged teeth; and an impressive fan-like crest of dark feathers. It is their role to threaten families, particularly children, requiring their obedience, cooperation, and the proper offerings of meat and cornmeal. Koyemsi, the Mudhead Kachina, adds comic relief to the serious kachina rituals, assuming many supportive roles as drummer, announcer, and assistant. Some believe that the original people, who emerged from the Sipapu, the earth opening in the Grand Canyon, looked like Mudheads.

The Powamu ceremony is a plea to the kachinas to bless the seeds that will be planted, and its Bean Dance is a celebration of germination. The kachinas dance into the plaza following the sacred cornmeal path that has been sprinkled for them by the priests. Their presence is powerful as it embodies the living spirits of the mysterious forces of nature so necessary for all Hopi life. They will live in the village for the next six months and dance for rain, fertility, and other myriad blessings.

On the last day of the Powamu Ceremony, Crow Mother Kachina walks through the village carrying a basket of fresh bean sprouts that were forced to germinate in the kiva, signifying the abundance to come. She is accompanied by her sons, the horned Hu' Kachinas called the Whipper Twins. With bared teeth and bulging eyes beneath wild, feathered tufts of hair, they carry long yucca fronds to ritually whip Hopi children, as part of their initiation into the kachina cult.

# HOPI YELLOW BEAN CAKES

*Varieties of Hopi beans are blessed at Powamu, and it is the one called* Sikya hatiko *that is sprouted in their kiva rituals, usually by the midpoint of their sixteen-day ceremonial cycle. These fresh young plants, with the pale yellow to orange mottled-black "mother bean" attached, are applied to kachina dolls, bows, and rattles and are given by Crow Mother Kachina to children throughout the village. The remaining sprouts are then chopped, boiled, and prepared for the feast.*

1 cup Hopi yellow beans or white beans, cooked and mashed

1/2 cup fine yellow cornmeal

1 teaspoon cooking ash or baking soda

1/2 teaspoon salt

1 tablespoon fresh epazote, finely chopped

1 tablespoon honey

1 tablespoon corn oil

2 eggs, well beaten and light

1 cup bean water, vegetable broth, or milk

oil for griddle

In a large bowl, combine the mashed beans and cornmeal, blending well. Stir in the remaining ingredients except the oil for the griddle, blending well, and allow to rest for 20 minutes or so. Add more liquid, if necessary, to thin the batter when ready to grill.

Warm griddle to medium-high, oil lightly, and drop batter by half-tablespoonfuls. Flatten and grill quickly, about 2 to 3 minutes on each side. Remove to broad platter lightly sprinkled with fine cornmeal. Serve warm with whipped bean butter and cilantro and epazote leaves.

**Makes 24 or more little cakes**

# WHIPPED RED BEAN–HERB BUTTER

*Another special variety of Hopi bean is the pala hatiko. These low-desert beans are solid red, sometimes streaked with black, and they are meaty, tasty, and very versatile. In this recipe, a little goes a long way, pleasingly.*

*We served this delicious creation as an appetizer for an opening-night menu of "American Indian Regional Specialties" for an American Indian audience at the Native American Film Festival at Lincoln Center in New York City. It was fabulous!*

1 tablespoon corn oil

2 tablespoons onion, diced

1/2 teaspoon chili powder

1 cup Hopi red beans, cooked and mashed (or pinto or kidney beans)

1/2 tablespoon fine cornmeal

**1 tablespoon apple cider vinegar**

**1 tablespoon epazote, diced**

**1 tablespoon cilantro, diced**

**1/2 teaspoon salt**

**1/2 teaspoon freshly cracked black pepper**

Heat the oil in a medium saucepan over medium heat. Quickly sauté the onion and chili powder, stirring well for 3 minutes. Add the mashed beans, cornmeal, and vinegar, stirring well after each addition. Simmer for about 5 minutes. Add remaining ingredients, balance tastes, and simmer for 3 minutes.

Remove from heat, stir, and cool.

Purée cool bean-herb butter, whipping briefly until fine. Place small half-tablespoonfuls on top of each small bean cake; barely flatten the butter, and place a fresh cilantro leaf on top.

**Makes 1 1/2 cups**

## Beans

*E*arly evidence of four domesticated species of native Phaseolus indicates that bean cultivation may have closely accompanied the cultivation of corn (maize), squashes, pumpkins, and chilies in the Americas. Scarlet runner bean, Phaseolus coccineus, which was called ayacotli ("red flower") in Nahautl, has probably been cultivated more than 2,000 years in Mexico, and its wild ancestors are dated at over 8700 B.C. in Oaxaca. Lima beans, Phaseolus lunatus, also show a range of early dates of 3000 to 6000 B.C. in the Andes highlands. String beans, Phaseolus vulgaris, date back to 5000 B.C. in ancient Mexico, and the northernmost tepary beans, Phaseolus acutifolius, date to 3000 B.C.

Native to the New World and cultured by ancestors of many of today's Native Peoples into numerous varieties distinguished by taste, color, and size, beans have had thousands of years to become woven into the traditions of earlier people. Rich in minerals, beans are also a traditional protein complement to corn and contain soluble fiber helpful in controlling cholesterol and diabetes. Beans are also valuable members of the legume family, fixing nitrogen from the air when appropriate soil bacteria are present. Native gardeners often inter-cropped beans with corn and other vegetables, and a number of the earlier varieties grow as perennial vines in their native tropical environments.

# HOT BLACK LAVA CHILI

*Spicing, smoking, and cooking meats were early techniques for preserving meat, preventing meat spoilage, and "masking" the taste of meats that were already becoming spoiled. Some of these techniques gave birth to our American "chile con carne" and its countless variations. Pure invention rules this field—recipes are limited only by one's imagination. The small Hopi black beans called "kumvimore" work deliciously in this, as will any favorite black turtle beans. Soak overnight and partially precook beans in preparation.*

3 strips of lean bacon, cut into small pieces

2 pounds lean venison meat, cut in bite-size bits

1 pound lean pork meat, cut in small cubes

6 cloves garlic, chopped

2 large yellow onions, chopped

3 Ancho chili peppers, roasted, chopped

2 Poblano chili peppers, roasted, chopped

4 cups black beans, partially cooked

6 tablespoons chili powder, toasted

4 tablespoons cumin powder

1 teaspoon salt, more or less, to taste

3 cups tomato sauce

2 cups hot water

1/2 cup epazote, chopped fine

1 teaspoon oregano

1 teaspoon paprika

3 tablespoons cider vinegar

1 jalapeño chili pepper, roasted, chopped fine (optional)

Heat and cook bacon, briefly, in a large skillet or deep stew pot over medium-high heat to render a small amount of fat. Immediately add the venison and then the pork, stirring continually to brown all surfaces. Lower heat to medium and spoon meat to one edge of pan. Add the garlic and onions, stirring well but briefly to just wilt. Then add the chilies, blending well. Next add the beans, chile powder, cumin, salt, tomato sauce, and water. Stir well to blend together; continue cooking for an hour at high-simmer. Stir well occasionally.

During the last 20 minutes of cooking time, add the herbs, paprika, and vinegar . Stir well, balance liquids, and adjust taste. Simmer for another 15 minutes.

Remove the chili from the heat and allow to stand for 1 to 2 hours or two so that flavors mingle. Reheat and balance liquids and flavors to your taste before serving. Add salt, chili powder, or optional jalapeño chili if desired.

Prepare fresh garnishes and condiments such as Rattlesnake Salsa (page 158), diced avocado, diced green onions, red onions, epazote, cilantro, white cheese, and sour cream. Small bowls clustered around the Hot Black Lava Chili make a hearty, colorful presentation, and then everybody can "season" their servings individually. Bake fresh cornbread or frybread to accompany this delicious classic.

**Serves 8 to 10**

157

# Rattlesnake Salsa

*Many popular recipe names give stylish color to respected, often-sacred native animals. Although rattlesnakes are "ranched" in a manner not unlike other large game animals and are meaty and delicious, this meatless, colorful salsa contains no rattlesnake. Some of its special essence comes from the little, round, rusty-brown cascabel (Spanish for "rattle") chilies and serrano chilies roasted for smoky charm and flavor.*

**3 cascabel chili peppers, roasted and chopped**

**2 serrano chili peppers, roasted and chopped**

**2 medium tomatoes, poached and chopped**

**4 tomatillos, husked, poached and chopped**

**3 cloves garlic, roasted and finely chopped**

**1 small onion, finely chopped**

**3 green onions, finely chopped**

**1/4 teaspoon ground allspice**

**1/4 teaspoon salt**

**2 tablespoons apple cider vinegar**

**1 teaspoon sunflower seed oil**

**1/2 cup water**

Assemble all ingredients near a food processor or blender. Briefly process a little at a time until you have the texture you desire for this salsa—coarse, medium, or fine. Balance seasonings to your taste. Serve at room temperature. This salsa keeps well for 3 to 5 days, covered, in the refrigerator. It accompanies many diverse dishes very well.

This can be served beautifully in several carved, peeled jicama bowls, which are delightful to eat afterwards!

**Makes 4 to 5 cups**

# O'odham Tash Indian Days
# Celebration

Casa Grande, Arizona, welcomes more than 250,000 people during mid-February for their nationally acclaimed "window into the Native American culture." Many popular activities draw visitors together at O'odham Tash "Indian Days" for such annual events as an all-Indian rodeo, an all-Indian powwow, all-Indian ceremonial dances, and Native American arts, crafts and demonstrations. More than 200 individual tribal dancers from all over North America are featured here. Visitors also have the pleasure of listening to and dancing to the vivacious sounds of colorful Chicken Scratch bands, so popular throughout the South.

Some of the best Native American cowboys and cowgirls vie for a $40,000 purse in such events as bareback riding, saddlebronc riding, bull riding, calf roping, team roping, steer wrestling, barrel racing, century roping, and breakaway roping. Exceptional Native American arts, crafts, and foods are arrayed in compelling proximity to the many memorable features here.

The O'odham, "The People" whom we have come to call Pima and Papago, have inhabited their desert homelands for millennia, including some of the hottest, driest terrain in North America. Their regions stretch from Phoenix, Arizona, to east-central Sonora, Mexico, where they are called Pima Bajo in the lowlands and Mountain Pima in the pines and oaks of western Chihuahua. Their desert farming is legendary and gives new meaning to xeriscaping. We continue to learn much from their horticultural and ancient dietary wisdoms.

*W*aila *music and dance of the O'odham is a wildly popular adapted polka that has been evolving among these tribes for more than a hundred years. Waila music absorbs elements of Mexican and European contributions through O'odham social interpretations. Waila was probably born from baile, the Spanish word for a social dance, and the instrumental music is clearly influenced by the Mexican norteño music, with a charming rural southern style that is popularly called Chicken Scratch. Perfect music for social gatherings like weddings, birthday parties, and traditional church feasts, waila can last from sundown to sunrise, warming the desert nights with gregarious sound and lively movement.*

*Tempos are usually beaten out on a single drum or two, accompanied by guitars, violins, and even button accordion and saxophone. Electric acoustics fill out this delightful tribal tradition. Along with the annual Waila Festival and appearances elsewhere, many waila bands and groups gather to perform at the Annual O'odham Tash. The San Simon Old Timers Band, the Joaquin Brothers Band, the Gila River Old Time Fiddlers Band, and the Alex Gomez Band are some of the regional musicians with national recognition, cassette tapes, and a growing following.*

160

# Barbecued Pork Spareribs

*The word* barbecue *can be traced back beyond the Spanish* barbacoa, *meaning "a raised platform for cooking," to the early pit-fire cooking (grilling, roasting, broiling) of the Maya, recorded in their* Popul Vuh *and in the Aztec* Codice Tudela. *Other food historians trace back through French settlers in Florida who roasted their goats whole,* de barbe en queue—*"from beard to tail." There is an old Indian recipe along these lines, that calls for an anthropologist . . .*

*Barbecues are big occasions at O'odham Tash, and at countless other Indian gatherings, where this generous, delicious cooking style fits well with the ubiquitous Indian frybread, tribal corn soups, game roasts, and medleys of beverages.*

*Begin these preparations the day before, as the sauce wants advance preparation for blending of flavors and the meat profits by marinating overnight for tenderness and tastiness.*

Place two racks of lean pork spareribs (6 to 8 pounds) in a large kettle over high heat. Cover with water. Add 2 bay leaves and 10 black peppercorns. Bring to a boil. Reduce heat to a simmer and cook for an hour, skimming the froth as necessary. Remove the spareribs and drain and dry. While the spareribs are simmering, assemble and prepare the barbecue sauce below.

## BARBECUE CHILI SAUCE

*A great barbecue sauce usually begins with the contribution of one or more cups of a great chili sauce (see page 163). The rest is a careful choreography of roasting, cutting, and cooking. The food processor and blender are great helps to those with sensitivities to the heat of chilies and alliums, though some purists still like to make this delicious preparation by hand.*

1 tablespoon corn oil

1 large onion, chopped

3 Poblano chilies, roasted and semi-seeded

3 New Mexican green chili peppers, roasted and semi-seeded (some seeds add great taste, heat, and personality)

1 jalapeño chili pepper, roasted and seeded

2 Pima Bajo chili peppers, roasted and seeded

3 garlic cloves

2 tablespoons apple cider vinegar

2 tablespoons brown sugar

1/2 cup hot water

1 tablespoon Worcestershire sauce

3 tablespoons tequila (optional)

1 teaspoon coarse salt

1 teaspoon freshly cracked black pepper

1/2 teaspoon ground allspice

1/4 cup fresh lemon juice

Heat the oil in a medium skillet over medium heat; sauté the onions in the hot oil until it is crisp. In the food processor, purée well together all of the remaining ingredients. Pour this mixture and crisp onions into a saucepan. Add 1 cup of Ferocious Barbecue Chili Sauce (next page). Simmer for 10 minutes, blending well.

To make the barbecued spareribs, place spareribs on a tray and coat generously with a portion of this sauce. Reserve the remaining sauce in a glass bowl, covered and chilled in the refrigerator until ready for further use. Cover and chill the spareribs overnight in the refrigerator to marinate and develop fuller flavors.

The next day, baste the spareribs again with the sauce and allow them to stand at room temperature for an hour. Prepare the barbecue and oil the grill rack. Build and season the barbecue fire. Set the oiled rack 6 to 8 inches above the glowing coals. Place the spareribs to grill on one side for 8 to 10 minutes, then baste with more sauce and turn. *Note:* It is best to only baste the last 15 minutes or so of cooking time, as cooking the sauce too long makes the spices bitter. Barbecue for an additional 10 minutes until done and the flavor and crispness you desire is achieved. Serve hot with additional barbecue sauce, which can be simmered again and served on the side.

**Serves 12**

# FEROCIOUS BARBECUE CHILI SAUCE

*Those with true courage and a hearty palate may wish to spice up the recipe for Barbecue Chili Sauce.*

**1 1/2 cups of Barbecue Chili Sauce**

**1/4 fresh lemon, seeded and very finely diced**

**1 teaspoon ground coriander**

**1/2 teaspoon ground ginger**

**1/4 teaspoon ground Spanish paprika**

**1/2 teaspoon ground cumin**

**1 small Pico de Gallo "Rooster's Beak" chili, roasted, seeded, and finely ground**

Combine all of the ingredients in a medium saucepan. Heat for no more than 5 minutes. Use as side sauce or as basting sauce.

**Makes 2 cups**

### *To Put Out the Fire!*

*Some of us who are diehard chili-lovers can develop "dragon's breath" or scorched palates, and while the intense "heat" does not last (and does have valuable medicinal benefits), it can be uncomfortable to tender palates. If you need to put out the fire from "chili heat," hold a teaspoonful of chilled plain yogurt or sour cream in your mouth for a few moments, or try a bite of bread, pasta, corn tortillas, potatoes, avocado, or banana. Don't try water!*

*Water cannot put out the fire.*

*If a dish gets too hot/spicy, you may be able to moderate it a bit by adding a teaspoon or two of cider vinegar, and simmering it for another 5 to 10 minutes. If too salty, peel and halve one or two raw potatoes and drop them in, stir them around, and cook for another 10 minutes. Then remove the potatoes and hope for the best.*

# Seminole Tribal Fair, Powwow, and Rodeo

Mid-February marks the big annual Seminole Tribal Fair, Powwow, and Rodeo in Hollywood, Florida. Dancers, riders, drummers and singers, vendors, and cooks converge here with thousands of visitors from all over North America for one of the most colorful four-day celebrations in the South. Thousands of Seminole and Miccosukee People work toward these events all year, and some of their business enterprises (like their Cattle and Range Program, Arts and Crafts Center, Aquaculture (Catfish Farm) Project, Hog Farm, and Citrus Groves) are geared up for this month's extra visitors. Many small home businesses, especially sewing and craftwork, thrive in these winter months. Indeed, the People have much to look forward to and celebrate. They have come such a long way from their turbulent, persecuted history of displacement and repression. The Seminole Tribe of Florida has much to celebrate, including their promising future.

Florida has been Indian Country far longer than we may know. The lush Florida peninsula covers 60,000 square miles of low, diverse land surrounded with an 8,500-mile coastline dotted with glorious beaches along both the Atlantic and Gulf coasts. Thousands of stunning islands in the Gulf of Mexico add to its beauty. Geologically, Florida is North America's "baby," being part of an area on this continent that was late to rise out of the ocean. The highest point of land is only 345 feet above sea level. Yet, Florida's pre-history stretches back more than 10,000 years to ancient burial and ceremonial mounds and archaeological evidence of ancient trade routes and intricate canals that indicate sophisticated prehistoric cultures.

Among the Seminole foods taken from old-time traditional dishes and still enjoyed along with thoroughly modern foods are panfried alligator tail, roast corn, turtle soups, crawfish, and catfish. The Seminole are famous for their awesome alligator wrestling, yet less is known about their alligator farming, which is a growing business due to a high demand for skins and the rich, white meat of alligator tails.

Alligator, *Alligator mississipiensis,* crayfish, *Cambarus diogenes,* and shrimp, *Crangon vulgaris*, are valuable native foods that together or individually work well to enhance countless Native dishes. Shrimp are valuable saltwater foods, and the state of Louisiana harvests almost 100 million pounds a year, making Louisiana the nation's top producer of this food. Both brown shrimp and the larger white shrimp are harvested from the Gulf Coast waters. The smaller brown shrimp are favored for southern gumbos, étouffées, and jambalayas.

## ALLIGATOR-CRAWFISH JAMBALAYA

*Native American foods have significantly influenced other cuisines around the world, and, contemporary Native American cuisines reflect strong influences from many other ethnic cuisines, especially, in the South, the colorful marriages with Cajun and Creole.*

*A cooked dish of Creole origins, jambalaya is basically rice with medleys of herbs, vegetables (especially tomatoes), and meat or shellfish. Creole influences are born of Spanish, French, West Indian, American, and American Indian cross-fertilizations, and Creole foods are understandably delicious.*

**2 slices of bacon, chopped**

**1 medium onion, chopped**

**1 tablespoon fine cornmeal**

**1 tablespoon Worcestershire sauce**

**1/2 cup hot water**

**1 cup tomatoes, chopped**

**2 Anaheim chilies, roasted, seeded, chopped**

2 cups alligator tail meat chopped in bite-size chunks

1 pound crawfish, partially cooked

3 cups cooked rice

1/2 cup chopped parsley

1/2 cup green onions, diced

1 tablespoon fresh basil, chopped

1 teaspoon thyme

Sauté over medium heat in a large saucepan the bacon, onion, cornmeal, and Worcestershire sauce; stir well as you add each ingredient. Now add water, tomatoes, chilies, alligator, and crawfish. Increase heat to bring all ingredients to boiling point. Stir in 3 cups cooked rice. Blend well, lower heat, and add parsley, onions, basil, and thyme. Correct and balance seasonings. Simmer over low heat for 15 minutes. Serve with additional condiments, herbs, and hot sauce.

Variations on this dish appear at many different festivals to feed many appreciative folks. The additions of spicy chorizo sausage, alligator sausage, Florida oysters, crab, or diced ham and chicken enlivens this recipe and takes it in new directions.

**Serves 8**

## Alligators Wrestle with a New Destiny

*The increasing desire for native game and finer, lighter meats and seafoods leads to fascinating farming and ranching alternatives with expanding economic opportunities for more people. One marvelous success story is the delicious alligator. Scarcely two decades ago alligators were removed from the endangered species list, and commercial trappers and hunters have not been able to keep up with the demand for the fine white meat, which has almost no fat and is classified as seafood. It actually tastes like a cross between catfish, chicken, and frogs' legs, but with a mild, distinctive flavor of its own. More than fifty alligator farms have opened in Florida. Gatorland Zoo, in the eastern part of the state, succeeds as an attraction for tourists as well as a profitable "farm" of more than 1,000 alligators a year.*

# TULSA INDIAN ARTS FESTIVAL    THIRD WEEKEND IN FEBRUARY

"Oklahoma is the heart, it's the vital organ of our national existence," Will Rogers wrote in 1926. This is certainly the ecological crossroads of our continent, where eastern and western species of plant and animal life mingle. Four historic national capitols are here: the Creek Council House in Okmulgee, the Cherokee capitol in Tahlequah, the Chickasaw capitol in Tishomingo, and the Choctaw capitol in Tuskahoma. The Seminole council house in Wewoka was destroyed by fire.

Home to more Native Americans than any other state, the arts and culture of sixty-four tribes add much to the fabric and color of life. Oklahoma, the name, comes from the Choctaw language, okla meaning "people" and homma (humma) meaning "red." The state tree (the Eastern Redbud, *Cersis canadensis,* an ancient Indian herbal resource), the state wildflower (Indian Blanket, *Gaillardia pulchella*), and the state animal (*Bison bison,* which once roamed the Great Plains in great herds) all pay tribute to Oklahoma's extensive Native heritage.

Honoring this heritage is the Tulsa Indian Arts Festival. "A celebration of art, education, dance, tradition . . . honoring the spirit of the American Indian" heralds the annual three-day event. More than 100 juried Native American fine artists gather in the Tulsa Trade Center to exhibit their best works and to give demonstrations and talks to thousands of area schoolchildren who come for educational programs along with more than 10,000 visitors converging on this major weekend event.

Grand Entry and Powwow Dancing competitions (especially Junior and Tiny Tot dance competitions) highlight each day's events, along with storytelling, stomp dances, gourd dances, intertribal dances, and traditional Indian foods. Ethnic food booths offer the finest corn soups, spicy meat pies, pumpkin frybread, grape dumplings, corn pudding, and Indian candy, along with many other favorites. Monetta Trepp, Creek businesswoman and one of the festival planners and civic leaders, is a driving force in pulling the best Indian cooks together to help cater this gala event. Choctaw, Osage, Kiowa, Creek, and Cherokee foods lend their best contemporary flavors to the celebration of Oklahoma's Native legacies.

# Rayna Green's Grape Dumplings

*Four native species of grapes flower in May and June and produce prodigious clusters of delicious grapes through late summer and fall. Fox grapes (*Vitis labrusca*), muscadine (*Vitis rotundifolia*), frost grape (*Vitis riparia*), and California grape (*Vitis californica*), each have their special regions, habitats, and unique personalities. Many of these vines live for over a century, climbing to the tree-tops in woodland environments.*

*Rayna Green is an Oklahoma Cherokee folklorist and cultural historian at the Smithsonian's National Museum of American History. A dynamic and passionate cook, she plans to open a "Cherokee Chili Parlor" on Pennsylvania Avenue. This is one of her treasured recipes.*

**2 quarts fresh muscadine or Concord grapes**

**1 quart water**

**3 cups sugar**

**2 cups flour**

**2 tablespoons vegetable shortening**

**2 tablespoons cold water**

Mash the grapes, removing the skins and seeds. Put them in a non-aluminum saucepan with 1 quart cold water. Add the sugar and boil gently, as though you were making jelly, until the mixture reduces by at least one-third. In the meantime, make the dumplings by mixing the flour, cutting in the shortening with a knife, and adding 2 tablespoons cold water. Make a ball of dough and roll it out. Cut into strips about 1 inch wide and 2 inches long. Use a little dry flour to roll out and cut them if the dough is too sticky. When the grape mixture reduces and begins to thicken, drop the dumplings in one by one. Cook for 6 to 7 minutes more. The mixture should thicken; the flour dumplings will have cooked and the whole should be just a little more liquid than a berry cobbler. You may serve as a dessert, as you would serve a cobbler, or with a meal, as Cherokees might eat them.

**Serves 10 to 12**

# Mary O'Brien's Apricot Blueberry Cookies

*Gifted Cherokee businesswoman, civic activist, and cook Mary O'Brien, of Tulsa, weaves folks together from her charming bookstore and throughout the country. Her gardening, literary, and gourmet activities inspired these delicious cookies, often brought to Native gatherings to sweeten the discussions.*

*These cookies stay wonderfully moist and have great keeping qualities—if they escape being eaten! Mary suggests numerous variations on this theme. Combine seasonal or favorite fruits in these ways: persimmon/blackberry, pumpkin/cranberry, apple/elderberry, pawpaw/gooseberry, or sand plum/strawberry. The results are delightful!*

**1 1/2 cups flour**

**1/2 cup white cornmeal**

**1 teaspoon baking soda**

**1 teaspoon cinnamon**

**1 teaspoon salt**

**1/2 cup butter**

**2/3 cup sugar**

**1 egg, beaten**

**1 cup apricot purée (use jarred preserves, or purée pitted fresh apricots in a food processor)**

**1 cup dried or fresh blueberries**

**1/2 cup chopped pecans**

Preheat oven to 350°. In a medium bowl, measure and stir together the flour, cornmeal, baking soda, cinnamon, and salt. In a smaller bowl, cream together until light the butter, sugar, beaten egg, and apricot purée. Add these wet ingredients to the flour mixture bowl and blend well. Then add blueberries and pecans. Blend all ingredients well together. Drop by teaspoonfuls onto a lightly greased cookie sheet. Bake for 15 to 20 minutes until just barely golden. Remove and cool slightly before serving.

**Makes about 3 dozen cookies**

# RASPBERRY SNOW CREAM

*A childhood favorite for so many of us is an "instant" classic, easily revisited anywhere there is sufficient fresh snow cover. Any fresh fruits, or none at all, add additional dimensions to this simple dessert. Generations of young and old "cooks" in our family enjoy this noncooked presentation each winter, and it has lots of delicious variations. This old fashioned treat is a wonderful, spontaneous celebration of each snowfall.*

*First, gather a fresh bowl or two of clean snow (the dryer the snow, the better the results). Working fast (this is an instant treat), dust 1/4 cup to 1/2 cup sifted granulated sugar over the top of the bowl of snow. Sprinkle 1 teaspoon, more or less, of vanilla extract over this. (Try other flavored extracts for a different character.)*

*Stir briskly with a fork or egg beater to thoroughly blend and fluff this mixture. Add 1/2 cup of fresh or frozen raspberries (optional) and blend in well. Serve immediately in small bowls. The simplest creation: It is basically a bit of sugar and a sprinkling of extract. It is so ephemeral that it seems like nothing at all, and by its very nature should disappear quickly!*

**Makes about 4 bowls**

# MARCH

*Brilliant sun shining through bare, glistening branches illuminates a crisp morning filled with bird songs and courting activities. Fertile with new promise, the winter world thaws and warms to renewed seasonal urgencies. The cycle of life quickens as we hurry out of winter, and strong winds blow us on toward spring.*

*Reaching across our great continent, this is the Moon to Cook Olachen of the Tsimshian, the Herring-Spawn Moon of the Nootka, and the Raspberry Sprouting Moon of the Kwakiutl along the Northwest Coast, the Buffalo-Calving Moon of the Sioux, the Little Frog Moon of the Omaha, and the Water Stands In The Ponds Moon of the Ponca across the Great Plains. Around the Great Lakes it is the Snow Crust Moon of the Ojibwa (Chippewa), and moving south, it is the Cactus Blossom Moon of the Hopi and the Strawberry Moon of the Cherokee.*

*Moving down through the Northeast, this time is the Maple Syrup Moon and Fish Spawning Moon of the Micmac, the Eagles And Owls Laying Eggs Moon of the Penobscot, the Time Of Catching Fish Moon of the Wampanoag, and the Moon When The River Ice Thaws of the Agawam, Abenaki, and Narragansett. March moods are diverse. Nature's urgencies are evermore apparent.*

ENDURING
HARVESTS

# Northwest Coast Potlatches

For more than 9,000 years people have flourished and evolved in settlements of the Pacific Northwest Coast region, which stretches 1,500 miles through lushly forested terrain. Among the region's special Native traditions is potlatch, from the Nootka-Chinook word *patshatl,* meaning "give away" or gift. At this festival gifts of property and foods are bestowed on guests in a show of impressive wealth-sharing, which guests later attempt to surpass. Fearfully misunderstood by missionaries and governments in the nineteenth century because of its lavishness, the Canadian government declared potlatch illegal in 1884. Periods of great distress, restrictions, and arrests threatened Northwest Coast lifeways until the prohibition against potlatch was finally dropped in 1951. Now these enduring feasts are gaining strength and giving some of the greatest gifts a culture can manifest—pride, purpose, and cohesiveness.

Over one hundred years ago, Franz Boas, as a young anthropologist, noted the events surrounding a Kwakiutl potlatch. Immense ceremonial canoes were carved from a single cedar log; ornately painted, they were often more than 70 feet long and could hold 20 to 30 people. Diverse villages of related tribes living along the Pacific Northwest Coast, within several days traveling distance, would stage their ceremonial arrivals. Each clan in their own canoe had a ceremonial dancer standing in the prow, representing the clan's totem. Large, stylistically painted paddles cut the water as the oarsmen chanted in unison with their strokes, while stationary drummers beat time within the canoe's interior.

The Tanana, one of eleven Athabaskan groups, who live in fifty-five villages along their Yukon River system, hold potlatches of three days that are usually hosted by people from one village who invite their relatives and friends from surrounding areas. More than 300 people may gather for these days of socializing, dancing and singing, feasting, and oratory. Much hunting and preparation is involved, and feast foods for these three days include fried, boiled, and roasted moose, moosehead soup, various preparations of duck, muskrat, and turkey, many kinds of fish, as well as favorite homemade pies, cakes, and doughnuts.

The Quinault of the Olympic Peninsula, the Skokomish of the Skokomish River, and the Hoh tribe of the Hoh River system, are all heirs to the rich cultural traditions of potlatch and naming ceremonies, with their traditional songs, dances, and foods. While Native American lifeways are constantly changing, the ceremonies are vital cultural threads constantly weaving people together.

The Quileute Nation of the Quillayute River watershed region of Washington's western Olympic Peninsula are part of the renewal of the cedar canoe culture, which augments their potlatching activities. These traditional feasts and gift-giving ceremonies mark many significant events in tribal life from name-givings and marriages, to funeral memorials and society rites and memberships, rekindling interests in their traditional social and spiritual lives.

Foods served at contemporary potlatches include herring roe on kelp or on hemlock boughs, clam chowder, fish and venison stews, seaweed, salads, smoked and salted eulachons, salmon cooked in many different ways, and many special baked goods. As Gloria Cranmer Webster, a Kwakiutl elder, reflects, "early in the morning, as many as twenty women gather to make about twelve hundred sandwiches." Considerable enthusiasm and energy continues to surround these events, as they evolve to suit the needs of the people who perform them.

173

Many potlatches were and are smaller affairs, serving a multitude of unique tribal needs, yet it is fascinating to reflect upon the legendary, elaborate potlatches with their dramatic gift-giving rites and complex rituals of initiation into Secret Societies, with extraordinary displays of feast foods and feasting protocols. Food preparation and presentation was masterfully calculated to match grand serving vessels, all designed to make impressive statements.

Potlatch also continues in many additional ways, as we use the word today to signify sumptuous events where both the foods and events go "beyond the ordinary." Cultural revitalization of such events as potlatch has been growing out of the sense of loss of some native languages and religious freedoms and perceived threats to natural resources and sacred sites. In addition, the critical depletion of salmon stocks in the Pacific Northwest and the depletion of many native fishstocks along the Northeast coast have brought a cohesion of talents and strengths. Smokehouses have been rebuilt in many Northwest Coast communities, and a dramatic revival of potlatches and winter spirit dancing is being experienced.

## Giveaways

Otu'han *is Lakota for "giveaway," which in their customs remains a lively, honoring practice for celebrating marriages, births, anniversaries, and other special occasions. The Otu'han, like the potlatch, is also a customary honoring of the memory of the dead. Lewis and Clark noted in their journals that the Lakota "had a custom of giving gifts in the names of those they wished to honor." These valuable customs continue among many diverse Indian People today.*

# GRILLED HALIBUT STEAKS WITH RASPBERRY-JUNIPER SAUCE

*Halibut,* Hippoglossus hippoglossus, *is a member of the family of large flat fish of northern Pacific and Atlantic waters. Huge bottom-feeders, halibut were so important in Northwest Coast Indian diets that they carved and fashioned strikingly beautiful, and effective, halibut hooks and clubs, designed to honor the inua (spirit) of the halibut. Numerous species of raspberries were collected for countless food uses, as were juniper berries,* Juniperus communis, *the aromatic blue-gray berrylike fruits valued with game meats.*

**3 (1-pound) halibut steaks, 1 1/2-inches thick**
**6 juniper berries, finely ground**
**1 cup of Raspberry-Juniper Sauce (below)**

Place the halibut steaks on a generous platter and lightly season them with the ground juniper berries by patting them onto both sides of the steaks.

Prepare the coals of the grill fire. Dampen with water 2 to 3 handfuls of alder bark and chips or other favorite wood. When the coals are ready, sprinkle the prepared wood chips over them and set the grill rack about 6 inches above this. Place the halibut steaks on the grill. Lightly brush the first side with the Raspberry-Juniper Sauce, then immediately flip each steak and lightly brush the sauce over the other side. Grill on each side for about 5 to 6 minutes per side. The halibut is done when the fish looks opaque. Test by poking a sharp knife tip into the thickest part of the steak and pulling the meat back slightly to check that it is opaque throughout. Remove to a heated platter, and serve hot with additional sauce.

**Serves 3 to 6**

# RASPBERRY-JUNIPER SAUCE

*Blackcaps,* Rubus leucodermis, *thimbleberry,* Rubus parviflorus, *and salmonberry,* Rubus spectabilis, *are three of the most abundant raspberries along the Northwest Coast and are traditional components of this sweet-sour sauce. As in the version below, any favorite raspberries will do to make this tart, tasty concoction. Keep in mind that mature juniper berries,* Juniperus communis, *are highly aromatic and should be used in limitation; they are strong and medicinal in action and can overpower foods. Less of them is always better.*

**1 tablespoon eulachon oil or corn oil**
**1 small clove garlic, minced**
**1 small white onion, diced**
**6 juniper berries, ground**
**2 cups fresh or frozen raspberries**
**1 tablespoon cornstarch**
**1 cup raspberry juice**
**1 tablespoon cider vinegar**
**1 tablespoon fresh parsley, minced**
**1 tablespoon fresh dill, minced**
**1/2 teaspoon each of salt, pepper, paprika, allspice**

Heat the oil in a medium saucepan over medium heat. Quickly sauté the garlic and onion for 3 minutes, shaking the pot and stirring often, until they are glistening. Add the juniper berries and raspberries, mashing them well into the garlic-and-onion mixture. Stir well.

In a small bowl or cup, dissolve the cornstarch in the raspberry juice, blending well.

Stir this into the hot ingredients. Continue to cook over medium heat, stirring well for 5 minutes, until it thickens; prevent from boiling. Add remaining ingredients, reduce heat, and simmer for another 5 minutes, stirring occasionally. This sauce can be made days ahead and stored in a covered container in the refrigerator to develop flavors.
**Makes about 3 1/2 cups**

# ALASKAN SALMON CAKES

*Pacific salmon normally return to their native rivers and streams to spawn after about four years at sea. After spawning, they usually die. The pinkish-silver coho salmon,* Oncorhynchus kisutch, *one of five native Pacific salmon species, is highly esteemed for use in this dish.*

1/2 cup corn oil or eulachon oil

1 cup cornmeal, crushed corn chips, or corn flakes

1 cup cooked or canned salmon (including bones)

2 cups cooked, mashed white or sweet potato or squash

1 egg, well beaten fluffy

1 clove garlic, finely diced

1 small onion, finely diced

1/4 cup parsley, finely diced

1/2 teaspoon celery seed

1/2 teaspoon dill weed

1/2 teaspoon paprika

salt and pepper to taste

Place the cornmeal in a large, flat dish.

In a large mixing bowl, blend the remaining ingredients well together, balancing the flavors and seasonings. Using a tablespoon and your hands, shape 12 to 15 small cakes, about 1 inch thick and 3 inches in diameter. Place each cake in the cornmeal. Pat and turn to coat each side.

Heat the oil in a large flat skillet over medium heat. Carefully place the cakes in the hot oil so that they do not touch each other. Sauté over medium heat for about 10 to 15 minutes on each side, until nicely golden brown. Serve hot with wild salad greens, peas, and wild rice. Whipped cloudberries or salmonberries make a tasty dessert to follow this meal.
**Serves 8**

*The trees that dominate the rocky Pacific Northwest forest regions have long provided materials for tools, medicines, foods, and ceremonies, as well as clothing, fuel, and shelter. Red cedar,* Thuja plicata, *and yellow cedar,* Chamaecyparis nootkatensis, *were and are vital to the people. This Kwakiutl woman's prayer of supplication to "Long Life Maker," recited before she would pull cedar bark necessary for utensils and mats, acknowledges the spiritual bond with the cedar tree:*

*"Look at me friend! I come to ask for your dress. You have come to take pity on us, for there is nothing for which you cannot be used . . ."*

*Kwakiutl festivals and ceremonies called for enormous feast dishes and boxes, and most of these were carved from cedar into special animal spirit forms. Large ceremonial raven and wolf ladles of cedar and mountain goat horn were paired with awesome feast dishes carved in the shapes of seals, sea otters, and killer whales.*

*Transformation feast dishes depict a grizzly bear and human form back-to-back and an eagle back-to-back with a wolf. One of the most intriguing specimens is a huge devilfish (octopus) bowl, with an immense oval mouth rimmed with great teeth. Considered a sea monster "bear of the rocks" by the Kwakiutl, the devilfish was treated as a supernatural being.*

*Masters of illusion, many Northwest Coast artists used ordinary materials to make remarkable feast accoutrements, dance masks, and spiritual regalia. Exquisitely carved, ornately detailed bentwood boxes for feast foods and beverages were often intricately inlaid with shiny opercula (the "trap door" of the Red Turban Sea Snail), polished pieces of pearl or abalone shell, and sometimes polished plates of copper. Even the smallest item seemed a celebration of the purpose of its use, and the spirit of the artist was well-woven into the spirit(s) of the article. Food provided under these circumstances certainly possessed greater power.*

# SHOOKS' PICKLED ICE FISH

*An elder Ojibwa Iroquois friend named Art Shook shared this recipe after a successful winter of ice-fishing. Actually, another fisherman out on the ice three years ago gave this recipe, verbally, to my friend, who adapted it for the plump white perch (a popular pan fish related to the striped bass) and the golden, vertically banded yellow perch. This is a great chilled treat in late spring and summer—it will bring the frozen winter lake to mind during the dog days of August.*

First, fillet, clean, salt, and pack into a crock 20 to 30 plump white perch (about 2 pounds). Use about 1/2 cup of pickling or kosher salt (not table salt) and salt each layer of fish fillets well. Cover and leave for 2 to 4 days in a cool place where they will not freeze. Stir occasionally.

After the 2 to 4 days, remove the fillets from the salt. Rinse and drain them. Prepare the pickling bath.

**1 cup fine, dry white wine**

**2 cups white vinegar**

**1 cup sugar**

**12 or more whole allspice**

**4 fresh bay leaves**

**salt and pepper to taste (optional)**

Combine all ingredients in a medium saucepan and bring to a slow boil. Simmer for 5 minutes over medium heat. Set aside, keeping warm on the stovetop. Cut the fish fillets into 1 1/2-inch pieces. Slice several large white onions very thinly. Pack into about 8 clean, sterilized pint jars a layer of fish pieces followed by a large, thin onion slice. Continue to alternate layers this way until each jar is almost filled. Pour about 1 cup of the hot pickling brine into each jar. Top off with a bay leaf and several allspice buds. Cover and refrigerate. Store for 2 to 6 weeks or a season. Invert the jars once or twice when you think of it. Chill before serving.

**Makes 8 jars**

# Indian Market

*Spread across the March calendar are some of the most exciting Indian Markets in the country. Events such as the big Indian Fair and Market at the Heard Museum in Phoenix, Arizona, and the Native Arts and Crafts Show and Sale in Scottsdale, Arizona, attract growing numbers of collectors and aficionados of Indian art. Visitors to these two-, three-, and four-day events can meet with and talk to the artists and their families and learn more about their varied works. Many contemporary Indian artists have built reputations that attract crowds of fans, so it is fascinating to watch the energies and excitement build as the finest jewelers, sculptors, basket weavers, painters, designers, dollmakers, and musicians gather to display their work and talk about their creative processes.*

*The Agua Caliente Indian Market in Palm Springs, California, and the American Indian Festival and Market at the Museum of Natural History of Los Angeles, bring together artists, musicians, dancers, storytellers, and foods, as well as films and videos, in such compelling ways that many folks plan their annual vacations and business trips around these major shows. The same is true for the Great Falls Native American Art Association Exhibit and Sale in Great Falls, Montana, and the Texas Indian Market in Arlington, Texas. Indian and American foods are served at these events, and modern recipes and presentations of traditional foods keep pace with modern trends in Indian art.*

# The Return of the Buzzards

The swallows return to San Juan Capistrano, California, on March 19, which is Saint Joseph's Feast Day. Pilgrims and locals alike gather to welcome them during this joyous, noisy, sacred occasion.

But Hinckley, Ohio, has its own similar pilgrimage—the Buzzards Return on the Ides of March! Those of us who were born in Ohio, an Iroquois word for "beautiful," understandably get worked up over this remarkable annual phenomenon which has been explained in Wyandot legend. A colorful series of festivals and "Buzzard's Breath" recipes help mark the day.

The Hinckley Buzzards are actually turkey vultures, which generally migrate south during the winter months, some going as far south as Cuba and South America. The Hinckley turkey vultures probably go to Kentucky and the Smoky Mountains, returning to Hinckley as daylight increases in early March. Perfect nesting and feeding conditions exist in Hinckley, and these massive gliding birds live for as many as twenty to thirty years.

# Buzzard's Breath Four-Alarm Revenge Chili

*The racy Road Kill Cafés all across the country pay special respect to the buzzards of Hinckley through this recipe. It's perfect for the celebrations of good faith that surround the birds' annual return.*

*Dedicated, with respect, to the vegetarians among us, as well as to the Hinckley turkey vultures and their kin, this volcanic meatless dish warms the palate. It also has been known to cancel a winter head cold by opening sinus passages you might have forgotten you had.*

3 tablespoons corn oil

2 large onions, diced

6 cloves garlic, diced

2 large bell peppers, coarsely chopped

2 cups water

5 celery stalks, coarsely chopped

3 medium poblano chilies, roasted and chopped

2 serrano chilies, roasted and chopped

1 jalapeño chili, roasted and chopped

6 tablespoons (or more) red-hot chili powder

1 tablespoon cumin, ground

2 teaspoons salt, or more, to taste

1 teaspoon black pepper, or more, to taste

2 cups cooked Anasazi beans

2 cups cooked cranberry beans

2 cups cooked black turtle beans

2 cups cooked navy beans

2 cups cooked tomatoes, chopped

1 cup tomato paste

4 cups, or more, water or vegetable broth

1/2 cup sunflower seeds, roasted

1/2 cup chopped pecans, roasted

1/2 cup chopped pumpkin seeds, roasted

1/2 cup fresh epazote, finely chopped

1/2 cup cilantro, finely chopped

1/2 cup green onions, chopped

1 teaspoon ground ginger

1 teaspoon oregano

**1 teaspoon thyme**

**favorite condiments: chilled sour cream, guacamole, diced**

**peanuts and sunflower seeds, raisins, and white cheese**

Heat oil in a very large, deep pot over medium-high heat. Quickly sauté the onions, garlic, and bell pepper, stirring often and blending well. Add 2 cups of water, celery, roasted chilies, and the next 4 dry seasonings. Stir well. Cook for several minutes. Add the 4 types of beans (or any combination to make 8 cups). Add the tomatoes, tomato paste, and the additional water or broth. Blend thoroughly and balance the liquids. Bring to a boil, then reduce heat to simmer. Add all of the remaining ingredients except for the favorite condiments. Blend and stir well; simmer for another 10 to 15 minutes.

Remove from the heat. Stir well and cover. Allow this chili to sit for several hours. Before serving, remove 1 or 2 cupfuls and pureé in a food processor. Return puréed batch to the original mixture and stir it all well together. Reheat. Balance seasonings and liquid to taste. Serve hot.

Spoon chili over a large, slit and steaming baked potato, and serve with hot corn bread, chilled sour cream (or yogurt), and more fresh cilantro, along with bowls of everyone's favorite condiments and additional hot sauces.

**Serves 8 to 10**

# Maple Sugaring Festivals

Time-honored urgencies of renewal are stimulated even during the turbulent weather and mood swings of March. The tree saps are surging, and maple sugaring events have been planned, accordingly, since February in southern areas and now in March in northern regions. "Sugaring camps" and sugaring festivals sweeten March activities from the central Plains to the Great Lakes to the Northeast.

Twelve species of maples are among the handsomest deciduous trees in North America, and though all produce quantities of sap, there is a great variation in sugar content and quality. The sugar maple, *Acer saccharum,* yields the highest sugar content, and it takes about twenty gallons of sap carefully boiled down to make two quarts of syrup. Further boiling will yield about one pound of pure maple sugar, a pale amber confection of distinct sweetness and texture.

The process begins well below ground in the sugar maples' magnificent roots, which absorb water and mineral essence from the earth. These gifts are mixed with stored tree sugars to form sap, which begins to run up inside the trunk when warm late-winter days are followed by freezing nights. Surging through the cambium layer just beneath the tree bark, this thin, watery fluid tastes faintly sweet. Though delicious just as a drink, sap is usually collected in pails or through tubes for the making of syrup and sugar.

This late-winter harvest, conceived millennia ago, produced rich rewards for industrious woodland Indians, and the oral traditions of many tribes spread this knowledge. The Mohican Indians believed that the melting snow caused the spring sap to run in the maples. Spiritually, this was considered the dripping oil of the Great Celestial Bear, their primary winter constellation, who had been wounded by the winter hunters (their interpretation of the Pleiades). Whole Indian families and clans would move to their "sugar bush"—sugar maple groves—for the sweet late-winter labor of sugaring, which lasted from three to six weeks, until the maple trees had budded and blossomed and the clear sap had turned to pale amber.

Maple syrup and sugar were primary seasonings for Indians and settlers, centuries before the present and long before the conventional use of salt as a seasoning and preservative. Maple syrup was added to wild berries, roots, nuts, vegetables, and various fish and game dishes. Maple sugar mixed with parched corn was carried in small leather pouches and eaten, for special energy, either plain, boiled into a gruel, or mixed into water or fruit juices.

Maple syrup still has a strong hold on our contemporary foodways. As a versatile sweetener and flavoring agent in everything from smoking tobacco to ice creams, maple syrup is produced to the tune of more than a million gallons annually, from the six leading states of New York, New Hampshire, Vermont, Pennsylvania, Ohio, and Michigan.

Wherever sugar maples and winter coexist, you will find sugarhouses, sugaring demonstrations, and maple sugar festivals. Indian reservations, nature and environmental centers, and museums and schools often sponsor these events so that folks can gather to celebrate the maples and honor an age-old legacy in North America. The processes of sapping, syruping, and sugaring are fascinating, and our observation of sugaring demonstrations helps to deepen our understanding of nature's gifts and the interdependence of all living things.

Maple sugaring festival menus often offer tastes of the fresh, icy sap straight-from-the-tree as well as dozens of maple syrup-laced treats both familiar and new. Maple-flavored breakfast sausages, maple-cured Canadian hams, maple-smoked bacon, maple-nut fudge, or maple-flavored cobblers or cakes, maple-nut ice cream, maple-caramel sauce, and maple-ginger tea are just a few of the possibilities. In the Northeast, you might find Indian Lollipops—a most delicious sweet made by pouring hot maple syrup into a birchbark cone surrounded with snow or crushed ice. At some festivals, huge dill pickles are served á la carte, to help quell the nausea that can sometimes occur after eating too much sugar. Hot cranberry tea and sumac tea is also often on hand to help stabilize a queasy stomach.

## Ojibwa Sugaring

Seensibaukwut *is an Ojibwa word for maple syrup, meaning "drawn from the wood." Among the Ojibwa/Chippewa People, "each family or group of two or three families had its own sugar bush . . . and the people went there in the early* spring to make the year's supply of sugar," *according to Frances Densmore, who lived and worked among these tribes. Ojibwa and Iroquois women owned the maple groves, which they inherited through their maternal lines.*

# CRANBERRY-MAPLE ICE

*Maple syrup, the sweet essence of our native maple trees, has been used as preservative and sweetening commodity for centuries. The tart, vitamin rich cranberry is also highly valued in Native recipes. This simple dessert is a perfect marriage of these two perennial resources.*

**2 cups fresh, washed cranberries**

**1/2 cup pure maple syrup**

**1/2 cup sugar**

**1 teaspoon fresh lime, orange, or lemon zest**

**1/2 teaspoon ground allspice**

**1 cup water or cranberry juice**

Place all ingredients in a small-medium saucepan. Bring to a boil over medium-high heat, stirring well. Cover and reduce heat to simmer. Cook, stirring occasionally, for 10 to 15 minutes. Cool slightly. Purée in a food processor and pour into a plastic container with a tight-fitting lid. Place in the freezer overnight. Serve by scraping scoopfuls off the top and placing rosy, sherbet-like scoops in small bowls with fresh fruits and cookies surrounding them. This same recipe is easily varied by using fresh, ripe blueberries, salmonberries, currants, or other favorite seasonal fruits. You can even serve medleys of colorful ices for a festive potlatch treat.

**Serves 6**

# MAPLE–GINGER TEA

*Both American wild ginger,* Asarum canadense, *and its Oriental sister are noted aromatic digestive aids. If an excessive enjoyment of maple sugar candy threatens to ruin your afternoon at a maple-sugar festival, a cup of this tea may help settle your stomach. American ginger is a protected species, so Oriental ginger is best used for this delicious tea.*

Pour boiling water into a tea mug or cup over a 1-inch piece of fresh or candied ginger root and a teaspoon of maple syrup. Cover, and infuse for 10 minutes, then sip and enjoy. To soothe a headache, add 1/4 teaspoon fine paprika and stir well. The paprika is also a flavor enhancer, as well as an appetite stimulant and digestive aid.

**Serves 1**

# Raspberry Flapjacks with Hot Maple Syrup

*Small, thin cakes are easiest for turning, and this simple recipe has many possibilities for variations. Replace the raspberries with raisins, currants, or any favorite seasonal, regional fruits. For added ecstasy, heat the maple syrup and add fresh fruits or butter, if desired.*

**1 1/2 cups fine cornmeal**

**1/4 cup sifted all-purpose flour**

**1/2 teaspoon salt**

**1/2 teaspoon baking soda**

**2 cups buttermilk**

**2 tablespoons raspberry jam or conserve**

**1 egg, well beaten (optional—if you omit the egg, the flapjacks will be lacy)**

Place the dry ingredients in a medium bowl. Warm the buttermilk in a small saucepan. Partially dissolve the raspberry jam by stirring it into the warm buttermilk, then carefully and swiftly stir the buttermilk/jam mixture into the dry ingredients with a few good strokes. The batter can even rest, covered, at this point for 1 to 2 hours, but refrigerate the batter if you decide to add the beaten egg.

Heat griddle, lightly greased, and drop the batter by tablespoonfuls, carefully spaced, onto the hot griddle. Make the cakes small for easier turning and handling. The batter tends to settle, so stir from the bottom and blend again before making each batch. Serve hot, topped with warm maple syrup, additional fresh berries, or a spoonful of jam smoothed between each flapjack in place of butter.

**Serves 6**

## Tapping Additional Resources

*N*ative Americans tapped other deciduous trees as well as sugar maples. The sap of the hickory, birch, beech, and elm was also sought, each within its own late winter-early spring window of opportunity. Pine and spruce trees were also slightly tapped, or wounded, for collection of their sticky pitch and resins, so valuable to chewing gums, external medicines, and numerous other applications.

Many of the Dakota People returned to their "sugarbushes," or groves, to collect the wild mushrooms that would grow on the healed wounds of their tapped trees—principally the elms and box elders. Melvin Gilmore recorded in 1919 that "some women were gathering . . . in a grove of box elder near the Missouri River . . . in decayed spots caused by tapping the trees for the purpose of sugar making, for these people still make sugar from the sap of the box elder." Wind-borne spores of wild mushrooms flourish in tapping scars, making the protection of our tree resources all the more important.

189

# Aztec Chocolate Nut Fudge

*The essences of two very different native trees, the maple and the cacao, have for centuries made a delicious impact on diverse foods around the world, yet almost never together in the same recipe! This and the following modern "sweet" appear at countless Native American gatherings and celebrations. Intense, concentrated sweetness personifies this first one, which some of my Native friends suggest is "industrial strength" chocolate. A good, accurate candy thermometer is invaluable for this creation.*

**4 (1-ounce) squares unsweetened chocolate**

**3 cups sugar**

**2 tablespoons light corn syrup**

**2 teaspoons allspice, finely ground**

**1 cup milk**

**4 tablespoons butter**

**1 teaspoon pure vanilla extract**

**1 cup pecan halves, broken**

**1 cup hazelnuts, coarsely chopped**

Melt chocolate over lowest heat in a 3-quart saucepan or in a double-boiler over hot (not boiling) water. Stir in the sugar, corn syrup, allspice, and milk. Increase heat to medium and cook, stirring, until the sugar dissolves. Wash crystals from the side of the pot by covering the pot briefly, then stirring again. Cook to 238° on candy thermometer—the soft ball stage. Remove from heat and add butter. Allow to stand without stirring until it cools to lukewarm. Add vanilla and beat until this mixture thickens. Stir in the nuts. Continue beating until the candy holds its shape.

Drop individual candies from a teaspoon onto buttered wax paper or pour the whole mixture into a buttered 10x10x2-inch pan. If you use the pan method, cool completely and cut into squares. Enjoy this with spicy hot cocoa, mulled cranberry juice, or hot mulled cider. **Makes 3 pounds of fudge**

# Maple Nut Cream Fudge

*Distinctive essence of sugar maple combines beautifully with our native black walnut, butternut, and hazelnut to yield a pale, gorgeous fudge. This rich, creamy confection profits by using the best quality ingredients and, as with all foods, by preparing it with lots of love!*

**2 cups light brown sugar**
**1 1/2 cups fine maple syrup, pale Grade AA**
**1/2 cup light cream**
**1 tablespoon butter**
**1/2 cup black walnuts, finely chopped**
**1/2 cup butternuts, chopped**
**1/2 cup hazelnuts, chopped**

Melt the sugar with the maple syrup over low heat in a 3-quart saucepan, stirring well until dissolved and well blended. Increase heat to medium. Stir in the cream. Cook and stir these ingredients slowly until they reach the firm-ball stage, 248° on the candy thermometer. Stir in the butter. Remove from heat. Add the black walnuts and beat them in with a spoon until the mixture is light. Pour the candy into a buttered 10x10x2-inch metal or glass baking dish. Sprinkle the butternuts and hazelnuts evenly and generously over the top, gently patting them into the surface of the fudge. Cool for about 30 minutes. Cut fudge into squares with a lightly buttered knife. Cool completely for 3 hours or more. Turn onto a plate or board. Separate previously cut squares.

**Makes about 2 pounds of fudge**

# SUGARED CRANBERRIES AND NUTS

*This late-winter/early-spring dessert enlivens dried berries and nuts left in reserves since their harvests. This is also a sweet holiday dish that appears at various Native gatherings and festivals. It makes a wonderful gift.*

**1/2 cup maple syrup**
**1/2 cup light corn syrup**
**2 teaspoons lemon or orange zest**
**1 teaspoon allspice, finely ground**
**1/2 cup cranberry juice**
**1 teaspoon butter**
**1 teaspoon pure vanilla extract**
**1 cup dried cranberries**
**1 cup pecan halves**
**1 cup hazelnuts**
**1 cup peanuts**

Combine the syrups, zest, allspice, and cranberry juice in a medium saucepan over medium heat. Cook, stirring, to the soft-ball stage (238° on the candy thermometer). Remove from the heat. Let stand a minute or two, then add the butter. In several minutes more, add the vanilla and remaining ingredients, stirring well until the mixture thickens and begins to hold its shape.

Immediately turn this out onto waxed paper or into a shallow glass dish. Work quickly to separate the nuts and berries, allowing them to cool and dry individually. Serve on a plate with fresh fruits, especially melons, fruit ices, or ice creams, or enjoy these treats alone as perfect snacks or desserts.

**Makes 4 1/2 cups**

# April

*Steady, soft penetrating rain—a female rain—fills the night with thunder and throbbing sounds of renewal. Soon frog songs begin, as amphibians re-create the spring nights with their mating calls. Cycles of fertile exchange awaken the spring earth from her long winter rest.*

*In the Far West this is the Moon When The Ravens Lay Eggs of the Kaniagmiut, the Wild Goose Moon of the Nootka, and the Bitterroot Moon of the Salish. Tribes across the Great Plains called this the Breaking Ice Moon of the Mandan and Hidatsa, the Planting Corn Moon of the Osage and Winnebago, the Green Grass Moon of the Sioux, and the Geese Lay Their Eggs Moon of the Cheyenne. In the Southwest, this is the Moon When The Leaves Break Forth of the San Juan and Tewa Pueblos and the Kiowa.*

*Native Peoples in the Northeast knew this period as the Moon When They Set Corn of the Wampanoag, Moon Of Smelts of the Penobscot, and Birds Lay Their Eggs Moon of the Micmac and Narragansett. The natural rhythms of nature varied widely all across the continent, as did the observations and the observers. The yearly cycles of sun, moon, stars, planets, and our earth's seasonal moods were intensely interesting to our ancestors. Close attention was given to natural events, into which periodic festivals, tribal rituals, and normal lifeways were set.*

*As we move from region to region around North America we appreciate the many levels and textures of the traditional world.*

# SHAD—A BUSH, A FISH, A FESTIVAL

In the Native American tradition seasonal harbingers are often eagerly awaited. Signs and signals fill the natural world for those who watch for them. In the east, the white blooms of the shadbush, or serviceberry, *Amelanchier canadensis,* scattered throughout woodlands and hedgerows, are heralded as harbingers of spring. Also called Juneberry, the shadbush is delicate yet hardy. Enthusiasts of wild edible foods look for this beautiful shrub or small tree in June for the first fruits in the eastern woodlands. Deep purple-blackish Juneberries are actually miniature apples, sought for many seasonal recipes. Many tribes, like the Cherokee, also used the fine gray bark as a digestive aid and as a tea with marvelous tonic affects.

Shadbush is also widely considered a good harbinger of planting time. Many Native farmers would say "when the first young shadbush leaves get the size of a squirrel's ear, it is time to set the first corn."

The shadbush blossoms also signal the annual migratory "run of the shad" up inland rivers and streams and, consequently, the annual Native tradition of shad fishing and shad festivals.

Shad are marine fishes, related to the herring, that migrate into rivers to spawn, usually in late March and April. The American shad, *Alosa sapidissima,* was originally found in Atlantic-related waters from the Gulf of St. Lawrence to the Florida Keys, and in 1871 it was introduced successfully to the California coast and has now extended its range to Alaskan waters. Though one of the boniest of fishes, shad is a very popular sporting fish, sought for its delicious shad roe and milt. The hickory shad, *Alosa mediocris,* and the skipjack herring, *Alosa chrysochloris,* are also favored by anglers; in Atlantic waters they can reach twelve pounds—more in Pacific waters.

Native old-timers recall shad runs in the 1920s, 30s, and 40s when town criers would race through the village streets with their lanterns at night calling, "The shad's up! The shad's up!" Regardless of the time of night or day, everyone would race to the river with whatever basket and cart they could find, because the shad ran so thick and fine that one could just scoop them out of the river with a fishnet or even by hand. Catching this dependable spring delicacy took precedence over all other chores. Folks worked quickly to get what they could when shad were so plentiful. The shad runs once signaled the time of regional shad festivals, drawing folks together to savor and share nature's largess. Now hydroelectric dams have changed our old rivers so much that the shad can't make it up as far as they once could. Fishermen still crowd to the shores awaiting their annual migrations, but shad festivals are only occasional now. Often they are small community events, or "socials," held in community halls, granges, or schools. Folks gather to cook and eat together, then visit, tell stories, and discuss tribal and community affairs. Shad is the chief celebration on the menu, but companion foods may include wild rice with hazelnuts and pecans, wild leeks, wild violet and watercress salads, steamed fiddlehead ferns, and sautéed spring morels.

Shad fish festivals are at risk in many Native reservations and fishing areas because industrial plants along main rivers have caused serious systemic poisoning at many levels in the food chain. Mohawk midwife Katsi Cook at Akwesasne, the St. Regis Reservation, along the St. Lawrence River, has helped me to understand the depths of problems coming out of their research on the Mohawk peoples health and environmental concerns. Research programs such as Mothers Milk, done for nursing mothers, and Early Childhood Learning, done for children with learning disabilities, indicate growing causes for concern. Pollution of earth, water, and air in many reservations greatly affects their contemporary world and has limited the enjoyment of many old festivals. Nevertheless, wherever and whenever a good shad run occurs, shad festivals still celebrate this gift.

# BAKED STUFFED SHAD WITH SORREL SAUCE

*This delicious spring fish possesses more than 300 labyrinthine bones, making it a challenge to bone and fillet. The best approach is as follows, in which the long, slow baking time yields succulent, flavorful fish whose myriad bones have softened to the point of nearly melting away. For the stuffing, use either Salsa Cornbread (page 20), Juniper-Sage Corn Sticks (page 81), or the Buttermilk-Green Chili Cornbread (page 198).*

1 (5-pound) shad, dressed

2 tablespoons fresh lemon juice

2 tablespoons corn oil or melted butter

1/4 cup fresh parsley, finely chopped

1/4 cup fresh wild onions, finely chopped

salt and pepper to taste

4 strips of lean bacon (optional)

Preheat the oven to 250°. Rub prepared shad inside and out with the lemon juice and then the oil. Sprinkle it well with the herbs, salt, and pepper. Lay the fish on a heavy foil sheet in a long, shallow baking dish (unless you have a tight cover for the baking dish). Carefully stuff the shad with your favorite cornbread-herb stuffing or one of the suggestions above. Lay the strips of bacon over the shad. Carefully fold and seal the foil over the fish.

Place the prepared shad in the preheated oven. Bake for approximately 6 hours. (Start this in late morning for your evening meal.) Much later, prepare the Sorrel Sauce (see next page).

To serve, carefully lift out generous portions of shad. Top-dress each serving with Sorrel Sauce, fresh parsley, and dill.

**Serves 8**

# SORREL SAUCE

*A variety of leaves and blossoms of little wild sorrels can be used for this lemony-sour sauce. Sheep Sorrel, Rumex acetosella, Yellow Wood Sorrel, Oxalis stricta, Violet Wood Sorrel, Oxalis violacea, or Common Wood Sorrel, Oxalis montana, are good singly or collectively. French sorrel or spinach can also be used. Sorrel, from the Old German word for "sour," indicates that this sauce gives a slight tang; it also enhances the fine flavor of shad and many other types of fish.*

**2 tablespoons corn oil or butter**

**1 small white onion, diced**

**1 cup sorrel leaves and blossoms**

**1/2 cup wild green onions, finely chopped**

**1/2 cup fresh parsley, chopped**

**1 tablespoon cider vinegar**

**1 tablespoon Worcestershire sauce**

**salt and pepper to taste (optional)**

Heat the oil in a medium sauté pan over medium-high heat. When oil is hot, quickly sauté the white onion for about 3 minutes, stirring well. Add the sorrel, green herbs, and remaining ingredients. Lower heat to medium. Cook for barely 5 minutes, stirring often. Serve hot or warm over or beside the baked shad.

**Makes about 2 cups**

# Buttermilk Green Chili Cornbread Stuffing

*This simple classic cornbread is delicious as a side dish, but it is also wonderful when used as a stuffing. For stuffing, use freshly baked or day-old bread, crumbling it coarsely and spreading it on a baking sheet to dry. Hot or mild green chilies may be used, depending upon your palate and preference.*

1 cup yellow cornmeal

3 tablespoons all-purpose flour

1 teaspoon each of salt, baking powder, and thyme

1/4 teaspoon allspice, finely ground

2 cups cooked fresh corn, cut from the cob, with reserved liquids (corn milk)

1 medium yellow onion, chopped

1 medium green chili pepper, chopped

1 ½ cups buttermilk

1/4 cup corn oil

2 eggs, well beaten

1 tablespoon honey

Preheat oven to 350°. In a large mixing bowl, measure the dry ingredients. Create a well in the middle. Add the remaining ingredients. Beat quickly and carefully, until well mixed. Pour into a well-greased cast-iron skillet or 10x10x2-inch baking pan.

Bake for 1 hour or until a toothpick inserted in the center of the loaf comes out clean. Cool briefly and serve as a side dish or cool completely and turn out on a broad board to dry somewhat for use in the stuffing for shad or other game fish or fowl.

**Serves 8 to 10**

# BROILED SHAD ROE

*This fine delicacy is best when the freshest ingredients are used and preparation is careful. You can catch your own shad or buy shad roe at a fishmarket. This recipe calls for two roe sacs.*

Prick each roe sac membrane several times with a sharp needle to prevent it from bursting and splattering the little eggs. Parboil the roe by placing it in a saucepan and covering it with boiling water. Add 2 tablespoons lemon juice and a pinch of salt. Simmer for 10 minutes, then drain.

To broil, place 2 pairs of parboiled shad roe on an oiled flame-resistant broiler dish or plate. Sprinkle with lemon juice. Add salt and pepper to taste (optional). Lightly dust with paprika. Lay a strip of lean bacon over each roe sac. Broil in preheated broiler for 5 to 8 minutes, depending upon size and thickness of roe sacs. Roe is done when it turns pale beige. Do not overcook.

Serve hot on a bed of parsley, fresh, chopped watercress, and chopped wild onions. Top with the following light butter sauce: sauté 1/4 cup of chopped wild onions or scallions (both green and white parts) in 3 tablespoons of butter for 3 minutes on medium-low heat. Add 2 tablespoons of lemon juice and a dash of paprika and thyme. Blend well and pour over the shad roe. Enjoy!

**Serves 4 to 6**

199

# CREE WALKING OUT CEREMONY

Its origins are lost in the mists of time, yet the walking out ceremony is one of the most important rites in a Cree's life. For the young child, it opens the door to the real world. "All our children have done it," says Luke McLeod of Mistissini, one of the most populous Cree villages located on the south shore of the vast Mistassini Lake at the heart of an evergreen forest in the mid-northern region of Quebec.

Cree children cannot walk outdoors freely before the ceremony—they must be carried. Although they are allowed to walk indoors, they must not cross the house threshold alone, until this early spring rite. At dawn on the chosen day, parents, family, and friends gather in a big tent around one or more young toddlers, and they move from east to west around the interior, "from the sun's rising to its setting, from birth to death, greeted by the guests."

"Then each child crosses the door's threshold, accompanied by his grandparents or parents. He (or she) follows a path strewn with fir branches to a tree, the symbol of nature, some twenty feet away from the entrance." The child circles the tree, then returns to be welcomed inside the tent again by the elders, who congratulate and celebrate the child. The occasion is well planned for both boys and girls to mirror their projected roles in life, strengthened and supported by their families and friends.

The feast prepared for this very special gathering reflects the principal foods of these noted hunters and trappers and may include caribou rib roasts, moose steaks and stews, bannocks, pemmicans, and wild berry jams and teas.

# CREE CARIBOU RIB ROAST

*American caribou,* Rangifer tarandus, *are dynamic migratory animals of the northern forests, tundra, and bog regions. Relative of the Old World reindeer, caribou are members of the great deer family. Unlike their other relatives, both sexes of caribou are usually antlered. Whether you plan to prepare this over an alder campfire or treat it as haute cuisine in your own country kitchen, this feast and festival dish celebrates the spirit of the caribou.*

1 (5- to 6-pound caribou rib roast (or buffalo, venison, or beef)

2 tablespoons Worcestershire sauce

salt and pepper to taste

3 garlic cloves, finely diced

1 large garlic clove, halved

3 tablespoons corn oil

4 medium Yukon gold or russet potatoes, quartered

4 medium red torpedo onions, quartered

4 large Danvers (or other) carrots, quartered

4 medium serrano peppers, cored and quartered

1 cup water or broth

1/2 cup cider or other vinegar

3 bay leaves

Rub the caribou roast well with the Worcestershire sauce and salt and pepper. Sprinkle it with the diced garlic and rub the garlic pieces in well. Season a large, lidded roasting pan by rubbing it well first with the halved garlic and then with the oil. Place the roast in this deep roasting pot and surround it with the medley of vegetables. Pour the water or broth around it and sprinkle the vinegar over all. Add the bay leaves and any favorite seasonings (you can also subtract any you do not like). Cover tightly and place the pot in the center of an oven preheated to 350°. Cook slowly for 2 1/2 hours.

While the roast sets and cools slightly, make a gravy from the broth, pan drippings, and the roasted vegetables: After removing the caribou roast, spoon out the potatoes and onions into a food processor or blender container, add 1 cup of the hot pan juices, and purée. Place the roasting pot on the stove and warm it over medium-high heat, deglazing the pot roast juices and scraping down the sides and bottom of the pot.

Stir well and add 1 cup of cut fresh mushrooms (morels or other seasonal favorites). Remove the bay leaves, balance the tastes, and add the vegetable broth purée. Stir well and actively simmer to reduce and intensify the flavors somewhat. You may add a flour or cornstarch thickener if you wish.

Carve the caribou roast. Serve with the pot gravy, fresh bannock or corn bread, and wild greens in salad or as pot herbs.

**Serves 10**

# April Powwows and Other Celebrations

Numerous powwows fill the April calendar. From coast to coast, at universities, parks, expo pavilions, and tribal cultural centers, Indian students gather to celebrate Earth Day and to attend American Indian Youth Conferences. Participation in walk-a-thons, heritage festivals, potlucks, and sobriety gatherings help Native Americans take stock of seasonal and yearly progress. Native American Cultural Awareness gatherings may take place one weekend, and Indian Market festivities may fill another. Each event accomplishes, in many instances, far more than it sets out to do, as networking, sharing, and breaking bread together builds a special unity.

It is always best to check local listings for clear details. Native foods at these celebrations can run an interesting gamut—simple-but-sensational buffalo burgers, turkey franks, fried corn, chili-smothered baked potatoes, Navajo tacos, myriad variations on Indian frybread, elk and venison meatloafs, sausages, bear roasts, game pot roasts, rib roasts, and barbecues. A full complement of herbal teas, fruit and berry drinks, lemonade, sumacade, sassafrasade, birch beer soda, and, of course, hot cocoa and coffee help wash everything down smoothly.

203

Native American chefs with specialties and signature foods and products may show up at these gatherings to try out their unique ideas. Serving and playing to eclectic audiences, they usually achieve outstanding results. In such cases you might encounter delicious Lizard's Breath Equatorial Guacamole, Butternut Ridge Biscuits, Grilled Bear Bits in Grizzly Hot Sauce, Copperhead Ridge Roadhouse Meatloaf, Green Mountain Wild Salsa Salad, Fiery Powwow Mix, and Maple-Pecan-Peanut Brittle. Great tastes with great humor is a modern calling card in Native foods today. Surely as many different salsas, chili sauces, and guacamoles exist as there are Native cooks to create them. Distinctive regional and seasonal flair is apparent at April powwows.

*E*very sort of wild game has long been hunted by Native Americans for meat, hides, sinew, bones, and, in some cases, antlers, hooves, and paws. Valuable beaver, deer, and buffalo hides helped establish the eighteenth- and nineteenth-century fur trade. Today, many game animals are being ranched and farmed, as renewed appreciation of their value has produced a growing demand for their meat and skins. Deer, buffalo/beefalo, elk, caribou, antelope, llama, and alligator top the list of larger four-legged game favorites, while armadillo, rabbit, quail, wild duck, and wild turkey comprise the list of smaller game. Trout, salmon, catfish, oysters, lobsters, clams, and scallops add even greater dimension to our nation's many meaty resources. You may enjoy hunting for these in your local supermarkets and specialty stores. Some ranches have mail-order businesses if you can't find some items locally. See the Source Directory for a list of such sources.

# SAVORY FESTIVAL NUTS WITH POPCORN

*Whether you choose to pop blue, black jet, strawberry, white, or yellow popcorn kernels, they all explode a beautiful white. This sneaky coyote seasoning adds a delicious element of surprise and might leave folks howling for more.*

1 cup of popcorn, popped

3 to 4 tablespoons of butter

1 cup shelled peanuts

1 cup shelled hazelnuts

1 tablespoon medium red chili powder

1 tablespoon fresh lime juice

1/2 teaspoon ground allspice

1/2 teaspoon lime zest

salt and pepper to taste

Pop the corn by your favorite method and keep warm while you season the nuts that will be sprinkled over the top. In a large sauté pan over medium heat, melt the butter. Add all of the remaining ingredients, stirring well to blend thoroughly.

Heat well for about 5 minutes, stirring constantly. Pour hot mixture directly over the fresh, hot popcorn. Toss well and serve immediately. Enjoy with chilled lemonade or spicy Chilly Chili Corn Milk (below).

**Serves 10**

# CHILLY CHILI CORN MILK

*This unique, thick beverage has a combined spicy/minty essence and goes well with any crunchy snack.*

**1/2 cup well-cooked white hominy**

**1/2 cup buttermilk**

**dash chili powder**

**dash ground ginger**

**several fresh mint leaves**

**salt and pepper to taste**

**1/2 cup shaved ice**

Purée all ingredients, including shaved ice, together in a blender for about 1 minute, creating a fine, frothy liquid. Pour over ice in a tall glass and serve immediately.

**Serves 1**

# FIERY POWWOW MIX

*This hominy-based treat is pure invention with countless variations, yet it assembles some old-time Native American classics in a crazy, comfortable snack that can be enjoyed at any gathering, from April powwows to a backyard picnic to a hike.*

**1 (16-ounce) can Nixtamal Blanco white hominy corn, drained**

**3 tablespoons butter**

**2 tablespoons peanut oil**

**1 tablespoon fine, medium-hot chili powder**

**12 cloves of garlic, sliced in half lengthwise**

**1 tablespoon fresh lime juice**

**1 tablespoon cider vinegar**

**1/2 teaspoon allspice, finely ground**

**1/2 teaspoon each of ginger, thyme, cumin, salt, and pepper**

**1 cup hazelnuts, shelled**

**1 cup peanuts, shelled**

**1 cup pecans, shelled**

**1 cup pumpkin seeds**

**1 cup sunflower seeds, shelled**

Preheat oven to 400°. Drain hominy corn and set aside.

In a large skillet, melt butter over medium heat and add the peanut oil, chili powder, garlic, lime juice, vinegar, allspice, and other seasonings. Blend well while sautéing for about 5 minutes. Add nuts and seeds. Blend well and add the drained white hominy corn. Stir well and simmer all together for about 5 minutes. Remove from the heat and turn out onto a broad, lightly oiled baking sheet. Shake sheet to spread mixture well apart. Bake at 400° for about 10 minutes. Cool slightly and serve.

**Serves 12**

# The Wild Onion Women Dancing in the Night

*Throughout North America, tribal traditions saw the "movement" of the Pleiades as a signal of important events in annual calendars. For many tribes, the fading disappearance of this star cluster in early spring sunsets signaled the time to plant seeds. The reappearance of the Pleiades in the predawn skies of mid-June signaled the final planting time of late-annual seeds if they were to mature before killing frost.*

*For the Monache Indians on the Tule River Reservation in central California, whose ancestors were hunters and gatherers of wild plants, the Pleiades symbolized the six Wild Onion Women, who were banished by their husbands because of their strong wild onion fragrance. Humiliated, the women collected their sacred eagle-down ropes and the little daughter of one of the wives and climbed up the ropes into the Sky World.*

*The six husbands soon grew sad and tried to follow their wives to the Sky World using the same magic, but they could never quite join them. The Young Men are the cluster of six bright stars we know as the constellation of Taurus, dancing just behind the six Wild Onion Women and the little daughter we call the Pleiades.*

207

Throughout the spring, regional salmon feasts and root feasts are scheduled among the Northwest Coast tribes of Oregon and Washington. Many are remarkable annual events honoring two major sources of native foods.

The Root Festival on the Umatilla Reservation in the foothills of the Blue Mountains in Pendleton, Oregon, is a major spring event for the Umatilla, Cayuse, and Walla Walla tribes who govern their confederation of more than 1,000 tribal members on about 240,000 acres of tribal lands.

Warm Springs Reservation hosts the traditional Root Feast and Root Feast Rodeo on the eastern slopes of the Cascade Range in north-central Oregon, where the Wasco, Paiute, and Warm Springs tribes have created a community of more than 3,000 people on their 640,000-acre reservation.

The Annual Rock Creek Root Feast and Powwow in Rock Creek, Washington, is hosted by the Yakima Nation, whose reservation also encompasses the eastern slopes of the glorious Cascade Range and covers 1.6 million acres. With their tribal center in Toppenish, Washington, fourteen tribes and bands comprise the confederation known as the Yakima Indian Nation. The Yakima Indian Nation in The Dalles, Oregon, on the Columbia River, hosts an annual three-day Salmon and Root Feast, where wild berries and spring roots are served along with salmon prepared in traditional ways.

The earth has always been providing, along with constant human nurturing, either refrigerator or oven for our benefit. Pit fires are the ovens of the earth, embracing and enhancing the gifts of field, forest, and water. New England lobster and clam bakes, Pacific Coast abalone and oyster bakes, Pueblo corn and bean roasts, and Northwest root feasts all have pit fire cooking in common.

Pit-roasted, long-slow-sweet-cooked foods are earthy-delicious in a way not achieved by any other means. The following recipe for camas and salmon offers a traditional way to celebrate the root and river bounties of April.

# ALDER ROASTED CAMAS AND STEAMED SALMON

*Like many other Native American recipes, this one is more to be spoken, almost sung, rather than fixed out in a formula like conventional recipes. The instructions here, however, should help you avoid mistakes.*

**1/4 bushel alder bark, or hickory bark, dampened**

**1/4 bushel fern fronds and sweetgrass (combined), dampened**

**2 bushels of camas bulbs, or combination potatoes and turnips**

**1/4 bushel small onions, peeled but whole**

**1 bushel sunchokes**

**1 bushel small squashes**

**3 whole salmon, or about 10 steaks and 10 fillets**

**1/4 bushel cattail and tule reeds, dampened**

**1 or more large baking potatoes (for the top)**

A cleared area is chosen, and a pit is dug to the depth, width, and length that will accommodate the food to be cooked. The bottom of the pit is lined with big rocks (smooth hard ones that are not likely to crack or explode; worn river cobbles are great). A good, deep hardwood fire is built, log cabin style, upon these rocks in the bottom of the pit, and fed for about 2 hours with additional hard and soft wood until a good bed of charcoal develops. Hardwoods like oak and ash burn hottest and make less ash than other types of wood. Seasoned, rather than green wood, is best.

The coals are then evenly spread on the pit floor using long sticks and metal rakes. A good amount of damp alder wood and bark (or hickory, apple, mesquite, grape, or corncobs—depending upon the region and season) is then sprinkled over the hot coals to a depth of 2 to 3 inches. Immediately this "bake-bed" is covered with fragrant ferns and sweetgrass layers between which the foods are placed for roasting. Several bushels or more of camas bulbs interspersed with tiny bulbs of nodding onions, corn-in-husk (in season), sunchokes, potatoes, or small squashes (if desired), and each pierced or speared once to allow its steam to escape.

Top this off with a layer of large or individual salmon steaks and fillets and any choice shellfish desired. Top this with a 2-inch layer of cattail and tule reeds, evenly spread. Place a fresh potato in the center. When it is baked—allow about 2 hours—your foods will be done.

All of this is covered over with a heavy, damp tarp and secured with large stones around the perimeter. While the festivities go on at great pace, and the sauces, salads, and drinks are being made, the earth oven slowly steams along, developing fine fragrances, and fabulous, succulent foods. Most are fully cooked in about 2 hours.

# MOUNT SAINT HELENS SALAD WITH VOLCANIC LAVA DRESSING

*Medleys of freshly picked or store-bought spring greens provide the basis of this substantial, delicious dish, and the smoked salmon is an elegant seasonal companion to the other earthy ingredients. The volcanic dressing can be heated or cooled to suit the palate, and it can be served on the side or tossed into the salad.*

*Mount Saint Helens Salad is so popular, with seasonal variations, at many festivals that it is also served in the Yakima Tribal Restaurant, where I first enjoyed it.*

**1 quart each of fresh spinach greens, bibb lettuce, romaine, violet leaves,
and radicchio, all washed and trimmed**

**1 large white onion, very thinly sliced**

**1 large red onion, very thinly sliced**

**1 large green bell pepper, very thinly sliced**

**4 sunchokes, very thinly sliced**

**1 cup morels, sliced and sautéed briefly**

**1/4 cup fresh parsley, finely diced**

**1/4 cup wild onions, finely diced**

**1/2 pound alder-smoked salmon fillet, sliced in julienne strips**

Arrange the medley of greens attractively in 6 or 8 large salad bowls. Carefully divide and layer the remaining ingredients on top of each bowl of greens. Refrigerate while you prepare the Volcanic Lava Dressing, then toss and serve.

**Serves 6**

## VOLCANIC LAVA DRESSING

**2 tablespoons sunflower seed oil**

**3 cloves garlic, finely chopped**

**1 red bell pepper, diced medium-fine**

**1 small red tomato, finely chopped**

**1 teaspoon paprika or red chili powder**

**2 tablespoons lemon juice**

**1 cup red currants or grapes, chopped**

**1/2 cup cider vinegar, or more, to taste**

**salt and pepper to taste**

**1 cup roasted hazelnuts, shelled and chopped**

Heat the oil in a large sauté pan over medium heat. When hot, quickly sauté the garlic, pepper, and chopped tomato, stirring well and frequently until ingredients are just glazed and slightly wilted. Add the paprika, lemon juice, and currants or grapes. Heat thoroughly, stirring well. Quickly add the vinegar and seasonings. Balance the seasonings to suit your taste.

Spoon hot dressing over the chilled salads and sprinkle each bowl with roasted hazelnuts. Serve immediately with hot, crusty bread and cold drinks or hot coffee.

**Makes about 1 cup**

# GLACIAL MISTS COOLER

*Many nonalcoholic fruit beverages are served at Native gatherings and festivals and are great with many kinds of foods. Present at both root feasts, salmon feasts, and many other festivals and private occasions, this sweet-sour drink also serves as a mild digestive aid—helpful when we are tempted to overindulge. Colorful, tasty variations are possible as the seasons change. Ripe melon slushes in late summer and cranberry-lime or mango-papaya slush in the fall are delicious combinations.*

**1 fresh lemon, the zest grated and the rest squeezed and chopped**

**squeezed juice of 2 more lemons**

**pinch of salt**

**1/2 cup honey**

**1 teaspoon finely ground ginger root**

**1 teaspoon lime zest, plus the juice of the lime**

**1/2 cup crushed ice**

Place lemon in the blender bowl. Add all other ingredients. Process for half a minute or so until you've created a fine, thoroughly slushed purée.

Fill 8 glasses with equal parts of crushed ice and sparkling spring water or seltzer (about 2 or 3 ounces in each glass). Add a fruity "glacial mist" to each glass. Perch a thin slice of lime or a fresh strawberry "fan" over the rim of each glass.

**Serves 6 to 8**

# Corn Dance Feast of the Hidatsa Women

*A*s we leave the root feasts and salmon feasts, with their rodeos and myriad special activities, it is important to reflect upon earlier feasts which were also governed by spring urgencies, tribal needs, and principal foods. Corn, so central in many tribes' survival, has been celebrated in countless ways. The Corn Dance Feast of the Hidatsa Women was a particularly spiritual and central event.

The Hidatsas and Mandans were primarily village farmers, who lived in earth lodges on high bluffs along the upper Missouri River regions. They shared many customs and rituals, in particular the Corn Dance Feast of the Women. Their cosmology relates how the Old Woman Who Never Dies sent the first seeds for their long-ago gardens. This is symbolized by the spring migrating waterfowl—wild ducks brought the first beans, swans brought the first gourd seeds, and geese brought the first corn.

Each spring, to honor the Old Woman Who Never Dies, the elder women of the tribe gather and suspend dried meat offerings on tall poles to feed her spirit. These are left throughout the growing season until harvest time. In spring the elder women perform a special dance celebrating the Old Woman Who Never Dies. During the dance the young women feed the older dancers special meat and receive corn to eat in return. Some of these special ceremonial corn kernels are also mixed with the tribe's garden seeds to further bless the planting time.

213

# EASTER WEEK CELEBRATIONS IN THE DESERT SOUTHWEST

Living in "the House of the Sun" among mountainous moonlike landscapes studded with huge standing saguaros in the Desert Southwest are the Yaqui. The newly arriving Spaniards gave the tribe this name almost 400 years ago, probably after the Rio Yaqui, which flows through Sonora, Mexico. The Yaqui know themselves as Yoemem, which means "The People."

Today the Pascua-Yaqui Reservation embraces 892 acres southwest of Tucson and the Catalina Mountains, site of the O'odham's Frog Mountain with its exquisite ancient petroglyphs and pictographs in black volcanic rock. Most Yaqui are trilingual, speaking their unique Yaqui dialect of the Cahita linguistic family, as well as Spanish and English. Tribal consciousness continues to grow and to weave their far-flung villages together. The American Yaqui maintain close ties with the Sonoran Yaqui in Mexico (the latter of which have been immortalized in the deer dance of the Ballet Folklorico and curiously exposed for more than twenty years in Carlos Casteneda's books revolving around the legendary sorcerer Don Juan Matus). Inspiration and endurance are certain pillars of Yaqui society.

During Lent and Holy Week, the Yaqui *kohtumbre*, "keepers of our most sacred traditions," take over the village on Ash Wednesday. Throughout the Lenten and Easter season, their two main societies, the *caballeros*, "horsemen," and the *fariseos*, "masked members," conduct all business and religious duties "with a good heart." These Lenten ceremonies are a fascinating hybrid of Yaqui beliefs and Jesuit Christian influences.

The annual Yaqui Passion Play expresses faith, endurance, and imagination through a reenactment of the Passion of Jesus, while beautifully overlaying the Christian theme is the Native celebration of the flower world and all of nature. On the Saturday before Palm Sunday, the Yaqui religious societies reenact the early seventeenth-century Easter Ceremony. The maestros, "church leaders," and pascolas, "the old men of the fiesta" act as ritual hosts, orators, dancers, and clowns, converging and dancing until dawn. Their marvelous dances and ceremonial protocol continue to draw the Yaqui together. Although no photographs or sound recordings are permitted, everyone is invited to share their ceremonies, at this time, "with a good heart." According to Raul Silvas, 1988 Pascua Yaqui chairman, the Yaqui People are always drawn together by their village church. This is true especially at Eastertime, which each year represents "a new beginning for everyone."

On the Friday following Easter, children's dance groups from the Tohono O'odham and Yaqui tribes gather at San Xavier del Bac Mission, founded in the early 1700s. Known as the "White Dove of the Desert," this is one of the finest architectural examples of old mission churches in the Southwest, just 10 miles south of Tucson. The Easter fiesta at San Xavier features a magnificent late-evening, torchlight procession as well as the children's dancing. Traditional Indian food booths open early for this special occasion. The following recipes are favorites here each year.

*The voice of the thunder*
*Within the dark cloud*
*Again and again it sounds,*
*The voice that*
*Beautifies the land!*

*—Mountain Chant of the Navajo*

# Empanaditas de Carne (Little Meat Pies)

*Similar to the* Empanadas de Fruta, *or little fruit pies, these savory little meat pies,* Empadinhas *in Brazil, are tasty finger foods wonderfully presented at festivals like the San Xavier Easter Fiesta. At Pascua-Yaqui, these pies are called popovers; at Tulsa's Art Festival they are simply called meat pies. Many variations on the pastry dough and fillings exist—you may enjoy creating your own or you can try some of the ideas suggested below.*

## SAVORY MEAT FILLING

1 tablespoon corn oil

1 small onion, finely chopped

1 pound lean ground beef, buffalo, lamb, or pork

2 green Serrano chili peppers, fire-roasted and finely chopped

1/2 cup pine nuts, roasted

1/2 cup currants or raisins

1 teaspoon finely ground allspice

salt and pepper to taste

Heat oil in a medium sauté pan. Quickly sauté the onion and then the meat. Stir well, then add the remaining ingredients. Stir and simmer together slowly for about 15 minutes. Balance seasonings to taste. Remove any excess liquid or thicken the mixture with a sprinkling of fine cornmeal stirred in well. Add just enough hot sauce or chili paste to give this filling a savory tang. Set aside while you prepare the dough.

# FRIED PASTRY DOUGH

**1 1/2 cups all-purpose flour**

**1/2 cup fine cornmeal**

**1 teaspoon each of salt, honey, lemon zest**

**2 tablespoons sunflower seed oil (do not substitute butter)**

**1/2 cup, or more, hot water**

Place the flour, cornmeal, and seasonings in a mixing bowl. Blend in the oil with a fork or your hands. Add the hot water, and mix to form the dough. Flour your hands lightly, and turn the dough several times to knead, but do not overwork it. Cover with plastic and let rest at room temperature for about 30 minutes.

To make the empanaditas, pinch off golf ball-size pieces of dough and dip each dough ball in flour or fine cornmeal. Pat dredged dough balls into small circles, then, using a rolling pin, roll each piece out into a 6- to 7-inch circle. Place a generous tablespoonful of the meat filling on each dough circle, just off-center. Barely moisten the inner edges of the circle with lemon water and fold in half. Crimp the edges of the half-moon pies to seal in the filling. Repeat this procedure for all the circles of dough until all become "moon pies."

In a large, deep frying pan, heat about 3 inches of oil to 375°. Ease 3 or 4 little pies at a time into the hot oil. Gently spoon the hot oil over them and move them around to cook quickly and thoroughly until just honey-golden. This should take 3 to 5 minutes—the shorter, the better. Remove finished pies with tongs or a slotted spoon; drain on layers of paper towels or brown paper. Repeat with remaining pies. Serve plain or dust lightly with grated cheese, chopped cilantro, or paprika.

Try these marvelous savory variations for this recipe, extending the range of these little meat pies to serve every taste: pork and apricot-raisin, grilled chili pepper and avocado, chicken and green chilies, refried bean and cheese, or lamb and pine nuts. For sweet "moon pies," you may try fillings of sweet potato and raisin, pineapple and pecan, and so on.

**Makes 12 to 14 pies**

# Fiesta del Sol Cookies

*Simplicity and lightness define these sunny little treats, which are easy to make and even easier to eat, especially with chilled, homemade lemonade or hot tea or coffee. They are inspired by the Easter Week Yoemem, or Yaqui, in "the House of the Sun."*

1 cup sugar

1/2 cup butter

1 egg

1 teaspoon vanilla

1 cup all-purpose flour

1/2 cup fine cornmeal

1 teaspoon cinnamon

1 teaspoon baking powder

1 teaspoon fresh lemon zest

1/4 teaspoon salt

cinnamon-lemon sugar

In a medium mixing bowl, cream together sugar and butter, then beat in the egg and vanilla. Add remaining ingredients (except for the cinnamon-lemon sugar, which is used to dredge dough balls). Blend together well. Cover and refrigerate for 2 or 3 hours until firm.

Preheat oven to 350°. Shape cookie dough into small balls, about 1/2 inch in diameter, and roll each one in the cinnamon-lemon sugar, which is made by stirring together 1/4 cup sugar, an additional teaspoon of fresh lemon zest, and another teaspoon of cinnamon.

Set cookie balls 1 inch apart on lightly greased baking sheet. Bake for 10 minutes or until just honey-golden. Cool slightly on baking sheet, then remove to racks to cool completely, or serve immediately, warm from the oven.

**Makes 6 dozen cookies**

# MAY

*A mackerel sky ripples overhead, moderating the bright golden heat of spring. Cries of the red-tailed hawk echo over the ravine, alerting its mate and young to prepare for a banquet. Hunting is good in this season of plenty, and food is to be celebrated.*

*The natural world reflects continual changes, echoed in Native American observations. This is the Frog Croaking Moon of the Micmac, the Alewives and Planting Moon of the Penobscot and the Corn Planting Moon of the Wampanoag in the Northeast. Moving west, it is the Moon of Flowers of the Menominee and Osage, the Hoeing Corn Moon of the Winnebago, and the Moon When The Ponies Shed of the Sioux. In the South, it is the Mulberry Moon of the Creek, the Great Sand Storm Moon of the Zuni, and the Baby Antelope Moon of the Jemez Pueblo. Along the Pacific Northwest Coast, this is the Moon of the Wild Eggs of the Tsimshian and the Getting-Ready-For-Whaling Moon of the Nootka. It is always fascinating to see the many ways we have of looking at the same old moon, in the same month, from the same continent.*

*The great cornucopia of cultures that make up North America can dazzle with a bewildering variety of choices but also deepen our perspectives on every region and season. Native foods are equally diverse and eclectically nurturing at every festival, fiesta, ceremony, and powwow.*

# SAN FELIPE PUEBLO FEAST DAY
# AND CORN DANCE

Well known among the Rio Grande pueblos for its beautiful, traditional ceremonials, San Felipe Pueblo welcomes visitors on their annual feast day celebrating their patron saint. One of the most conservative of the Keresan villages, its soft-cornered adobe dwellings, and smooth beehive-shaped bread ovens called *hornos* seem to anchor the village in another period of time. On the first of May hundreds of participants gather in the village's broad bowl-shaped earthen plaza for the glorious Corn Dance. A magnificent ritual prayer for rain, generous harvests, good health, and general well-being, the Corn Dance is so important in Pueblo Indian life that it can be performed at various times of the year, celebrating religious or political events. Similar spring pageants are held at the Acoma Pueblo (Santa Maria Feast Day), the Taos Pueblo (Santa Cruz Feast Day), and the Cochiti Pueblo, where classic hollow log drums resonate at their Corn Dance (also performed in July in honor of St. Bonaventure).

Hours and days and generations of preparations go into the Corn Dance: clothing, regalia, accessories, prayers, and rehearsals. In the public dance, you can sense the sacred dimensions and "read" the emblems of the natural world in the dancers' clothing and accoutrements. Throbbing drumbeats, chanting, moccasined feet massaging the earth, and leg bells and rattles weave hypnotic rhythms as the multilayered musical fabric simulates the sounds of steady rain falling on sturdy corn plants and soft earth. The Creator must be pleased with this lovely and careful pageantry. So much depends upon it.

Symbols of sky and clouds, wind and prayers, longevity and fertility, are woven into the costumes and other regalia. Some of the female dancers wear ornate towering tablettas on their heads, which are adorned with images of the sun, moon, stars, and clouds, and the arching rainbow. Through symbol and pageantry, the San Felipe people pay homage to their patron saint as well as the Earth and Creator. As is true in much of Pueblo life, spiritual dimensions are an integral part of the festivals and the foods themselves and extend to their concept of the whole scheme of the universe.

# Soft Corn Clouds

*This pillowy corn vegetable dish may resemble a pudding, yet it is meant to be savory rather than sweet. A wonderful accompaniment to Cochiti Lake trout or any favorite main dish, it is inspired from Pueblo food gifts. Try it adorned with tasty Pumpkin Seed Point Sauce (next page) or pungent Green Chili Paste (page 82).*

**2 tablespoons butter**

**1 teaspoon fresh garlic, minced**

**2 cups apple juice or cider**

**3 tablespoons unsweetened pumpkin purée, fresh or canned**

**1/2 cup fine cornmeal**

**1/2 cup fresh corn kernels (or frozen, thawed)**

**1/4 teaspoon finely ground allspice**

**1/4 teaspoon finely ground cayenne**

**salt and pepper to taste**

**2 tablespoons wild onions or chives, finely chopped**

Melt the butter in a medium saucepan over medium heat and sauté the garlic for 3 minutes. Pour in the apple juice and add the pumpkin purée. Stir well. Bring this mixture to a quick boil, then lower the heat and sprinkle in the cornmeal, corn kernels, and seasonings. Blend and smooth well; simmer for 6 to 10 minutes, stirring occasionally. Cover and remove from the heat. Keep warm for 20 to 30 minutes before serving.

Spoon or scoop generous corn clouds onto the serving plates and top with the wild green onions. Accompany with Pumpkin Seed Point Sauce or Green Chili Sauce.

**4 servings**

# PUMPKIN SEED POINT SAUCE

*Inspired and named for a special place at Hopi, this tasty, savory sauce develops yet another personality of the green, shelled or shell-less pumpkin seeds, or pepitas—so versatile a pure-energy source that many of us eat them plain and raw and others find them more digestible when slightly cooked. Glorious in pumpkin seed butter, salsas, syrups, vinaigrette, and pipian sauce, they accompany all favorite foods, whether sweet, savory, or salty.*

**2 cups green, shell-less pumpkin seeds, raw**

**1/2 cup apple cider vinegar**

**2 tablespoons balsamic vinegar**

**1 teaspoon garlic, minced**

**1/2 teaspoon finely ground allspice**

**1/2 teaspoon annatto seed (achiote), crushed**

**1/2 cup peanut oil**

**1/4 cup unsweetened pumpkin purée, fresh or canned**

**salt and pepper to taste**

Spread the pumpkin seeds on a baking sheet and lightly toast in a preheated oven at 350° for 10 minutes. Remove and cool.

Heat the vinegars, garlic, allspice, and annato seed in a small saucepan over medium heat. Add more than half of the toasted pumpkin seeds (save the rest for garnishes to be used last). Simmer, stirring well, for 5 minutes. Add the oil, pumpkin purée, and remaining seasonings. Balance the seasonings to your taste and simmer for another 3 minutes. Cool slightly, then purée this mixture in a blender for about a minute. Keep warm until ready to serve, using the remaining pepitas as garnishes. This sauce keeps well in a covered glass container for a week. It is great hot or cold and even better after its flavors have a chance to develop and mingle.

**Makes about 3 cups**

# CINCO DE MAYO

Centuries of foreign domination in Mexico crested on the fifth of May in 1867 in the city of Puebla when the French forces of Napoleon were defeated by Mexican General Ignacio Zaragoya and his troops. Fiestas and folk plays reenact the Batalla de Cinco de Mayo each year in small plazas and major cities, from villages in Mexico to the city of Portland in Oregon. Liberation and freedom are compelling themes around which people easily gather, and Hispanic origins, politics, and foods enhance the victory celebrations.

May Day has traditionally been celebrated in many different cultures as a time to honor labor, religion, or politics in various ways. Cinco de Mayo, correspondingly, fits a special niche and reinvents itself annually, embracing more and more of the early May calendar. Now, Cinco de Mayo festivities can stretch for three days in some towns and cities, providing ample opportunities to explore the many delicious foods that originated South of the Border.

Five hundred years ago the New World opened a valuable culinary universe to the Old World, yielding graciously its many gifts that continue to nurture, inform, and surprise international cuisines in countless ways. The spice trade influenced the many winds of discovery. Imagine the value of "finding" allspice, for instance. Derived from the dried reddish fruits of an evergreen tree in Mexico and Central America *Pimenta officinalis* and *Pimenta dioica* (and ancient in Mayan and Aztec cuisines), it was called "allspice" by its "discoverers" because it so closely mimics the aromatic qualities of cinnamon, cloves, and nutmeg. Allspice flavoring is widely used today beyond our personal kitchens in many baked goods, ice creams, candies, beverages, and chewing gums.

Annato, *Bixa orellana,* also known as *achiote* (for the thick red paste it is worked into), is the small red-orange seed of a shrub or small tree native to Central America. A noted Mayan and Aztec orange dye, its ancient versatilities to dye cloth and skin, as well as to color and flavor foods, established its value in ancient cultures. Today annatto continues to provide the colorful essence in many Caribbean and Mexican foods.

Arrowroot, *Maranta arundinacea,* refers to the starchy underground stem, or rhizome, of another plant native to the Caribbean, especially the West Indies. Its starchy abilities to thicken cooked foods, cosmetics, and glues has long proved valuable. American Angelica, *angelica atropurpurea,* is an aromatic member of the parsley family, whose fragrant seeds, stems, roots, and leaves have also benefited foods, medicines, and fragrance products for countless centuries.

Avocado, *Persea americana,* wild pineapple, *Ananas comosus,* and circumtropical coconut, *Cocos nucifera,* continue to be some of the tastiest and most valuable plants of the New World tropics. The economic destiny of these indigenous plants has provided powerful incentives for medicine, farming, and food research. In their most delicious incarnations each of these fruits and spices turns up in varieties of wonderful foods at many Native American festivals. At Cinco de Mayo celebrations and other spring festivities, they are flavorful ingredients in beverages, snacks, desserts, salads, and main dishes. Here we offer several special recipes that go beyond the "typical" festival foods you will encounter.

# RICH COCONUT CREAM

*Coconut fruits and their handsome palm trees are common in the tropics, and there all the plant parts are used in thousands of unique ways. Here are two ways you can enjoy this New World tropical treasure.*

**1 ripe coconut, with a brown, hard shell**

**4 cups of very hot water**

Clean and examine your ripe coconut. Find its three "eyes," and, using a long carpenter's nail and small hammer, tap the nail halfway into each of these soft "eye" spots. Wiggle the nail a bit and remove it. This provides "breathing holes" so the coconut will not explode when you bake it. Be careful not to slosh out the milky water (flower sap) inside. Tip the pierced coconut upside down over a broad jar or glass, allowing most of this coconut milk to drain out. If it smells fine, you may strain and use this in recipes or you may just want to drink it all up.

Bake the coconut in a 400° oven for 20 minutes or more, when it cracks. Remove it and allow it to cool for 10 minutes.

Hold the roasted coconut firmly and give it several hard whacks with a hammer or crack it on a hard cement floor. *Be careful!*

Using a dull knife, carefully pry away the thick white coconut meat from the hard outer shell. Peel away the brown "skin" that protects the white meat from the shell. Cut the meat into thin 1-inch strips.

Place 2 to 3 cups of coconut meat in a blender or food processor. Cover with the hot water. The less water, the richer the coconut milk. Process for about 1 minute. Pour the liquid through a fine strainer. Collect the coconut "cream" to drink or to use in breads, desserts, or other foods. Save the processed coconut for snacks and other food uses. This can be stored, covered, for 2 to 3 days in the refrigerator or frozen for future uses.

Any remaining coconut can be shredded or sliced using simple hand tools. The broken shells can also be used in many ways. Some people make planters and other unique containers and tools from these woody resources.

**Makes about 1 cup coconut "cream"**
**and 3 to 4 cups coconut meat**

# CARIBBEAN GARIFUNA COCONUT BREAD

*Many variations on this delicious classic come out of the numerous Garifuna villages, each with its own distinct personalities and specialties. Variations on this one are served in hotels and haciendas in Honduras and Central American Caribbean coastal regions. Village and market specialties set each little region apart within each country, further enhancing the salient points of extended travel through MesoAmerica.*

1 tablespoon dry yeast

1/4 cup warm water

1 teaspoon sugar

3 cups flour

1 cup warm coconut milk

2 tablespoons corn or coconut oil

1 teaspoon salt

1 egg, well beaten

1 tablespoon butter, melted (to brush in middles)

1 egg white, well beaten (to brush on tops)

Sprinkle the yeast over the warm water in a measuring cup or small bowl and stir slightly to dissolve. Sprinkle with the sugar, stir, and let stand for 5 minutes.

Place the flour in a large mixing bowl and make a well in its center. Pour into this well the remaining ingredients except the butter and the egg white. Pour the yeast water over all. Blend thoroughly, then knead on a floured board or surface to make a moderately stiff dough. Shape into a smooth ball and place dough in a greased bowl. Cover and allow to rest for about an hour in a warm place until it doubles in size. Punch down dough and divide in half. Roll each half on the floured board to make two 12x8-inch rectangles. Brush with melted butter.

Combine the following ingredients for the filling, and let them stand at room temperature for an hour before using.
(The bread dough will also rise again during this time.)

1 cup shredded coconut

1/2 cup sugar

1/2 teaspoon allspice

1/2 teaspoon vanilla extract

1/2 teaspoon lime zest

Blend these ingredients well and divide in half. Sprinkle generously over each "buttered" rectangle of dough. Carefully roll up the filled dough lengthwise. Smooth and seal edges.

Cover with a warm, moist towel and allow to rest and rise in a warm place until double in bulk, about 1 hour.

Finally, brush the tops and sides of the dough rolls with the beaten egg white. Bake in a preheated oven on a lightly greased bread sheet for 20 to 30 minutes at 350°. Cool slightly and serve hot, plain or with a coconut butter or guacamole.

**Makes 2 loaves**

# FESTIVAL GUACAMOLE

*This ancient pre-Columbian dish is continually reinventing itself in ever-wider circles of appreciation. it seems in itself a fiesta of flavors and fine tastes. Ripe avocados can be puréed to a fine, thick butter or spread, thinned somewhat, to a delicious dip for raw or sizzling finger foods, or coarsely chopped for a fabulous salsa or salad accompanying grilled meats, other vegetables, or fresh tacos or tortillas. Guacamole can be very spicy or very mild. In its mild version, it is valuable to "put out the fire" of spicy accompaniments. Guacamole does not keep well or long and is best eaten right away—which is never a problem with a great guacamole! Many recipes exist for this classic festival dish, which you will find at Cinco de Mayo and countless other Native gatherings.*

2 medium ripe avocados, scooped out of skin (rind)

1 jalapeño chili pepper, roasted, or 1 Chipotle

1 medium ripe tomato, roasted and blackened

1/4 cup fresh cilantro, chopped

1/4 cup red onion, sautéed and chopped

1 tablespoon fresh lime juice

1/2 teaspoon salt

1/2 teaspoon freshly cracked black pepper

1/4 teaspoon finely ground allspice

Place all ingredients in a food processor or blender and purée briefly until well blended. You may choose the texture you wish to achieve. Serve at room temperature or chilled.

**Makes 1 1/2 to 2 cups**

*Spring Prayers*

*We call upon our Mother Earth,
in thanksgiving for our home,
we ask Her to teach us and show us the way.
We call upon the creatures of the fields,
forests, and seas,
we ask them to teach us the way.
We call upon those who lived on this earth,
our ancestors,
we ask them to teach us the way.
In thanksgiving, we call upon the
Creator to teach us the way.*

—from a Chinook Blessing

# Nipmuck Planting Moon Observance and Potluck

The Chaubunagungamaug Council of the Nipmuck in Webster, Massachusetts, holds their annual Corn Planting Observance on the second Saturday in May on the Chaubunagungamaug Reservation. The Nipmuck People, named for their "freshwater fishing place," were originally many different bands and villages of eastern Algonquians whose homelands were central Massachusetts and regions of the Berkshire Hills.

Chief Wise Owl speaks about the traditional prayers and observances on this day, designed to draw folks together to honor the old ways and bless the future. Everyone gathers around mid-day for a social, bringing a covered dish to share for the potluck later. After all the greetings are exchanged, the Circle opens and the Medicine Man lights the Sacred Fire, gives the blessings, and "feeds" cornmeal to the sacred fire as he prays for good health and good harvests in the whole community. Then everyone is invited to pray and to feed the sacred fire their own offerings of cornmeal or squash seeds. Perhaps 150 to 200 people converge here for the Planting Moon Observance, staying to enjoy the dancing, singing, and generous foods of the Potluck that ends this joyous day.

Favorite traditional foods enjoyed during the Planting Moon gathering are baked beans, succotash, red beans, corn chowders, cornbreads, Johnnycakes, and venison burgers in gravy. These socials bring folks together in many special ways to celebrate the people, the past, and especially the future.

# Nipmuck Venison Burgers and Gravy

*Chief Wise Owl in West Brookfield, Massachusetts, shares his recipe, as some of us, if we are lucky, still have in May a little venison left after the long winter. Ground venison is fabulous in chili, sausage, meat loaf, or just this way.*

**1 pound of lean venison, ground**

**2 small onions, chopped**

**1/2 cup bread crumbs or cornmeal**

**1 egg, well beaten**

**salt and pepper to taste**

**chili pepper sauce to taste (optional)**

**2 tablespoons bear fat, lard, or corn oil**

**1/2 cup flour**

**2 cups of hot water**

In a medium bowl, mix together the venison with half of the chopped onion, the bread crumbs, egg, and seasonings. Shape into 4 patties.

Heat the fat or oil in a medium skillet over medium-high heat. When hot, quickly sear and brown the patties for about 5 minutes on each side. Remove the venison patties and place them in a square baking dish. Now add the rest of the chopped onion to the hot skillet, lower the heat slightly, and sauté for about 5 minutes. Spoon the cooked onion over to the side of the skillet and add the flour, stirring to brown it. Carefully pour in the hot water. Scrape the skillet to deglaze it and stir drippings, water, flour, and onions together until smooth. Season to taste. Pour this hot gravy over the venison burgers in the baking dish. Cover with foil, and bake in a preheated oven at 350° for 30 to 40 minutes.

Serve hot with potatoes and cooked wild mushrooms and greens.

**Serves 4**

# Nipmuck Corn Chowder

*Classic chowders have many unique regional variations, and some are personal "signature" dishes because of their unforgettable flavors and tastes. Chief Wise Owl shares his favorite recipe, which can become a delightful springboard for seasonal variations, additions, and subtractions.*

**1/4 pound of salt pork, cubed in 1/2-inch pieces**

**1 large onion, finely chopped**

**4 cups of hot water**

**3 large potatoes, cubed in 1/2-inch pieces**

**1 can of cream-style corn**

**4 cups milk**

**salt and pepper to taste**

Place the salt pork in a large, deep chowder pot over medium-high heat. Quickly brown, stirring often, for 3 to 5 minutes. Add the onion; sauté for about 5 minutes. Add the hot water, stirring well, and bring to a slow boil. Drop in the potatoes. Bring back to a slow boil, then reduce heat and simmer for 30 to 40 minutes. Stir occasionally and salt lightly to taste.

When the potatoes feel soft when pierced with a fork, drain most of the water from the chowder pot and add the milk and corn. Simmer the chowder for 15 to 20 minutes, stirring occasionally. Balance the seasonings.

Serve with favorite garnishes and crackers or Johnnycakes.

**Serves 4**

Taos Pueblo celebrates their "Blessing of the Fields" in mid-May, along with their traditional foot races and perhaps their Corn Dance. Tesuque Pueblo holds their Blessing near the end of May or early June, along with their Corn or Flag Dance. Time-honored ceremonies protect the vital essence of tribal society, and, as always, the Governor's office at each pueblo will have the exact dates and times of all special events.

The magic and power of seeds are celebrated by all farming people. Tiny envelopes of life, seeds hold our promise of tomorrow's survival and good foods. Throughout Indian Country, horticultural people, and many who are not, are blessing, celebrating, and planting their annual seeds in planned sequences from early to late spring, based upon maturation, ripening needs, and observations of the moon, sun, and weather signs to ensure success. The many grains, and root crops, and fruits of the vines and trees and shrubs that contribute to our varied diets today are given new birth in spring, and we are each a compelling part of this cycle of life.

232

## San Ysidro Feast Day:    May 15

*In many parts of the Southwest, especially through New Mexico, you will encounter small handcarved statues of Saint Isadore, the peaceful husbandman usually depicted tending a small plot and surrounded by birds or an angel. Special blessings of successful gardening are embraced within the annual celebration of this patron saint of farmers and all who cultivate the soil. His festival, commonly called San Ysidro Feast Day, is May 15. Like that of Saint Francis, Saint Isadore's goodness extended to all creatures. This patron saint also possessed the gift of finding fresh water.*

# COCHITI STUFFED BAKED LAKE TROUT

*Pueblo streams and lakes help to feed the fields as well as the people, and this delicious offering is just one example. Rainbow trout are perhaps the most widely known and sought of the many species of trout, and this hardy, fast-growing native species is successfully farmed. Individual fish can reach more than twenty pounds in four years under good conditions.*

**1 (4- to 5-pound) whole trout, cleaned**

**the juice of one lemon**

**1 tablespoon sunflower seed oil**

## STUFFING

**2 tablespoons corn oil**

**1 large onion, chopped**

**3 cloves garlic, finely chopped**

**1 teaspoon each of salt, red chili powder, oregano, zest of lemon**

**1/4 cup epazote or cilantro, chopped**

**pepper to taste**

**1/2 cup fine cornmeal, divided**

**1 cup hot water or vegetable broth (more if needed)**

Prepare cleaned trout by rubbing inside and out first with lemon juice and then oil. Lay the trout in an oiled baking dish and prepare the stuffing.

Heat the corn oil in a large skillet over medium-high heat. Quickly sauté the onion and garlic, stirring thoroughly, for about 3 minutes. Add the chili powder (gently roast or sauté it first to enhance its flavor). Add the other seasonings, including pepper to taste. Sprinkle 1/4 cup cornmeal over all and stir well. Add half of the hot water or broth; stir well. Lower heat and simmer together for about 5 minutes. Add the remaining hot water or broth and more water as needed. Remove from heat and spoon this hot stuffing into the prepared trout, spreading it evenly. Dust stuffed trout with the 1/4 cup cornmeal. Cover trout with foil and seal. Bake in preheated 350° oven for 1 to 1 1/2 hours, until trout flakes apart easily.

Serve the steaming trout by slicing it in generous vertical portions and spooning it onto plates spread with chili-fried cabbage and onions or julienned raw jicama and green peppers. Top with Pumpkin Seed Point Sauce (page 222). Accompany this with Corn Cloud Pillows (page 221) and Pueblo Posole (page 40).

**Serves 4 to 6**

# Upper Mattaponi Spring Festival     Last Saturday

The beginning of the Memorial Day Weekend brings thousands of folks together in King William, Virginia, for the annual Spring Festival on Upper Mattaponi tribal grounds at their historic Sharon Indian School, about 19 miles from Kingston. Ethel Adams, Upper Mattaponi committee woman, says it is usually very hot on this weekend, so the foods served on this special day are fairly cool and light: everyone's favorite frybreads, tacos, trout and other fish, chilled salads, cold sodas, and iced teas. From the start of the festivities at noon, crowds gather for the foods and refreshments, storytelling, arts and crafts, Native American powwow dancing, children's games and rides, and the various educational programs that fill the day.

The state of Virginia recognizes eight tribes from the original Powhatan Confederacy, first encountered by English settlers in 1607. Powhatan, meaning "at the falls" or "People of the Land," according to Shirley Little Dove, was an early Algonquian Indian confederacy uniting about 30 bands and more than 200 native villages throughout the greater Tidewater regions that came to be called Virginia. The Pamunkey Reservation, headed by Chief William "Swift Water" Miles, borders the Pamunkey River and has a fine museum welcoming visitors. The Mattaponi Reservation borders the Mattaponi River in King William County. The Chickahominy are centered in Charles City County. The Eastern Chickahominy are located in New Kent County. The Upper Mattaponi are located in King William County. The Monacan are the westernmost group, centered in Monroe, Virginia. The Nansemond are quite spread out, with many tribal members living on the edge of the Great Dismal Swamp, ancient hunting territory in the Bowers Hill and Deep Creek areas. The United Rappahannock are centered mainly in King and Queen County. Proud traditions continue to interweave these beautiful people together, and many have become leaders in all walks of life.

*B*orn about 1595 in Werowocomoco *village in what is now the Chesapeake Bay region,* Pocahontas *was also known as* Metoaka, *"Little White Cloud," and she lived her short life on the forefront of recorded history in the "New World." In the early sixteenth century, everything in her world was changing forever. She and her powerful father and the Powhatan People helped sustain the early English settlement, as Captain John Smith, writing in 1607, noted that the settlers of Jamestown would have starved if the Indians of that region had not brought them corn, squash, beans, and other foods. It is estimated that Pocahontas was about eleven years old when she interceded to rescue Captain John Smith from having his head smashed at her father's orders.*

*Pocahontas married colonist John Rolfe in 1614 in a celebrated Jamestown wedding, notably the first "mixed marriage" so well documented in the new colonies and apparently the first marriage-of-state, intended to forge close bonds between the powerful Algonquian Confederacy and the fledgling English settlement. Pocahontas sailed to England with her new husband in 1616 and was perhaps one of the first American ambassadors to England presented to the royal court. She died in England of smallpox on March 21, 1617, and was buried in Gravesend Church cemetery, leaving an infant son, Thomas Rolfe, and his grieving father. In 1635 young Thomas Rolfe sailed to Virginia and inherited his father's considerable tobacco business.*

*I am just one of many thousands who can chart direct descent lines back fourteen generations through Thomas Rolfe to Pocahontas and Chief Powhatan. The considerable legacy of this young Powhatan woman is that her name continues to be used and commemorated all across America in both Indian and non-Indian "Pocahontas" Societies that usually stand for civic and philanthropic works, making quiet but important accomplishments that might otherwise not be done. From the Connecticut Mohegan areas to the Pawnee Tribal Center in Pawnee, Oklahoma, I have been surprised, impressed, and touched by their achievements!*

236

# Braised Frog Legs with Wild Mushrooms

*This great southern delicacy now turns up at many northern Indian festivals and powwows, even though these once-plentiful amphibians are certainly declining in numbers. Cricket frogs, chorus frogs, spring peppers, barking tree frogs, squirrel tree frogs, pickerel, leopard, crawfish, mink, wood, and red-legged frogs are all valuable, but the biggest, choicest gourmet treat is the Bull frog, Rana catesbeiana. Frog legs are most similar in taste to chicken; in the Leeward islands of the West Indies, these delicacies are called "mountain chickens." Prepare frog legs in a closely covered skillet so they cannot hop out!*

3 tablespoons hazelnut oil

2 tablespoons sunflower seed oil

8 pair large frog legs, cleaned and skinned

1 cup seasoned fine cornmeal (mix cornmeal with small amounts of your favorite seasonings, such as chili powder, cumin, dried parsley, basil, oregano, marjoram, or thyme, epazote, or a favorite mint)

1 small onion, finely chopped

1/2 cup hot broth or water

1 cup fairy ring mushrooms or morels, chopped

salt and pepper to taste

1/4 cup wild onions greens, finely chopped

1/2 cup hazelnuts, chopped

237

Heat both oils in a large skillet over medium heat. Roll frog legs in the seasoned cornmeal. Place them in the hot skillet with the onion. Cover skillet and sauté, shaking skillet gently but frequently, for 8 to 10 minutes. Remove lid and turn the frog legs. Lower heat slightly and add the hot broth or water and the mushrooms. Stir well to blend thoroughly. Simmer for another 5 minutes. Add seasonings to taste. Spoon frog legs and fairy ring mushrooms onto plates. Garnish with the wild onion greens and chopped hazelnuts. Serve with chilled fresh greens and violets.

**Serves 4**

# Raspberry Fool

*This chilled dessert is inspired by the genius of Bill Neal and his classic cookbook,* Southern Cooking. *The cross-fertilization of many unique cultural gifts has brought us delicious desserts like cobblers, crisps, bombes, grunts, crumbles, frushies, buckles, and trifles, along with fritters, nogs, possets, slips, and fools. Fools were essentially seventeenth-century custards of dairy cream or coconut cream, and a fool, as we know, is simple. As with everything in life, this profits from the use of the best possible ingredients. Seasonal fruits, alone or in combinations, give this a broad range of use.*

*This is just one of many simple, cool desserts likely to please folks at the Upper Mattaponi Spring Festival and other warm-season festivals.*

1/2 cup sugar

1/2 teaspoon allspice

2 cups fresh raspberries or strawberries

1 teaspoon fresh lemon zest

1 cup heavy cream

Place the sugar and allspice in a medium saucepan. Heat until it is just hot to the touch. Save some of the raspberries for the garnish, and add the rest, plus the lemon zest, to the hot sugar. Cover and shake well over the heat for a minute, then remove. Stir to blend thoroughly and dissolve the sugar.

If you wish, rub this cooling mixture through a fine sieve to remove the seeds, but this is not necessary. Refrigerate this fruit purée until cold.

In a medium chilled bowl, beat the cream to form stiff peaks. Stir about 3 tablespoons of the whipped cream into the chilled fruit until light and fluffy, then fold in the remaining cream. Return to the refrigerator, covered, and chill well before serving. Garnish with remaining berries and fresh mint leaves.

**4 servings**

# JUNE

*Brilliant sunlight streaming through breaks in the rain clouds dissipates the cleansing thunderstorm and welcomed rains. Now follows another surge of strong growth in all living things. As the summer solstice approaches, festivals, feast days, socials, and powwows draw people into the celebrations of Native America.*

*This is the Summer Blossoms and Leaves Full Moon of the Micmac Indians in the Northeast and the Grubbing Hoe Moon of the Penobscot. It is the Moon When They Hill The Corn of the Wampanoag and early Agawam and the Summer Moon When Women Weed the Corn of the Narragansetts. Moving westward, this is the Eggs Hatching Moon of the Eastern Cree, the Moon of Buffalo Rutting of the Omaha, and the Moon of Making Fat of the Sioux. In the Pacific Northwest Coast regions this is the Bead Stringing Moon of the Nootka, and the Salmon Moon of the Tsimshian. Natural cycles and urgencies are so different from one region to the next, and yet all share common needs.*

*Across this land from Maine to California are place names that testify to the rich, diverse larder that is our continent: Menahga (Minnesota) is Ojibwa for "blueberry," Sapulpa (Oklahoma) is Creek for "sweet potato," and Topeka is Kansa for "good potato place." The earth's food gifts were indeed of central importance to Native Americans, and they continue to be, turning up at Native festivals and gatherings in many traditional and modern ways.*

The first Saturday in June draws many Choctaw families and friends together in Skullyville, Oklahoma, near their tribal headquarters in Durant, for a historic "awareness" day commemorating the forcible removal of the Choctaw Nation from their eastern homelands in Mississippi and Louisiana. Thousands of Choctaw people died during this relocation in 1830, and their descendants honor their memory by holding this annual reenactment of their walk. Guest speakers, special events, Indian foods, and dancing help mark the day.

The Choctaw are descendants of the ancient Mound Builders. Skilled farmers, plant gatherers, fishermen, hunters, artists, and weavers, the peaceful Choctaw were among the first to be relocated to the west in 1830, suffering great losses along the way. Today the eastern Choctaw have a reservation near the Pearl River, Mississippi, and the western Choctaw hold trust lands centered in Durant, Oklahoma. Some of the finest cane-plaited baskets were woven by the Choctaw, especially their food- and corn-refining baskets and herbal infusion baskets in the shapes of hearts, elbows, and canoes. Exceptional old basket patterns are eye-dazzlers much like later quilt patterns, and some have charming names like deer-tracks, rattlesnake trails, and going-snake. Many of the fine old basket patterns' names have been lost, but the patterns remain as imaginative geometric gifts from earlier artists.

Choctaw foods, especially festival foods are flavorful companions to their fine old baskets—colorful, nurturing, and generous. Vona Loper, at the tribal headquarters in Durant, recalls some of the older, traditional foods like *pashofa* (a hominy-pork stew), *banaha* (boiled cornmeal tied in cornshucks), *tanchi labona* (a thick hominy-pork dish), and crawfish.

242

# CHOCTAW CRAWFISH STEW

*Clear streams and rivers are the natural habitat for the miniature lobster-like freshwater crustaceans known as crawfish, crawdads, or crayfish. They taste best after being caught fresh by hand, but that can be quite a challenge. Moving closer to the Gulf Coast, shrimp are the tasty substitute. The Choctaw have countless crawfish recipes; this one generously feeds a good-size crowd. A forerunner to gumbo, this stew is thickened at the very end with filé powder, which is made from ground young sassafras leaves.*

6 cups hot water or broth

1 pound Jerusalem artichokes (sunchokes), thinly sliced

3 cups whole kernel yellow corn

1 teaspoon each salt and pepper

3 tablespoons sunflower seed oil or hazelnut oil

2 large onions, chopped

4 cloves of garlic, chopped

1 medium red bell pepper, chopped

1 medium green bell pepper, chopped

6 scallions, green and white parts, chopped

2 stalks celery, chopped

1 1/2 pounds fresh crawfish (or shrimp)

2 teaspoons dill seed, slightly crushed

1 teaspoon dried thyme

1 teaspoon dried oregano

1 teaspoon ground allspice

3 teaspoons filé powder, dissolved in 1/2 cup water

1/2 cup fresh parsley, finely minced

1/2 cup scallions, finely chopped

dash of cayenne or hot sauce to taste

Bring the water to a slow boil in a large enamel pot. Add the sunchokes, corn, and some of the salt and pepper. Simmer, stirring occasionally, for about 15 minutes.

Heat the oil in a large sauté pan over medium heat and sauté the onions and garlic, stirring well, for about 2 minutes. Add the chopped peppers, scallions, and celery. Stir well and sauté for 4 to 5 more minutes, adding a spoonful or two of the hot broth from the stew pot, if needed, to keep the vegetables from sticking. Remove cooked vegetables from the heat and add to the stew pot.

Return the stew to a boil. Add the crawfish.

Stir well. Lower heat slightly and simmer, stirring occasionally, for 5 to 8 more minutes, or until done to your liking. Do not overcook. Remove from the heat, and add the dill, thyme, oregano, and allspice. Blend well, and season with remaining salt and pepper to taste. Balance the flavors. Add the filé powder, stirring until well blended. Serve immediately, and top each bowl with the parsley and scallion garnishes. A dash of cayenne or hot sauce may also be added to individual servings.
*Note:* Filé is a thickening agent, but it will become "ropy" if reheated, so be sure to add this at the very end!

**Serves 12 to 15**

*S*assafras, Sassafras albidum, *is a native eastern deciduous tree, and all plant parts are used by Native Peoples in various culinary and medicinal ways. The roots and root bark contain flavoring agents similar to anise, fennel, and cloves, and the young green leaves contain a mucilage and flavoring desirable for thickening stews and gumbos. Like arrowroot, cornstarch, and flour, it is selectively used in short-term thickening of particular dishes. Sassafras flavorings were originally used in root beer and in the chicle gum patented by Thomas Adams in 1871. Now the* safrole *in sassafras is considered to be toxic when released under high-heat methods of cooking and manufacturing. It is now advised that sassafras not be boiled, and in most food*

*and beverage recipes it is not. Yet the toxic cautionary listing must be applied. Very small amounts of* safrole *also occur in basil, black pepper, mace, and nutmeg.*

*Sassafras plant parts were used in various ways by Native Peoples for food, beverage, medicinal, and ceremonial needs. Young sprouts of green leaves were steeped to make eyewash, a reliable "spring tonic," and a flavoring to enhance medicinal formulas. Green leaves were also rubbed on the skin for insecticidal values and roasted or dried and crumbled into foods as a lemony, aromatic seasoning. We can buy this seasoning now as filé powder, the essence of gumbos and Creole cooking.*

# CORPUS CHRISTI FIESTA AT PALA MISSION    EARLY JUNE

The first Sunday in June is devoted to an annual pageant and procession celebrating the Corpus Christi Fiesta at Pala Mission in Pala, California. Serving as a fund-raiser to benefit the mission school, the festival features games, music and dancing, and the ubiquitous Indian food booths that make this occasion truly memorable. The Pala Band of Mission Indians includes the Luiseno, Cupa, and Ipai Indians, and almost 600 members live on the 11,892 acres set aside for them in 1875 in the lovely valley filled with groves, streams, and tourmaline mines.

California has the largest, most diverse Indian population in the United States, with a prehistoric Native presence that goes back at least 15,000 years. Many different tribes, speaking more than sixty-five different languages, were encountered first by the Spanish and then later settlers during a long, turbulent recorded history. Today about 600,000 acres of Indian lands are set aside for more than 300,000 indigenous tribal people, and California is a patchwork of numerous reservations and tiny rancherias.

245

The Los Angeles region is home to more than 20,000 Native Americans, a greater pan-Indian population than New York City or Chicago. Los Angeles boasts Indian Markets, festivals, pow-wows, art demonstrations, dance, and storytelling events scheduled almost every weekend. Most events are further graced by Indian foods and food booths serving the broad, colorful range of contemporary "fast foods" and California foods. Local berries and fruits dominate many food preparations and drinks, pit beef barbecues are highlights at some festivals, and the broad influences of Spanish/Mexican foods are woven generously into most celebrations.

## Roundhouses

*Through* central and northern California the distinctive Native roundhouses appear, most being semisubterranean structures with their entrance porticos facing east. Roundhouses are similar to Hopi kivas in many respects; both are sacred centers of native ceremonial dances and special gatherings, and neither is usually open to the public. Outside some roundhouses are sweatlodges used for purification and prayers, as well as ancient mortars and grinding rocks for processing acorns, the essential staple for Native Peoples in these regions for countless centuries.

Miwok and Shoshone descendants gather to use their roundhouse and sweatlodge in California's Yosemite National Park in June and at other important times during their ceremonial year. Sometimes their dances go on all night in the roundhouse, as dancers seek to invoke the spirits to bring good health and safety to their people and lands.

# CALIFORNIA PATHFINDER BREAD

*Acorns were to the California tribes what corn was to the Southern tribes. More than sixty species of oaks are distinctive native trees, and those indigenous to California ecosystems provided abundant foods for people and animals. Tanoak,* Lithocarpus densiflorus, *California white oak,* Quercus lobata, *and California black oak,* Quercus kelloggii, *produce prodigious amounts of oil- and carbohydrate-rich acorns during good years, and these became staples in the Native diets.*

*California Indians wove incredibly fine food processing baskets and bags, especially for their nutritious acorns, which had to be processed through several changes of water to leach out the constipating tannins. Pouring hot water over them repeatedly or submerging cracked, shelled acorns in bags in clear-running streams for half a day was vital for digestibility. All oaks can be divided into two main families: The black oaks have the more bitter acorns than white oaks, and these acorns require more water baths.*

*All acorns are delicious meat substitutes, tasty for acorn meat loafs, acornburgers, acorn sausages, and acorn chilies.*

*Now we principally find acorn flour and starch in the Korean markets in our major cities. This modern bread is inspired from earlier California Indian acorn breads.*

1 cup boiling water

1/4 cup maple syrup

1 tablespoon Anaheim chili pepper, roasted and finely chopped

1 package dry yeast

1/2 teaspoon salt

3 tablespoons hazelnut or sunflower seed oil

1 1/2 cups all-purpose flour

1/2 cup acorn meal flour or ground hazelnuts

1/2 cup buckwheat flour

1/2 cup fine yellow cornmeal

Pour the boiling water over the maple syrup and the chili pepper in a medium bread bowl. Stir well. Cool to about 100°. Sprinkle the yeast over this warm water and stir in gently. Allow to rest for about 5 minutes, then sprinkle the salt over the surface. Add the oil and stir well. Carefully add the flours and cornmeal one at a time, stirring well with a wooden spoon until the dough begins to get thick. Turn the dough out onto a floured bread board. Knead for 5 to 10 minutes until no longer sticky, adding more flour if necessary until it reaches a satiny texture.

Place dough in a lightly oiled bread bowl and turn it over once to make sure that the whole surface of the dough is just glazed with oil. Cover with a clean towel. Let rest and rise in a warm place for 1 to 1 1/2 hours until nearly double in size.

Punch dough down and knead it briefly on clean, lightly floured dough board. Divide in half and shape into 2 oblong loaves. Place each in warm, clean, well-oiled tin cans (1-pound coffee cans are perfect) or 8-inch clay flowerpots. Cover again and allow to rest in a warm spot for another hour, to rise and double in volume again.

Preheat oven to 350°. Bake the 2 loaves (uncovered) for about 45 minutes until the bread sounds hollow when lightly tapped on top. Breads should be a deep brown. Remove from the oven and place on racks to cool for 10 minutes. Loosen and remove after 10 minutes. Cool further on bread racks. The bread will cut best when cool, but it is so good you may want to serve it warm with hazelnut butter and fresh berry jams.

**Makes 2 loaves**

# Papaya Coconut Frost

*Fruit drinks, hot or cold, increasingly replace soda pop and conventional coffee at Native festivals for a variety of healthful reasons, as well as for flavorful and thirst-quenching virtues. Papaya, Carica papaya and Carica candicans, is a fabulous native fruit with ancient uses among the Yucatan Maya and early Peruvian Incas. Papaya has tenderizing enzymes, and like the wild native pineapples, valuable digestive enzymes, making these particular fruits evermore desirable in the common diet. This is just one of many delicious drinks likely to be encountered at the Corpus Christi Fiesta and other Native American festivals.*

**1 cup chilled papaya juice, canned or fresh**

**2 tablespoons coconut milk or coconut cream**

**1 teaspoon fresh lime juice**

**1/2 teaspoon fresh lime zest**

**1/2 teaspoon finely ground allspice**

**1/2 cup cracked ice**

**1/2 fresh papaya, trimmed and cut in long, thin wedges**

**16 ounces crushed ice**

**1 cup chilled sparkling springwater**

**4 large fresh strawberries**

**honey or sugar (optional )**

Place the papaya juice, coconut milk, lime juice and zest, and allspice in a blender jar with 1/2 cup cracked ice. Purée until well blended and frothy, about 30 seconds.

Place a long spear or wedge of fresh papaya in each of four 8-ounce glasses. Add 4 ounces of crushed ice to each glass. Pour the frothy papaya frost equally into each glass to about two-thirds full. Top with the sparkling springwater. Half-cut the tip of each fresh strawberry and perch 1 on the rim of each glass. Serve immediately, with straws.
**Serves 4**

# Otsiningo Powwow and Indian Craft Fair

EARLY JUNE

Numerous powwows fill the early June calendar, as everyone looks forward to busy, full seasons on the summer "powwow highway." The first weekend in June many folks head for the Otsiningo Powwow and Indian Craft Fair at the Waterman Conservation Center in Apalachin, New York. Native American artists, craftspeople, and food vendors throughout the Northeast attract thousands of buyers, appreciative visitors from the public, and many Native Americans who gather for intensive days of networking, visiting, trading, and eating. Three meals a day and continual snacks and "pick-me-ups" keep seasoned food vendors stepping.

Predawn visits over the first, freshmade coffee of the day draw "early birds" together for chatter before the crowds of the day begin arriving. Various native cooks prepare the legendary powwow breakfasts, showing off their famous particular specialties or re-creating the traditional range of powwow breakfast favorites. Fried corn and potatoes, home fries with chilies, refried beans, quesadillos filled with scrambled pepper-eggs and cheese, huevos rancheros, sausage and eggs, blue corn and blueberry flapjacks, hush puppies, venison sausage, buffalo sausage, andouille and chorizo sausages, and alligator sausage are just some of the breakfast delights that may be encountered at a June powwow like Otsiningo.

249

## Breakfast Hush Puppies

*Light cornmeal fritters or quick-fried "clouds" are easy accompaniments to many dishes or great on their own. Whether using blue corn or white, red or yellow cornmeal, with or without a bit of seasonal fresh fruit stirred into the batter, the hottest, crispest hush puppies should not be overcooked or overbrowned, as they will become bitter. When serving many hundreds of hungry breakfast folks, you can develop quite a deft flair for turning these out quickly.*

JUNE

corn or peanut oil for deep frying

1 1/2 cups fine blue or yellow cornmeal

1/2 cup all-purpose flour

2 teaspoons baking powder

1 teaspoon baking soda

1 teaspoon salt

1/4 teaspoon freshly ground black pepper

dash of cayenne pepper

2 eggs, well beaten

1 cup buttermilk

1 tablespoon honey

2 tablespoons corn oil or rendered bacon fat

1/2 cup green onions, finely chopped

Preheat 2 to 3 inches of oil to about 365° in a deep cast-iron skillet over medium-high heat.

Sift together all of the dry ingredients, making a well in the center. Add the beaten eggs, buttermilk, honey, corn oil, and green onion. Beat well together. Drop batter by rounded tablespoonfuls, 3 or 4 at a time, into the hot oil. The hush puppies will immediately sink to the bottom, but as they boil in the hot oil they rise to the top and roll over. Lift out with tongs or a slotted spoon after 3 to 5 minutes. The hush puppies will be golden. Drain on absorbent paper. These can be wrapped in brown paper and kept in a warmer for a few minutes, but they are best served as soon as you make them.

Hush puppies are great with powdered sugar, honey, or hot, spicy pepper jelly. Serve them beside eggs, refried beans, and home-fried potatoes. In midsummer these same creations can be enlivened with wild blueberries, strawberries, huckleberries, or Juneberries added to the batter. Serve these "sweetberry hush puppies" with powdered sugar and Juneberry syrup.

**Makes 2 to 3 dozen hush puppies**

## Buttermilk

*B*uttermilk was originally the somewhat soured residue from the butter churn, and I remember getting to help my grandmother make this on the farm in Tennessee. Our modern buttermilk is made from pasteurized skim milk to which a culture has been added to produce a more flavorful, heavier texture while also boosting the amount of lactic acid. Buttermilk is more readily digested than regular or skim milk and contributes to finer textures in baked breads or cooked sauces. Similar to yogurt in many ways, buttermilk is easy to make, but as you must do in preparing yogurt or sour dough, always save enough starter to get your next batch going.

**1 quart skim milk, at 70° to 80°**

**1/2 cup cultured buttermilk, at 70°**

**pinch of salt**

Combine ingredients in a glass or ceramic pitcher. Stir well and cover. Allow to stand in a warm place at about 70° until clabbered. Stir until smooth. Refrigerate.

# HUEVOS RANCHEROS

*This spicy Southwest and South-of-the-Border dish combines flavorful favorites in a beautiful presentation. Accompany this with plenty of fresh cilantro and epazote, and the old standard egg breakfast becomes a fine banquet of taste sensations as highly esteemed in the Northeast as in the Southwest. Side dishes of refried beans and venison sausage make this an unsurpassable breakfast hit.*

**4 tablespoons lard or corn oil, divided**

**1 large onion, chopped**

**2 green bell peppers, roasted and chopped**

**1 jalapeño pepper, roasted and chopped**

3 garlic cloves, finely chopped

2 (30-ounce) cans of plum tomatoes, chopped

1 teaspoon honey

1/2 teaspoon each salt, pepper, oregano, thyme, cayenne

6 large eggs

6 blue corn tortillas

2 tablespoons fresh cilantro, chopped

Heat 2 tablespoons of the lard or oil in a large pot over high heat. Quickly sauté the onion, peppers, and garlic, stirring briskly for about 3 minutes. Lower heat. Carefully add the tomatoes, honey, and seasonings one at a time, stirring in well. Lower heat again and simmer, stirring occasionally, for about 25 minutes.

Stir sauce well and make 6 little wells in its surface with the bowl of the spoon. Carefully break an egg into each well. Dust each egg lightly with an extra pinch of cayenne and salt. Cover the pot and simmer for 2 to 3 minutes.

While the eggs simmer, heat the other 2 tablespoons of lard or oil in a small skillet over medium-high heat. Quickly fry the tortillas for 20 to 30 seconds on each side. Drain them on absorbent paper towels, then arrange them on warm plates. Carefully spoon a cooked egg and sauce onto the center of each tortilla. Garnish with cilantro.

**Makes 6 regular-sized servings or 3 huge ones**

Barrie, Ontario, is a scenic, thriving city on Kempenfelt Bay, part of the westernmost finger of Lake Simcoe, north of Toronto. Originally Huron Indian territory, Huronia was first visited by European explorers in the fifteenth century, and lively fur trading ensued for several hundred years with countless conflicts. The Hudson Bay Company erected a storehouse here in 1812, and settlement pressures quickened. Now Barrie is a large metropolitan city.

The Barrie Native Friendship Centre hosts its big annual powwow and art exhibit on the second weekend in June, drawing thousands of folks together for further networking. The centre was founded in 1987, inspired by another native friendship centre 40 miles north of Midland, Ontario. Barrie serves its own growing native population, and six surrounding reserves of Mohawk, Cree, and Ojibwa Indians.  Darleen Baldwin, Development Coordinator and one of the founders of this friendship centre, has helped to implement an Ojibwa language retention program, a Native Way Training curriculum, and a Native Culinary Consortium of traditional foods in conjunction with Georgian College. Her mother, Ernestine Baldwin, is one of the teaching Elders in several of these programs, as well as one of the leaders in the Native Healing Lodge.

253

Favorite regional foods served at the Barrie Powwow include Hominy Corn Soup, Fried Salt Pork and Kidney Beans, Buffalo Burgers, Indian Tacos, fish and venison dishes,  raspberry-cranberry drinks, and much, much more.

## BUFFALO BURGERS WITH WILD MUSHROOMS AND ONIONS

*Commonly called buffalo,* Bison bison, *the American bison is the largest terrestrial animal in North America and by far the best suited for our native rangelands and plains. An estimated 75 million bison roamed the broad prairies before the seventeenth century, yet through much of the nineteenth century white hunters exterminated the great herds, reducing their numbers from 50 million to 1,500 before laws were passed in Canada and the United States in the 1890s to save the precious few remaining.*

*Captive breeding programs have brought the buffalo back to more than 100,000 today, and a number of ranches, including one at the Cheyenne River Sioux Reservation in Eagle Butte, South Dakota, have developed good businesses in selling buffalo meat. It is a remarkable point of reflection that the buffalo were hunted to the brink of extinction in part to subdue the Native American tribes dependent upon these majestic free-ranging bison herds. Now, more than a century later, Native cooks are serving buffalo gourmet meats to ever-growing, wildly enthusiastic crowds hungry for more. Many people who enjoy it at powwows say they prefer it to beef.*

**3 tablespoons sunflower seed or corn oil**

**2 large onions, sliced in generous rings**

**1 large green bell pepper, sliced in rings**

**2 cups sliced bolete caps or favorite mushrooms**

**1 1/2 pounds buffalo meat, ground**

**chili pepper sauce (optional)**

**salt and pepper (optional)**

**hot water or broth**

Heat the oil in a large skillet over high heat. Quickly sauté the onions and pepper rings, then spoon to one side and add the musrooms, stirring well. Lower heat slightly. Shape the ground buffalo meat into four generous patties and make a nest among the mushrooms so each patty can be slipped in and sautéed quickly for about 5 to 6 minutes on each side. Add chili pepper sauce and salt and pepper, if desired, to suit your taste. Cook to preferred degree of doneness. Lift out the finished buffalo burgers and place each one on a bun or plate. Continue to cook the mushroom, onions, and pepper accompaniment, if necessary. Add a little hot water or broth to the skillet and scrape up the pan juices. Spoon this over the buffalo burgers or serve alongside them. Treat the buffalo meat like fine steak. It is great rare.

**Serves 4**

# RED EARTH FESTIVAL

Flying in to the Will Rogers International Airport or driving in from all over the country, we converge in Oklahoma City in late spring just before the summer solstice at Red Earth for one of the world's largest Native American cultural festivals. Hundreds of dancers don their stunning regalia for the annual parade in the center of Oklahoma City to the enormous Myriad Plaza Convention Center and Exhibit Halls. More than 2,000 American Indian competition dancers, drum groups, tribal leaders, Indian Princesses, and hundreds of top artists, jewelers, musicians, and film and video people gather here for three days, from early morning to midnight.

Energizing drumbeats and ever-changing rhythms call these special dancers together in gorgeous, colorful choreographies of spirited, precise movements. Ancient traditions are danced and celebrated here, fueled with renewed awe and appreciation.

The Red Earth Indian Center is a new museum and cultural organization dedicated to increasing appreciation of American Indian cultures. Located in the 10-acre Kirkpatrick Center Museum complex in Oklahoma City, the Red Earth Indian Center welcomes visitors throughout the year and especially during this big weekend.

Red Earth Festival foods reflect the eclectic range of modern pan-Indian powwow "fast foods" like Navajo tacos and frybread, and medleys of favorite tribal specialties surround these. Boiled, buttered corn-on-the-cob, little meat pies, grape dumplings, pumpkin frybread, and seasoned popcorn, raisin, and seed mixes are popular at most intertribal socials, powwows, and celebrations.

Older traditional tribal foods are less likely to catch the mainstream festival circuit, as many of them take considerable time to prepare and fewer folks remember how to make them for casual consumption. Regional, tribal, and general public tastes do not take readily to the tastes, fragrances, and appearances of some of the older traditional foods. Gritted breads, sweet potato breads, bean breads, and Indian shuck breads are somewhat more common. Peach bread, huckleberry dumplings, and Indian pudding are enduring favorites you see at many southern socials.

# Spicy Cornmeal-Fried Catfish

*Connoisseurs like my cousin Audene will argue whether pond or channel cats taste best, but the farmed catfish enrich most festival and powwow cuisines and it is hard to tell the difference. Smothered in crisp, spicy cornmeal crust, these delicious white-meat fillets are perfect served whole for socials and home dinners or cut into bite-sized nuggets for powwows and festivals. A savory range of sauces can be chosen to accompany this dish—try smoky chili barbecue sauce, the Red Earth Chili Salsa (page 257), or tartar sauce.*

4 catfish fillets, about 6 ounces each and 1/2-inch thick

peanut or corn oil sufficient for frying

1 large egg, well beaten

1/2 cup buttermilk

1/2 cup fine yellow cornmeal

1/4 cup all-purpose flour

1/2 teaspoon salt

1/4 teaspoon each of cayenne, allspice, chili powder

1 teaspoon freshly cracked black pepper

1/4 teaspoon white pepper

Red Earth Chili Salsa

fresh scallions, chopped

lemon wedges

Cut catfish fillets into 1/2- to 1-inch cubes or chunks.

Heat oil (about 1 1/2 inches deep) in a large iron skillet or fryer over medium heat (about 350°). When a fresh bread cube browns in about 20 seconds, the oil is ready.

Mix the beaten egg with the buttermilk in a shallow bowl; set aside. Mix the cornmeal, flour, and seasonings in another shallow bowl. Dip the catfish chunks in the buttermilk-egg mixture. Roll them in the spicy cornmeal mixture. Ease them carefully into the hot oil. Fry briefly, turning them often, for 4 to 5 minutes or until golden and crusty. Do not overcook. Lift catfish chunks out with long-handled tongs or slotted spoon. Drain on absorbent paper towels or brown paper. Serve hot with a selection of favorite sauces such as the Red Earth Chili Salsa (below). Garnish with the fresh scallions and lemon wedges.

**Serves 4**

# Red Earth Chili Salsa

*Inspired by the annual Red Earth Festival in Oklahoma City, this savory hot chili sauce is pure invention and may be slightly varied to suit the more delicate palates.*

**3 large ripe tomatoes, roasted until blistered and soft**

**3 jalapeño chilies, roasted until blistered and blackened**

**1 large Anaheim pepper, roasted and chopped**

**3 cloves garlic, pan-roasted until brown**

**1 medium red onion, chopped and roasted**

**1/2 teaspoon Mexican oregano, toasted**

**1/2 teaspoon red chili powder, toasted**

**1/4 teaspoon cumin seeds, toasted and ground**

**1/4 cup apple cider vinegar**

**1/4 cup balsamic vinegar**

**salt to taste**

Combine all ingredients in a food processor bowl or blender and purée. Balance flavors to suit your taste. This is best served at room temperature. It can be stored up to 3 to 4 days, but it rarely ever lasts that long!

Add 1/2 cup water to make this mixture into a fine sauce. Simmer about 15 minutes over medium-low heat.

**Makes about 3 cups**

# CREEK NATION FESTIVAL AND RODEO

The early Creek were village farmers, hunters, and artists, probably descendants of the Temple Mound Builders of the prehistoric Southeast. The Alibamu, Coushatta, Muskogee, and other Creek bands made up the original Creek Confederacy, whose villages were usually located along creeks and rivers. Forced removal from their homelands in 1836, following the Creek Wars of 1813–1814, caused many to die. Today their tribal centers are in Alabama, along with scattered groups of Creek people living throughout the Southeast. Three main groups also live in Oklahoma—the Creek Nation, the Kailegee Creeks, and the Thlopthlocco Creeks.

The Creek, or Muskogee, Nation, in north-central Oklahoma is nonreservation, yet has jurisdiction of all or part of eight counties, with its capital in Okmulgee. Sixteen traditional ceremonial grounds are located throughout the Creek Nation, and are sometimes used for ceremonial stomp dances that celebrate life, give thanks to the Creator, and serve as important events for cleansing, purification, and renewal. Held at selected times in the summer, Stomp Dances usually begin late Friday night and end early Saturday morning, and are repeated again on Saturday night.

The third weekend in June, the three-day Creek Nation Festival and Rodeo are held at the Creek Nation Complex. Stomp dances and other dances, a parade, and a rodeo are major events, along with a Little Olympics competition, softball tournaments, volleyball, horseshoe pitching, golf and tennis tournaments, and fine arts and crafts exhibits. Food concessions help sweeten and fuel these activities with favorite summer foods.

Seasonal Creek Indian foods vary considerably from one region to another and from one family to another. Individual cooks create unique variations and styles of their own, which are then shared and changed. Drawing upon the help and inspirations of Creek friends and family (and a few precious written accounts, like *Corn Recipes From The Indians,* by Cherokee Publications), one can illuminate a small selection of special Creek foods.

Abuskee is a Creek roasting ears corn drink, similar to posole in many ways. Cold Corn Flour Drink (soffkee) is another of the many Creek corn drinks made with roasting ears and a wood-ash lye base to soften, split, and help remove the heavy, often indigestible outer corn kernel skin. *Ah-gee-chum-buh-gee* is a mixture of boiled cornmeal, dried fruits, and brown sugar, wrapped and tied in cornhusk packets to make little dumpling-like tamales. As with other Native foods, traditional Creek dishes embrace the seasons with delicious, earthy warmth.

# SIMI CHUMBO

*This delicious custard-like dessert is inspired by the recollections of noted Creek artist Acee Blue Eagle, among others. This recipe is a great vehicle for nutritious hickory nuts or pecans. Shagbark hickory,* Carya ovata, *by the way, has the sweetest nuts.*

**1 pint sweet, whole milk**

**4 heaping tablespoons fine yellow cornmeal**

**2 tablespoons honey or maple syrup**

**1 cup hickory nuts, finely chopped**

**1/2 cup pecans, coarsely chopped**

**1/4 teaspoon each of salt and allspice**

**2 tablespoons sweet butter or walnut oil**

**3 large eggs, well beaten**

Place the milk in a medium saucepan over medium heat and bring almost to a boil. Sprinkle the cornmeal over the top; stir it in well. Add the honey, nut meats, seasonings, and butter or oil. Simmer, stirring, until it thickens, about 15 minutes.

Remove from the heat and cool. Whisk in the well-beaten eggs. Pour this mixture into a 10x10x3-inch buttered baking dish. Bake in a preheated oven at 350° for 30 to 40 minutes.

Cool slightly. Cut into squares or bars and serve. This is good with pecan or maple-nut ice creams or fresh whipped cream and seasonal berries like Juneberries and strawberries.

**Serves 4 to 6**

### *Native Nuts*

*Diverse wild nuts were eagerly sought by Native Peoples as part of their time-honored seasonal harvests. Although most nuts were eaten and enjoyed raw during autumn and winter harvests, flavors were improved through drying, roasting, cooking, and processing in various ways. Nut butters, milks, and oils were pounded, ground, and rendered to get the rich nut meats; many were pounded into flour for* gruel, breads, and cereals, providing greater digestibility for the young and elderly. The carbohydrate-rich nuts of the American beech, Fagus grandifolia, American chestnut, Castanea dentata, Allegheny Chinkapin, Castanea pumila, Black Walnut, Juglans nigra, *and* Butternut, Juglans cinerea, *are just some of the many nuts seasonally harvested from nature's wealth and bounty.*

# Yukon International Storytelling Festival

SUMMER SOLSTICE

Pushing north toward the "roof of the world" beyond the Arctic Circle, one can drive on the famous Dempster Highway over mountains and across sprawling plains and rolling tundra to Aklavik, the oldest community in the MacKenzie Delta. Yukon's First Nations draw on more than 10,000 years of history in these regions.

Today People of three cultures live in timeless harmony across these stunning environments. The Gwich'in of the boreal forest and the Inuvialuit of the open tundra, are joined by other Canadians and many visitors at the edge of the treeline, where beluga whales frequent the waters of the MacKenzie estuary near Herschel Island, site of one of the last whaling stations until the early 1900s and for more than 1,000 years a resting point for the Thule culture, ancestors of the modern Inuvialuit People.

Each June near the summer solstice, the First Nations Peoples gather to celebrate their culture and traditions over three days of festivities filled with social and cultural events and entertainment and foods. The storytelling festival usually follows the People Gathering, as it draws together storytellers, drummers, and dancers from all over the circumpolar world.

Travelers come to Fort McPherson and Arctic Red River historic Gwich'in communities and traditional camps to see their drum dance, distinctive arts and craftworks, and unique clothing styles. Here too, one can savor the Native heritage by listening to the Elders' stories, legends, and folklore. The Elders still hike up Old Crow Mountain to speak with the spirits. Life breathes at a different pace in these primal regions.

The special gatherings and celebrations of the Yukon villages are savory, multisensory experiences. Many are drawn to the delectable regional foods of grayling, Alaska King Crab, Yukon and Taku River Salmon, Arctic Char, caribou, and musk ox. Young fireweed shoots, with fresh raspberries, mossberries, dewberries, wild strawberries, and bearberries are assembled into delicious salads, along with the young leaves of mountain avens and arctic willow. Tombstone

Mountain teas are blends of raspberry leaves, Labrador tea leaves and blossoms, and Arctic willow shoots. Subsistence hunting, fishing, and trapping continue to sustain Yukon's First Nations Peoples through their profound understanding of this land and how to live on it.

The Yukon International Storytelling Festival is always steeped in abundant inspiration and descriptive excellence, and the foods there feed the imagination. And, like their Yukon Native Arts Festival and Native Folklore and Yukon Indian Days, it is hosted by the Yukon First Nations Peoples with warmth and hospitality.

ENDURING HARVESTS

# WILLOW-GRILLED ARCTIC CHAR
# WITH WILD MUSHROOMS

*Silvery with blue-green backs flecked with pink specks when it is at sea, the migratory Arctic char,*
Salvelinus alpinus, *undergoes a glorious transformation when it enters northern rivers to spawn.*
*Then its colors flush and deepen to bright orange-reddish hues. Yukon People treat this succulent,*
*meaty fish like salmon. It is excellent grilled with a light vinegar and oil dressing over dry alder*
*and willow stems brushed with spicy hazelnut oil.*

**2 to 3 cups of alder and willow stems and bark, dampened**

**1/2 cup hazelnut or walnut oil**

**1/4 cup apple cider vinegar**

**1 tablespoon diced onion**

**dash of salt and pepper to taste**

**1 (5-pound) Arctic char fillet**

**6 small white onions**

**12 medium young mushroom caps**

Gather fresh willow or alder withes (stems) to skewer small onions and mushroom caps. Prepare the campfire or grill by building a fine bed of coals. Spread the alder and willow pieces over the prepared coals and place the grill about 6 inches above the coals. Lightly oil the grill with a small amount of hazelnut or walnut oil. Combine in a small saucepan the 1/2 cup of oil, the vinegar, the onion, and salt and pepper. Warm over medium heat at the edge of the grill. Place the Arctic char fillet in the center of the grill, skin side down, and brush top well with the warm grill sauce. Quickly skewer alternately the onions and mushroom caps on the fresh willow stems. Place these beside the char fillet. Brush well with the same sauce.

Grill the fillet for 5 to 10 minutes on each side, turning once and brushing often with the sauce. Check and turn the vegetables more often to grill evenly. Grill lightly; do not overcook. Serve on a bed of steaming wild rice and hazelnuts.

**Serves 6**

# YUKON MORNING GLORY STORY MUFFINS

*These large, generous, moist and crunchy muffins are an inspiration from the Yukon Storytelling Festival. They are in themselves a festival of delicious ingredients, resembling small individual cakes when baked. Create your own stories around the ingredients you assemble. Each muffin is a powerhouse of goodness and almost a meal in itself. Great for breakfast or along with any meal, they make especially nice companions for the Arctic char and other game preparations.*

3 eggs, well beaten

2 tablespoons sunflower seed oil

1 cup buttermilk

1 cup whole wheat flour

1/2 cup fine cornmeal

1/2 cup rolled oats

2 tablespoons bran

1/4 cup warm honey

1 cup grated carrots (about 2 medium carrots, packed)

1/2 cup currants or raisins

1 tablespoon chopped ginger root

1/2 cup pecans, black walnuts, or hazelnuts, chopped

1 tablespoon orange zest

1 teaspoon baking soda

1 teaspoon each of salt, allspice, baking powder, vanilla

allspice-granulated sugar mixture (equal parts of each)

Preheat oven to 375°. Line large-cup muffin tin with muffin papers. Set aside while you lightly blend the batter.

In a medium bowl, whisk together the eggs, oil, and buttermilk. Carefully add the remaining ingredients except  allspice-sugar topping.

Stir until just combined; do not overwork the batter. Divide the batter evenly among the 12 lined muffin cups, filling each about two-thirds full. Sprinkle the tops lightly with the allspice-sugar mixture. Bake for about 20 minutes until the tops are golden. Remove to wire rack and cool completely. Turn muffins out and serve, or wrap each muffin individually to save for trail snacks or to enjoy the next day with hot tea or strong coffee at sunrise.

**Makes 1 dozen muffins**

## *J u n e b e r r i e s*

*R*ipening berries of the native Amelanchier *shrubs and trees, widely distributed across North America, were a major food of numerous tribes beginning in June in southern regions and later in the north. These enduring members of the rose family were harbingers of spring and of the shad fish runs earlier in the year. Now in June, they bear some of the first delicious fruits of summer. More than twenty colloquial names and countless Indian names stress the vital importance of this slim, beautiful perennial called* hazshutsh *for its red berries by the* Winnebago *and* zhon-huda *for its gray bark by the Omaha and Ponca. All plant parts were valuable; some had medicinal importance and some had ritual significance. This continues to be true.*

*Blackfoot feasts often included a favorite dessert soup made of Juneberries and buffalo fat and blood. They also made a boiled sausage containing equal amounts of these berries and animal fat. Pemmicans and other Native foods also made use of this generous June gift.*

The Connecticut River Powwow Society, established in 1985 "to maintain and preserve the spiritual, cultural, educational and artistic traditions of Native Americans," hosts their annual Strawberry Moon Powwow in late June in Somers, Connecticut. This is a special time of healing and friendship and celebrating spring and is popularly attended by over 10,000 visitors. The circle of dancing, drumming, and singing is always blessed with the sacred fire and prayers, and various Native vendors fill the greater circle outside the dance ground. Strawberry Moon Tea (see page 274), made with frozen and fresh strawberries and sassafras and served chilled or hot, is their most popular drink, followed by lemonade, sumacade, the mints, and sassafras and black birch teas. The food is usually provided by the Society's own "Cook Shack," started almost ten years ago by friends and volunteers who felt a great need to feed and celebrate the 300 participants and volunteers who were instrumental in making these powwows happen each time. Those early "Whatchamacallit" Stews were so good, people kept asking for more.

Today's menus are deliciously filled with buffalo chili, buffalo stew, buffalo ribs and burgers, corn fritters, Three Sisters Rice made with a black Canadian rice, and succotash made with whole kernel corn, kidney and butter beans, salmon cakes, Strawberry Pan Cake (see page 136), and layered berry puddings. Generosity and good hearts have worked to create great foods nurturing ever-growing crowds.

# Woodland Teas: Black Birch, Sassafras, and Sumac

*These wild woodland beverages are easily made and are enjoyed hot or chilled, served over ice in tall cups. Each ingredient can be taken from the wild or purchased and is good when used fresh or dried. All three beverages are offered at Strawberry Moon gatherings and other Eastern powwows. (Note: Sumac tea is commonly referred to as sumacade.)*

**black birch bark or twigs**

**sassafras bark, root bark, or twigs**

**ripe sumac red berries**

For 1 cup of tea, use 1 teaspoon dried or 1 teaspoon fresh of any *one* of the above ingredients. For a pot of tea, use 1 cup dried or 2 cups fresh of any one of the above materials.

Select *one* of the tea ingredients (do not use all three for the same cup or pot of tea) and place appropriate amount in a clean teacup or 1-quart pot. Bring fresh water to a boil. Pour the hot water over the tea ingredient, then cover and steep for 5 to 10 minutes to infuse the volatile oils. Uncover, strain, and drink, or cool the tea and serve chilled. Tea may be sweetened with raw honey or pure maple syrup, but each of these three classic teas is tasty, aromatic, and refreshing on its own. Each is also great added to fresh or frozen strawberries, raspberries, blueberries, or cranberries for delicious wood/fruit teas. Try your own variation at home, and try some of the pleasant offerings at your next local powwow or Native American festival.

# Sun Teas

*A subtle variation on the above teas is sun tea. Simply place 1 cup of a dried tea ingredient in a large clear glass quart jar and fill it with fresh cool water. Cover tightly and place in the sun for 2 to 4 hours.*

# Sun Vinegars

*Substitute your favorite apple cider or rice vinegar for the water in the above recipe. Seal in a clear glass bottle or jar and let it stand in the sun for 4 hours or half a day. There is no need to strain off the vinegar if it is used within the next few weeks.*

# JULY

*Hot July nights are filled with cricket choruses, rasping swells from the gardens and meadows. Coyotes offer their own chorus of yipping and howling over by the heron pond. Then brief quiet, and a screech owl calls. Just before dawn, carbirds claim the cherry trees, and with the sunrise they commence to imitate all the other songbirds in order to dominate the breakfast feasts. Cardinals and bluebirds call their first broods off the nests, and fledglings give voice to their own concerns.*

*In the Pacific Northwest Coast region this is The Porpoise Moon of the Tlingit. Across the southern regions this is the Corn In Tassel Moon of the Cherokee and the Little Ripening Moon of the Creek. Moving up through the Great Plains and across the prairies, this is the Corn-Popping Moon of the Winnebago, the Buffalo Bellows Moon of the Omaha, the Deer Shed Their Antlers Moon of the Kiowa, and the Moon Of Ripe Cherries for the Mandan and Sioux Peoples. This is the Moon When Women Hill The Corn for the Narragansett, the Ripening Berries and Maize Moon of the Penobscot, the Birds Shed Their Feathers Moon of the Micmac, and the Ripening Moon of the early Agawam Peoples in the Northeast.*

*Observations about the natural world once governed vital activities, and this continues to be the case in many areas. The moon, Earth's natural satellite, influences the fluctuation of tides as well as our moods and the fluid changes within our bodies, and planting by the moon phases has long proved successful.*

Since late June, folks have been traveling north to Odanak in Quebec, Canada, to celebrate July 1, Canada's Independence Day, and to prepare for their own special annual gathering. Odanak (St. Francis) and Wolinak (Becancour) are the two primary Western Abenaki Reserves in the original Abenaki homelands surrounding the greater Lake Champlain region. Here family band-based traditions continue to embrace resurgent nationalism, and, along with French and English, their language survives. Abenaki arts are enjoying a renaissance—the fine ash-splint and sweet-grass baskets, beadwork, graphic arts, music, and storytelling share many facets of Native imaginations.

Traditional ceremonies, powwows, drumming, singing, and dancing draw many Abenaki people and their families back to this gathering each year for political and social discussions, storytelling, music, and favorite foods.

270

## BATTER-DIPPED SQUASH BLOSSOMS

*Dale Carson, in researching her Abenaki heritage, wrote a book entitled* Native New England Cooking. *She loves developing tasty recipes like this one. Freshly picked male blossoms on long thin stalks, which greatly outnumber the fruit-producing female blossoms on squash and pumpkin, (Cucurbita spp), plants, are the best choice for this delicacy. Be careful to check for bees and other pollinating insects inside each blossom.*

**1/2 cup all-purpose flour**

**1/2 cup fine cornmeal**

**1 teaspoon cornstarch**

1 teaspoon baking powder

1 egg white, well beaten

1/4 teaspoon each of salt, pepper, allspice, parsley, sugar

1/4 cup ice water, or more, as needed

sunflower seed or corn oil

24 to 36 male squash blossoms

Pick the male blossoms in late afternoon after most pollination has occurred.

In a broad, medium bowl, mix together batter ingredients with just enough ice water to yield a fine pancake batter consistency (start with about 1/4 cup and add more as necessary).

Pour corn or sunflower seed oil in a medium cast-iron skillet to the depth of 1 inch. Heat to about 375° for fast, hot frying.

Dip each squash blossom briefly in the batter and ease each one into the hot oil, without crowding. Fry until golden (about 2 minutes) then turn, if necessary, for another minute. Remove to drain on absorbent paper towels Serve hot as snacks or appetizers or as accompaniments to other vegetables and main courses.

Daylily buds and blossoms can also be used in this recipe, as can dandelions, elderberry clusters, and pink clover blossoms.

**Serves 4 to 6**

Mashpee, on the southeast coast of Cape Cod, is about 10 miles east of Falmouth and barely 70 miles south of Boston. Home to more than 1,000 Wampanoag descendants of Massasoit and his son Metacomet (also known as King Philip), this growing, scenic town is also home to more than 10,000 year-round residents and another 20,000 during the summer. It seems as if they all come to Mashpee Powwow.

Originally these annual summer powwows gathered tribes together around their chiefs and religious leaders for days of special festive, healing, and trading rites. These rites were enriched by coastal harvests, so feasting was, and continues to be, a savory virtue of the summer powwow. Archaeological evidence suggests that Wampanoag Indian ancestors have inhabited the region of southern New England for more than 12,000 years, evolving countless hunting, fishing, and food gathering strategies. Managing abundant wild resources, they evidently moved to horticulture and early pottery more than 3,000 years ago. It was the Wampanoags who shared their thanksgiving harvests with the Pilgrims in the 1620s, after giving them native Indian corn, beans, squashes, venison, and other seasonal wild harvests, thereby ensuring the survival of this new colony. From boiled lobsters, steamed clams, raw oysters, smoked mussels, and herring to diverse wild mushrooms, fish, and game, Wampanoag food traditions continue to enrich North American diets.

Today the Mashpee Powwow celebration embraces the Fourth of July weekend, drawing together hundreds of tribal peoples from all over the Northeast and beyond. Many thousands of Cape Codders and vacationers come for the colorful dances, drumming and singing, handcrafts and demonstrations, arts, storytelling, jewelry, and legendary Wampanoag foods!

The summer menu of coastal Wampanoag foods includes shellfish, bluefish, Three Sisters Rice with tasty sausages, quahog fritters, baked stuffed quahogs, quahog breads and cakes, codfish

272

with cornmeal dumplings, and fine medleys of coastal and woodland teas—blackbirch, sassafras, sweet fern, spicebush, sumac, and delicious blends like Strawberry Moon Tea.

A great old-fashioned Cape Cod Clam Bake concludes the major events on Sunday afternoon. Thousands of visitors savor the fabulous fragrances of these classic earth-baked foods as they perfume the crowds around the huge Dance Circle.

Many friends and visitors also allow time to visit the Old Indian Burial Ground nearby and the Indian Meeting House built in 1684, where the Mashpee Tribe continues to worship and meet for civic and social gatherings. The Mashpee Wampanoag Indian Museum on Route 130 elaborates Wampanoag history in a quaint nineteenth-century building.

## *Fireball and The Fireball Maker*

*Like a comet in the night, the burning fireball flies across the dark field as the men chase it, slapping and kicking it as it crisscrosses the broad field. One of the vital cornerstones of the Mashpee Powwow, Fireball is a traditional "medicine game," played for hundreds of years—but only once a year—on this particular night. Like a primal type of soccer—but freer and more dangerous—Fireball is played with a flaming ball wound of leather strips soaked for days in whale oil. According to Martin "Bruzzy" Hendricks, the current Fireball Maker, this ancient medicine game was played by men who had chosen to give their participation, strength, and consideration for a sick relative or friend in need of healing. The bruises, burns, and wounds suffered during this strenuous game were believed to take away or minimize a loved one's illness. Today many still believe there is great healing in and about this highly charged display of manhood and bravado. Standing in the masses who crowd together at Memorial Park to watch this haunting spectacle, I am convinced of its mystical powers.*

# Strawberry Moon Tea

*This is one of the "signature" beverages at Northeast gatherings. At Mashpee Powwow thousands of glasses of this chilled ambrosia are consumed each day and evening of this major weekend. Joan Avant Tavares, "Ohwamasqua," is noted for her delicious traditional Wampanoag cookery as she travels along the Powwow Highway throughout the Northeast. She serves this recipe at many festivals and educational gatherings. The evergreen strawberry and fragrant sassafras are natural companions.*

**1 pint strawberry juice or about 1 1/2 pints of strawberries,
crushed and covered with water
1 cup chilled sassafras tea (see page 267)
1/2 cup fresh or frozen chopped or sliced strawberries**

Mix all ingredients together in a large pitcher or bowl. Chill or serve over ice.

These ingredients, and this tea, have long been associated with healing and wellness. This tea is great cold or hot. Delicious variations on this tea can be made with regional, seasonal fruits linked with lightly brewed sassafras tea for robust taste and flavoring. Try Black or Red Raspberry Moon Tea, Salmonberry Moon Tea, Blackberry Sass, Huckleberry Sass, or Possum Apple Sass, a wild Southern variety made with frost-kissed persimmons and sassafras bark during the full moon.

**Makes about 1 quart**

# Quahog Fritters Mashpee-style

*Quahog,* Mercenaria mercenaria, *and Ocean quahog,* Arctica islandica, *are two of the primary clams that enrich our history and our cuisines. From the rich clamming banks around Mashpee on Cape Cod, many other fine shellfish are also harvested, yet the quahog is preferred for this and many other traditional recipes. Joan Avant Tavares shares this classic recipe of hers—a favorite at Mashpee and other Eastern powwows and socials. Joan is director of Indian Education in the Mashpee schools, author of* Wampanoag Cooking, *and a popular chef for Native gatherings.*

**3 cups all-purpose flour, sifted**

**2 1/2 teaspoons baking powder**

**dash of salt and pepper to taste**

**2 eggs, well beaten**

**2 cups quahogs, ground or chopped fine**

**about 1 cup quahog juice**

Combine all ingredients except quahog juice in a large mixing bowl. Mix well and add enough quahog juice to make the batter heavy enough to hold the other ingredients together. Batter should be a little thicker than pancake batter.

Drop by generous tablespoonfuls into deep fat preheated to 350°. Turn them over while briefly frying. Cook evenly for about 3 to 5 minutes. Remove with tongs or slotted spoon to drain on absorbent paper towels. Serve immediately.

These are so great and tasty alone that they need no sauce. Delicious variations can be made by adding sweet corn kernels, red clover blossoms, diced peppers, or a half cup of fresh salsa or herbs. Great as snacks, appetizers, or as the main dish, one of these is never enough!

**Makes about 30 fritters**

# APACHE GIRLS PUBERTY SUNRISE CEREMONY

As socials, Johnnycake festivals, homecomings, and powwows are peppered across July calendars in the East, many Apache families and friends head west to Arizona for the annual four-day Sunrise Ceremony celebrating Apache girls' womanhood. One of the oldest, most sacred of Apache ceremonials, the Nai'es, "getting her ready," ceremony is an "affirmation of power in the Apache universe," When a young woman reaches puberty, the entire community "dances her into adulthood." Not every Apache girl wants or has this ceremony, but those who choose it believe it is a powerful, life-affirming, transfiguring gift.

*Ndee,* the People, whom we call Apache, believe that their earliest ancestors emerged from the underworld by climbing up a cane stalk behind the Red Ants, the First People. Life-Giver created the Universe into which Changing Woman and her sons, Child Born of Water and Killer of Enemies, prepared everything for the *Ndee.* The mythic powers of Changing Woman are transferred to the Apache girl during her puberty ceremony, and she briefly becomes Changing Woman, or White Painted Woman. During this precious time she has the power to heal those blessing her. A beautiful piece of abalone shell tied above her forehead represents the shell in which Changing Woman survived a great flood to become the First Apache. Long song cycles of the Creation Story are sung for the girls' puberty ceremony. Each girl is blessed with sacred cattail pollen during the Sunrise Dance and painted with earth on the final morning to give her earth power. She and her symbolic accoutrements absorb ceremonial power.

The Apache *Gaan* Dancers, or Crown Dancers, are impersonators of the Mountain Spirits, who come to the girls' puberty ceremonies to dance with the girl. At night the bonfires cast their startling shadows beyond the gathering circles. Fantastic headdresses representing the Gaan spirits tower above their black-hooded faces and ghostly bodies painted and adorned with harness bells. The Gaan come from their home on sacred Mount Graham, source of medicinal herbs and healing as well as the marker of the southern horizon of San Carlos Apache territory.

Traditional foods for Apache ceremonies like this one would have included wild onions, the shoots, stems, and blossoms of yucca, the roots, shoots, and pollen of tule, countless wild greens, the pads, blossoms, and fruits of prickly pears, saguaro fruits, strawberries, chokecherries, sumac and juniper berries, wild potatoes, groundnuts, pine nuts, acorns, sunflower seeds, and numerous native grass seeds, wild herbs honey, and much more. To varying degrees, these foods are still present in Apache cuisine, but large gatherings and festivals tend to serve more contemporary Native American fast foods for convenience. Modern tastes are reflected in seasonal foods as well in this region noted for fine game hunting and fishing. Wild turkey, bear, and elk are hunted with permits in season, though the fish and bear are taboo for the Apache.

Notwithstanding the use of convenient, modern recipes, some traditions remain. Like early Mayas and Aztecs, Apaches have long used the fresh leaves of the amaranthus, *Amaranthus retroflexus*, or pigweed, *Amaranthus graecizans* so ruggedly widespread throughout the arid West. These plants are well known for their tiny, mineral- and fiber-rich blossom clusters and seeds. Delicious raw, roasted, or steamed, they are used in many Apache foods. It is impressive to note that amaranth is being grown more extensively as an agricultural crop and comes to market today in various cereals, breads, crackers, and pastas.

# BEEBALM PIÑON PASTRY BARS

*Beebalms,* Monardas fistulosa, pectinata, punctata, didyma, *and* citriodora, *have long been used by Apache and other tribes throughout the range of these rugged, perennial native mints. Also known as wild bergamots, beebalms can vary greatly in taste depending upon the variety, locations, and times of year the various plant parts are harvested. All parts of the beebalms are useful, but the recipe below requires just the leaves. In addition to beebalm, this sweet treat celebrates a variety of other summer resources.*

## PASTRY

**1/2 cup sweet butter**

**1/4 cup honey**

**3 tablespoons sunflower seed or hazelnut oil**

**1 egg, slightly beaten**

**1/2 teaspoon vanilla**

**1/4 teaspoon baking powder**

**1 cup all-purpose flour**

**1 cup fine cornmeal, lightly roasted**

**1/4 cup amaranth seeds, roasted in a dry, hot, cast-iron skillet**

**1/4 cup fresh beebalm leaves, finely chopped**

**dash of salt to taste**

Preheat oven to 350°.

In a large mixing bowl, cream together the butter, honey, and oil. Stir in the egg; blend well. Add remaining ingredients and just blend—do not overmix. Pat this dough into a 10x10-inch glass baking dish. Prick with the tines of a fork all over. Bake for 12 minutes, while you prepare the topping.

## TOPPING

**1/2 cup sweet butter**

**1 cup brown sugar**

**1 cup honey**

**3 tablespoons amaranth seeds, roasted**

**3 fresh beebalm leaves, finely chopped**

**1 cup piñons (pine nuts), shelled and lightly roasted**

**3 tablespoons apple juice or cider**

Combine all of the ingredients in a medium saucepan. Bring to a slow boil. Simmer, stirring constantly, for about 3 minutes.

Remove the pastry from the oven. Spread this topping over it evenly. Return to the oven.

Continue to bake for about 25 minutes until topping is lightly brown on top.

Remove baking dish to wire rack. When slightly cooled, cut into slim squares or bars. Serve immediately or freeze for later use.

279

**Makes about 2 dozen bars**

# Buffalo Days and the Plains Sun Dance

Buffalo Days Pow Wow and Tipi Village cover the third weekend in July with an extravaganza of colorful events and Native American dance competitions, as well as tours of a traditional tipi village in a broad, beautiful outdoor setting near the remarkable Head-Smashed-In Buffalo Jump Interpretive Center and site in Alberta, Canada. Designated a World Heritage Site by UNESCO in 1981, this is one of the oldest, largest, and best preserved buffalo jump sites in North America and predates by more than 500 years the first pyramid built in Egypt, as well as England's Stonehenge. The interpretive center chronicles the rich prehistory and history of highly sophisticated Plains Indian culture.

Buffalo Days Pow Wow is a great social event, full of singing and dancing, drumming, feasting, playing, trading and sharing, and conversation. Many people travel great distances to participate in this three-day gathering and enjoy the range of Indian foods made for the event. Ranched buffalo (somewhat parallel to the "managed wild resources" of ancient nomadic hunters) and other wild game meats are central in feeding great gatherings like this.

Prohibitions against American Indian religious traditions during the past three to five hundred years, depending upon when and how various tribes were "missionized," has in the last part of the twentieth century given way to growing popular appreciation of Native spirituality. The Medicine Lodge and Sun Dance continue to be central to many Plains Indian Peoples as the major tribal ceremonies in historic times. "Such tribal ceremonies are described as Rites of Intensification because they serve the social purpose of binding the loosely organized tribal bands together," according to the Blackfoot of Southern Alberta at Head-Smashed-In Buffalo Jump.

In midsummer, when the Saskatoon berries were ripe, the bands came together for the Sun Dance, and communal hunts of bison provided necessary foods for these gatherings, especially the bulls' tongues which were necessary offerings at the ceremony. For many tribes, this was the only time of year when all people assembled at the same place. Today's spirit lodges, sweat lodges, ghost feasts, naming ceremonies, and handgames, which were usually strictly religious, reflect some of the many traditional practices.

# GRILLED RACK OF BUFFALO RIBS

*The true barbecue demands a large piece of meat—a whole rib cage or shoulder of buffalo, beef, mutton, pork, goat, or other meat from the broad range of game. Whole, halved, or quartered, it must be slow cooked over glowing coals outside. Techniques vary for this centuries-old Native American tradition, but the usual method calls for long, slow pit cooking (roasting or grilling) over a deep, oblong stone-lined pit filled with hardwood like ash, hickory, or oak, burned down to coals before the cooking really begins. Fragrant woods such as apple, grape, or mesquite or corncobs can be added in various regions, depending upon ceremonies and plans. Today, barbecue traditions can be adapted to charcoal grills or home ovens, yet the time-honored pit roast is for great outdoor feasts to feed summer homecoming friends and crowds. To obtain the buffalo rib rack, contact the National Buffalo Association, P.O. Box 580, Fort Pierre, SD 57532 (604–223–2829). They will tell you who your nearest supplier is.*

*Prepare the cooking pit, as described on page 209, based upon the size of the meat to cook, and start the fire about an hour or two before cooking time begins.*

**20 pounds buffalo ribs (a trimmed rack)**

**salt and pepper to taste**

**3 cups barbecue sauce (see page 161)**

**2 cups Barbecue Mist, (see page 282) to spray on during grilling**

Arrange and light the barbecue pit coals and let them get hot while you prepare the meat. Rub the ribs with salt and pepper to taste and brush generously with the barbecue sauce. Let the ribs sit for at least 30 minutes. Place rack of buffalo ribs on the grill about 12 to 20 inches above the coals, depending upon pit and wind situations. Long, slow grilling for an hour to 1 1/2 hours (depending upon your taste) is best. Baste with additional barbecue sauce and/or mist with Barbecue Mist (below). Turn frequently for even cooking. Add damp alder or hickory bark over the coals if you wish to add their flavoring.

**Serves 20 to 30**

# BARBECUE MIST

*This is my pure "lite" invention after many years of watching and tasting pit-fired grilled meats, chicken, game birds, fish, and shellfish prepared at festivals all over North America. Some of the tastiest barbecues I shared were sprayed with melted butter, but this simple counterpart is a lower-calorie, lower-cholesterol alternative. It is best made a day or more ahead and refrigerated. It has good keeping qualities, but it's so tasty that it won't last long.*

**1 cup apple cider vinegar**

**3 whole garlic cloves, roasted**

**1 small whole Chipotle chili pepper**

**1/2 cup sunflower seed or olive oil**

**3 tablespoons peanut oil**

**1 tablespoon honey**

Place ingredients in order in a large, preferably glass, spray bottle sufficient in size to hold them (1-pint and 1-quart glass and plastic spray bottles can be found at hardware, gourmet, and five-and-dime stores). Shake vigorously, briefly before each use. This keeps for several days at room temperature, but it is best to refrigerate it. Mist the grilling meat each time it is turned or to your taste.
**Makes about 2 cups**

# Herbal Seasoning

*Many folks need to curtail or limit their intake of salt, a situation that may seem like a loss, since salt is a primary flavor enhancer and preservative. Here is a tasty salt-substitute seasoning mix based closely on the American Heart Association recommendations. I make this in small amounts and use it right up, as the flavors break down quickly. This works well in place of conventional salt and pepper in all recipes. Use a small nut or spice grinder (electric or manual) to create this to suit your taste. Place the mixture in a glass jar that can be tightly sealed for best results.*

**basil**

**garlic**

**onion**

**black pepper**

**allspice**

**marjoram**

**parsley**

**sage**

**savory**

**sea dulse**

**thyme**

**lemon zest or rind**

**lemon balm or verbena leaves**

Grind to a fine powder 1 part of each dried herb and seasoning.

This wonderful zippy seasoning can be enhanced further by adding several drops of apple cider vinegar.

# SPICY PEPPER SEASONING MIX

*This variation on conventional pepper is a fine companion to many game meats and wild foods. Like Herbal Seasoning, it is best made in small amounts, with the idea of using it right up and then making more for your next recipe. You can add or subtract your own favorite ingredients to this basic recipe. Store in a glass jar, tightly sealed, for best results. These ingredients perk up the tastes of most vegetables, pastas, meats, fish, and mushrooms. Consult the Source Directory for places to obtain the less common ingredients.*

smoky Chipotle chili pepper

garlic

onion

lemon zest

orange zest

red sumac berries

thyme

allspice

black pepper

cayenne pepper

sea dulse

celery seeds

cumin

Grind to a fine or coarse powder 1 part of each dried herb and seasoning.

In July, wild plums are ripening all across North America, enriching the larders and recipes of Native America. More than 400 species of shrubs and trees in the Prunus family include almonds, apricots, cherries, nectarines, peaches, and plums. In midsummer, Beach Plumbs, *Prunus maritima*, along the East Coast, Canada Plums, *Prunus nigra,* in northern thickets, and Allegheny Plums, *Prunus alleghaniensis,* in Eastern thickets are prominently producing their delicious and distinctive yellow, red, or dark purple fruits.

American or Osage plums, *Prunus americana,* Chickasaw or Sand plums, *Prunus angustifolia,* and Oklahoma or Kiowa Plums, *Prunus gracilis,* are ripening around homecoming times, along with the Wild-Goose Plum, *Prunus hortulana,* and Hog Plum, *Prunus reverchonii,* which flourish in thickets in many western regions. Captain William Clark, on the Lewis and Clark Expedition, extolled their virtues repeatedly, as on July 11, 1804, when he wrote extensively about seeing and eating many Osage plums in the region destined to become southeastern Nebraska.

Famous Indian painter George Catlin wrote enthusiastically about finding plum thickets in 1837 near what is now southern Oklahoma, near the Red River, where the plum thickets were over 6 feet high and closely interlocking for "hundreds of acres," forcing travelers to ride miles around them, as Catlin noted that "every bush that was in sight was so loaded with the weight of its delicious wild fruit, that they were in many instances literally without leaves on their branches, and bent quite to the ground." Fleshy, oval, yellowish-red or reddish-purple, depending upon species and location, each 1- to 2-inch fruit has a single, flattish oval seed. Seeds have turned up in prehistoric archaeological sites in the West, proving extensive ancient Native uses for these prodigious fruits. There were also many uses for the seeds, which were often pounded into pemmicans, soups, and fruit patties or used in crafts and games.

Some Dakota ceremonies called for the use of wild plum branches as wands, and for Lakota People the Red Plum Moon between July and August occurred during the plums' ripening times.

In April and May, early wild plum blooms signaled planting time for the Omaha, and by the time the tiny white petals had fallen like thick spring snow, the Omaha corn, beans, and squashes were planted. There is ample evidence that various Indian tribes dispersed plum seeds, spreading one of their favorite food sources as they moved about, especially during the last two hundred years of major removals and displacements.

# COMANCHE CHICKASAW PLUM BARS

*Diverse wild plums sweetened, spiced, and extended the foods of so many tribes. The Cheyenne called them "mak-u-mins," meaning greatberry, the Pawnee called them "Niwaharit," the Omaha and Ponca called them "Kande," and the Comanche called them "yuseke." Plum bushes do not always produce big crops each year, so many tribes would dry great quantities of plums, pitted or not, much as we do today. This hermit-like dessert can be made with cooked, pitted plums. These festive and delicious fruit-nut bars are served at many gatherings, and as winter desserts, they remind us of the ripe, hot days of July and August in the plum thickets.*

**2 eggs, well beaten**

**1 cup light brown sugar**

**1/2 cup buttermilk**

**1 teaspoon vanilla extract**

**2 cups all-purpose flour**

**1/4 teaspoon each of salt and allspice**

**1 cup cooked wild plums, mashed (pits removed)**

**1 cup chopped pecans or hazelnuts**

**powdered sugar to sift over baked plum bars**

Preheat oven to 325°. Grease a 13x9-inch baking dish or pan.

In a medium mixing bowl, cream well together the beaten eggs with the brown sugar, buttermilk, and vanilla. Add the flour, salt, and allspice, beating well together, then stir in the cooked plums and chopped pecans. Pour this batter into the greased baking dish; spread evenly. Bake for 35 to 40 minutes until golden.

Remove and cool on wire rack completely. Cut into about 30 bars and dust them well with fine sifted powdered sugar.

**Makes about 2 1/2 dozen bars**

The Aluets call their homelands *Alyeska,* meaning "the Great Land"—the majestic landscapes that stretch more than 580,000 square miles, embracing 3,000 rivers and more than 5,000 glaciers. Alaska is one fifth of the total area of the continental United States and encompasses arctic tundra, glacier-crested mountains, and lushly forested islands. Bordered by two oceans and three seas, this land of awesome beauty, famous dog-sled trails, ultramarathons and mountain running races, crab festivals, frostbite music festivals, sourdough rendezvous, and even the Cordova Iceworm Festival in February, is also host of the World Eskimo-Indian Olympics each July in Fairbanks, in central Alaska, just south of the Arctic Circle.

Native Peoples and their living legends, ancient arts, dances, and traditional athletic contests converge here from circumpolar regions around the Arctic Circle. Eskimo, Aleut, and Indian Peoples compete in nearly forty categories demanding strength, endurance, speed, and skill in games that include centuries-old traditional contests. The knuckle hop originated in northern lifeways' hunting acumen, imitating the seals' movements and requiring participants to balance on the knuckles of their fingers and toes and to hop as far as they can.

The toe kick's objective is to jump forward while kicking a target backward and landing on both feet. Agility and dexterity are crucial to much of Native life in the Far North. Hunting skills also gave birth to the two-foot-high kick contest in which the athlete must use both feet together to kick a suspended sealskin ball—and land in a standing position. This contest recalls the time when returning whalers would do high kicks on the beach to signal their good fortune to villagers and encamped family to come help in the harvests.

The blanket toss, *nalukatuk,* one of the most popular competitions, evolved from ancient entertainments. As many as forty native "pullers" encircle and hold on to a heavy reindeer-hide "blanket" on which each individual contestant is tossed up to 50 or 60 feet in the air and must land on both feet on the reindeer hide. Each contestant is judged for height and form.

Native dancers, drum songs, distinctive Native clothing, masks, and dance paraphernalia are also compelling aspects of the Olympic competitions, as Native judges work to choose the most authentic and artistic presentations. Many of these fabulous performances are born from pot-latches and other valuable ceremonial traditions, wherein host villages provide generous food and lodging for guests from surrounding villages, who would in turn share performances of origi-nal dances and songs to honor special occasions. Traditional dances, such as those performed at the *kivgiq*, a special messenger feast, accentuate the sharing, socializing, and trading relation-ships between villages when people gather in celebration. In many respects, the organizers of the World Eskimo-Indian Olympics help to keep many of these vital, valuable traditions alive and well appreciated, enabling Arctic Peoples to strengthen and preserve their cultures.

## Ulu — "The Woman's Knife"

*The crescent-shaped blade of the Eskimo woman's knife, with a sturdy wood or bone handle, makes quick work of skinning seal, splitting and filleting fish, and slitting birds for cooking. The ulu is an ancient tool with more than 3,000 years of traditional uses among Arctic Peoples. Through cultural traditions, the ulu was made for a young woman by her father or uncle, or perhaps her husband, as a wedding gift. Today, these treasured, useful heirlooms are passed from mother to daughter, and from father to son, and contempo-rary ones fetch a fine price depending upon the ulu maker. Ulus in art and jewelry expand our appreciation of these ancient tools.*

# BLUEBERRY ICE

*More than fifty kinds of wild berries grow in Alaska's rich riverine and glacial soils, including abundant sweet blueberries and cranberries, the* Vacciniums, *which thrive in many varied environments from Alaska to the Andes. Countless preparations (aside from the "black-bear method" of eating as many as possible, raw, right away) show the delicious versatilities of these choice fruits. This simple, favorite dessert is served at many festivals.*

**4 cups of fresh blueberries**

**3 cups water or apple juice (or 1 1/2 cups of each)**

**1 cup sugar or maple syrup**

**1 cup honey or corn syrup**

**1/4 teaspoon each of salt, allspice, vanilla**

**1/2 cup orange juice**

**1/4 cup lemon juice**

In a medium saucepan, combine the fresh berries, the apple juice or water, and the sweeteners. Crush the berries as you mix these together with a wooden spoon. Bring to a boil over medium heat. Stir and blend thoroughly, then cover and simmer for 10 minutes. Remove from the heat. Cool.

Process this mixture in a blender or food processor to a fine pulp. Blend in the seasonings and citrus juices. Pour the mixture into a freezer storage container. Cover tightly and freeze for 2 hours or overnight (but *not* too much longer—this ice is best when served shortly after preparation).

Scoop or spoon sweet Blueberry Ice into chilled glasses or onto fresh fruit. For an especially attractive presentation, shave into small balls with an ice-cream or melon-ball scoop and top with fresh lime zest and powdered sugar. This recipe also can be made with elderberries, huckleberries, and salmonberries.

**Makes 7 or 8 one-cup servings**

# Hopi Niman Kachina Dance LATE JULY

In the six months following the appearance of the Soyal Kachina and the celebration of the New Year, many kachinas come to the Hopi villages performing dances and ceremonies to bring the blessings of fertility, well-being, and rain. Whole Hopi villages have been swept up in private preparations and public dance ceremonies prerequisite to the Hopi planting needs. The last ceremony follows the summer solstice, and in July the *Niman,* or "Home Dance," celebrates the first ripening corn. In culmination everyone gathers to dance the kachinas home to their sacred San Francisco Mountains, where they will reside until time for the earth's renewal again in late December.

The Hemis Kachina appears at Niman Ceremony wearing a tall, glorious headdress, or tabletta, representing thunderclouds, rain, and the standing rainbow. He carries wooden, stylized lightning bolts in one hand, with spruce bows, and he shakes a large gourd rattle in the other hand, beckoning and simulating welcoming rains. This last dance is deeply moving with a dramatic, powerful farewell, as the masked gods leave the village with reverence and fervent prayers. Hopi rain dancers, prayers, village ceremonies, and hard work continue through the harvest times. Although the kachinas are absent, they have been charged to continue seeking nature's blessings. It is not surprising that the Hopi endure with so much dignity and strength! The kachinas infuse every aspect of Hopi life with spirituality and resilience.

# Hopi Amaranth Spinach

*For thousands of years, Natives in the Southwest have grown and eaten the annual amaranths, as have the early cultures south of them in what is now Mexico and Central America. The young leaves are rich in iron and calcium, and the tiny grains are high in lysine. Each has countless food and dye uses. Hopi Red Dye Amaranth,* Amaranthus cruentus, *can grow to 6 feet tall and produces prodigiously. Harvest young leaves to use for this spinach-like dish, but do not take more than half the leaves of a single plant. These are bright, delicious greens, fresh or steamed.*

*Seeds for this amaranth and many other valuable plants, as well as information about their backgrounds and nutritional value, are available from Native Seeds/SEARCH, 2509 North Campbell Avenue, Tucson, AZ 85719, and at the Tucson Botanical Gardens. Good folks there have been devoted to research on native botanicals for more than a decade.*

**6 cups fresh amaranth leaves or spinach (or 3 cups of each)**

**1/2 cup water or apple juice**

**1/2 cup fresh epazote leaves, finely chopped**

**1/2 cup fresh cilantro leaves, finely chopped**

**1/2 cup pine nuts, roasted and chopped**

**1 tablespoon sunflower seed oil**

**1 tablespoon apple cider vinegar**

**salt and pepper to taste**

Place the amaranth or spinach leaves and water in a medium pot. Cover and bring to a low boil over medium heat. Lower heat, shake pot to toss leaves, and steam for 6 minutes or until well wilted but only briefly cooked. Add the remaining ingredients, in order, and stir well. Remove from heat. Serve hot or chilled with additional vinegar dressing to suit your palate.

**6 servings**

# AUGUST

The searing heat of August seems to melt all ambition, and days crawl by like molasses. Yet the "Dog Days" include some of the finest Native American events of the year, particularly the green corn festivals. All are shaped and influenced by ageless traditions that continue to hold great relevance for us today.

This is the time of the Red Plum Moon for the Lakota People of the Plains, the Yellow Flowers Moon of the Osage, and the Corn Silk Moon of the Ponca. This is the Big Ripening Moon of the Creek and the Black Butterfly Moon of the Cherokee. In the West, the Maidu call this the Acorns Begin To Ripen Moon, and farther up the Northwest Coast, this is the Humpback Salmon Moon of the Tsimshian. The Northeast knows this period as the Fruit Ripening Moon of the Micmac, the Flying Bird Moon of the Montagnais, the White Chubs Moon of the Penobscot, and the Ripening Beans and Squash Moon of the Wampanoag. The Narragansett call this the Feather Shedding Moon, and the early Agawam knew this as the Eating Ripe Corn Moon.

While green corn festivals, ceremonies, homecomings, and powwows are being celebrated throughout the Americas and much delicious sweet corn is eaten with great relish, the diverse, versatile night-shades—tomatoes, peppers, eggplants, and potatoes—also appear at most events. These ancient foods have been feeding peoples of the Americas for millennia, and they continue to nourish us in evermore creative recipes.

ENDURING
HARVESTS

The staple grain and favorite cereal and bread throughout much of Indian Country has always been corn. Many farming tribes celebrated green corn both in advance of and during the first ripening of the sweet corn, when the young corn was full of milk (the milky fluid essence in underripe corn.) The annual green corn ceremonies, dances, and foods have unique meanings for every different tribe who celebrates.

Steamed corn, boiled sweet corn on the cob, sweet corn dumplings, shuckbread, corn fritters, roasting ears of corn on the wood fire or grill, and cornmilk are some of the myriad festival corn foods of green corn feasts. *Yokeag* (parched corn) is the favored dish of the Mohegan people, along with their succotash and numerous other traditional and contemporary festival foods.

The midsummer Green Corn Feast of the southeastern tribes was called the *busk,* and among the Creek Indians it was planned according to lunar phases and usually lasted four days. The Creek Indian Nation today embraces about nineteen towns in Oklahoma. Originally from the regions of Georgia and Alabama before tribal removal to the West, the Creek organize their towns near or around ceremonial grounds with the sacred fire in the center.

Purification and renewal are the central threads of Green Corn feasts and ceremonies. Honoring especially the renewal of the long partnerships between supernatural forces and humans, appropriate rituals were followed before any of the ripening crop could be eaten. Women and children traditionally cleaned the Creek dwellings, extinguishing their household fires, which had burned continuously since last year's busk. The men cleaned and prepared the ceremonial grounds, choosing four great new logs to mark the four directions in the fresh ceremonial fire in the center. When this was consecrated, each family would take live coals from this fire to relight their new year's fire at home.

Forgiveness, understanding, and harmony dominated this period, as these were considered crucial to a successful harvest. An important part of the purification rites has been the ceremonial Black Drink made from Yaupon holly. For centuries, the holly leaves were roasted and brewed and then used in important cleansing ceremonies to cement friendships and promote communications. Remains of beautifully inscribed shell cups used in ceremonies accompanying the drinking of this brew have been found at the Temple Mound Culture site of Spiro, in Oklahoma, and other sites in the Southeast such as Etowah, Georgia. Days of dancing and singing follow the purification rites, and prayers, ritual bathing, feasting, and celebrations concluded this important annual festival.

## *Pueblo Green Corn Dances*

*Corn Dances performed at most pueblos are time-honored rituals designed to ensure corn propagation and growth, the very basis and healthy underpinning of pueblo life. Opened with prayers and ceremonies in the underground kivas, usually in August when the first corn ripens on the stalks, pueblo leaders give thanks to the corn spirits and ask the rain spirits to come, assuring good harvests. As the dancers converge outdoors in the pueblo plaza, the entire village becomes a part of these honored ceremonies. The music of the drums, rattles, bells, and chants accompany the dancers' movements until after sundown, when the feasting begins.*

# Steamed Green Corn

*Soft, milky-fresh green corn, the sweet corn of midsummer, is one of our most sought-after and versatile vegetables. This recipe has universal appeal and is enjoyed at Creek, Choctaw, and Cherokee celebrations.*

**6 ears of green corn**

**1/4 teaspoon each of salt, pepper, and thyme to taste**

**enough fresh green corn shucks for wrapping the 6 ears**

**enough hot water for steaming**

In a medium, shallow bowl, grate or cut the fresh, sweet corn off the cob, scraping downward to get all the milk and pulp. Carefully mix this well with the seasonings, to taste. Spoon this into thin layers of fresh green corn shucks, making little "packets" by folding over and tying them up with fine cotton string or the peeled corn shuck "strings" from the husks themselves. Place these little green corn packets in a single layer, close together in the bottom of a broad, flat steamer or skillet. Add about 1/2 inch of hot water around this. Simmer slowly over low heat for about 30 minutes or until done to taste.

Serve with chilled cornmilk, sunflower seed butter, and other favorite August foods.

# Cornmilk, or Soffkee

*Cornmilk is very similar to posole and atole (see pages 40 and 69), but the Creek make their own distinctive soffkee, which begins as prepared, boiled corn and is then "rested" until an agreeable sourness develops after several days, making this soup/beverage tastier and more digestible.*

296

# MOHEGAN WIGWAM POWWOW AND GREEN CORN FESTIVAL

"Each year, the arrival of the first corn reconnects our people to the Great Spirit, *Gunche Mundu* . . . At this time, we renew our connection to the earth." This weekend we conduct an ancient ritual of art, history and sacred remembrance," says Ralph W. Sturges, Lifetime Chief of the Mohegan, in Uncasville, Connecticut. Corn, *Weewachermunch,* is sacred to the Mohegans and is considered food for both body and spirit. Native People converge at Fort Shantok State Park in eastern Connecticut for a busy weekend of storytelling and celebration in this annual cycle of honoring corn and Mother Earth. These Mohegan homelands reflect more than 2,000 years of settlement patterns, peppered with sacred sites and striking features that are the touchstones of Mohegan legends and Creation stories, especially those of the *Makiawisug* (the Little People) Mounds, and Moshup's Rock. *Moshup* was a formidable giant who once roamed the territorial Northeast in ancient times and was so powerful that he left his footprints in the granite ledges and outcroppings.

297

Like the Mashantucket Pequot Tribal Nation's Schemitzun (Green Corn Feast and Dance) in mid-September, the Mohegan Green Corn Festival embraces a broad array of contemporary activities, foods, and traditions and breaks new ground in sharing rich histories.

## *Yokeag—Traveling Food*

**Y**okeag *has always been one of Gladys Tantaquidgeon's favorite foods, and at the fullness of her beautiful ninety-five years she recalls: "Corn kernels were parched, then ground to a fine meal called yokeag, or ' traveling food.'*

*Hunters and travelers would carry a small sack of this, which would serve as food until they could stop to cook. Today at our annual festival, yokeag is very popular because visitors like it sprinkled on ice cream, and some eat it as cereal."*

# FRIED GREEN CORN

*This is one of my uncle Earl McLemore's favorite foods, and, with slight variations such as seasonal herbs of choice, this has long been a family favorite. Many enjoy their fresh boiled or steamed and buttered corn on the cob, but this recipe just seems easier and is, for some, more digestible.*

**8 ears of fresh green corn, shucked**

**3 tablespoons butter or corn oil**

**1/2 teaspoon each of salt, pepper, and cumin**

**1/2 cup boiling water, (or more, if needed)**

Over a broad, flat bowl, use a sharp knife to score each row of corn kernels to release their sweet cornmilk. Cut or scrape the corn kernels off with a downward motion to remove all the pulp and juice.

Heat the butter or oil in a skillet over medium heat, then add the corn kernels, stirring often to sauté evenly for about 5 minutes. Add the seasonings and boiling water, and blend well. Lower the heat slightly and cover, simmering for an additional 10 to 15 minutes or until done to your liking.

**Serves 6 to 8**

High in the Bighorns, The Shining Mountains, on an alpine plateau on Medicine Mountain rests an immense circle of stones more than 70 feet in diameter, with 28 spokes of stones radiating from its 12-foot center. Was this magnificent Medicine Wheel also a solar/lunar clock and calendar? From here you can look out across hundreds of miles of rolling hills, broad prairies, and lush valleys. Retracing the winding roads down the mountain, you head north to the Wyoming border with Montana, and follow the Bighorn River as it cuts through the "Greasy Grass" heartland of the Crow Nation in southeastern Montana.

Crow Agency, 25 miles northeast of Saint Xavier on the Little Big Horn River, is the capital of the Crow Nation. During the third week of August, this becomes the "Teepee Capital of the World." Crow families and friends pitch their teepees in a giant homecoming village for this intense week of visiting. Powwow festivities, competition dances, evening dances, a rodeo, and a road race converge at the Crow Fairgrounds to celebrate more than 90 years of traditional summer meetings. Native dancers, drummers and singers, rodeo riders, artists, jewelers, and craftspeople gather here from all across North America, providing feasts for the eyes and souls, as well as for the palates.

Favorite Crow Fair foods are the universal crowd pleasers of frybread and Indian tacos and the traditional *menudo,* which is a delicious mixture of chili and tripe. This and much more is eagerly washed down with ice cold lemonades and soda pop, or hot coffee, and chased sweetly with selections of buffaloberry pudding or blueberry pudding. In addition, wild mushrooms, especially the ephemeral white puffballs, have long been important Crow foods as well as valued medicines. Mushroom dishes still abound, yet rarely at festivals (unless behind the scenes). The following recipe is inspired by early Crow uses of puffballs in foods.

# Puffballs with Wild Rice and Hazelnuts

*August harvests bring together three compelling native foods in this recipe. Wild rice,* Zizania aquatica, *is the long, dark, ripe seeds of a unique aquatic grass found growing along many of our rivers and lakeshores. Two native species of hazelnut,* Corylus americana *and* Corylus cornuta, *grow wild on thick shrubs in open woodlands and hedgerows. And puffballs have us all surrounded. In Crow Indian cosmology, puffballs were thought to be fallen stars that landed on the prairies for the people's needs.*

**3 tablespoons hazelnut or sunflower seed oil**

**1/2 cup scallions or green onions, chopped fine**

**1 cup fresh puffballs, cut in bite-sized pieces**

**3 cups water or stock**

**1/2 teaspoon salt (optional)**

**1 cup wild rice, rinsed**

**1/4 cup fine maple syrup**

**1 cup chopped, roasted hazelnuts**

Heat the oil in a medium pan over moderate heat. Add the scallions and sauté for 2 minutes; then add the fresh cut puffball pieces, stirring well, and sauté for another 5 minutes. Set aside.

Bring water or stock to a rolling boil in a large pot over medium-high heat. Lightly salt the water and carefully sprinkle the wild rice over the boiling water; add the maple syrup, stirring well. Cover pot and reduce the heat to a simmer. Continue cooking for about 45 minutes, until almost done. Uncover and stir in the puffball mixture. Simmer for another 5 minutes, then stir well and turn out into a big serving bowl. Top with the roasted hazelnuts.

This may be served hot or cool as a side dish or salad over summer greens and herbs. **Serves 6 to 8**

## August Puffballs

*A* "puff" of smoky spores issues darkly from the tiny hole on top of an old puffball, sowing future puffballs on the wind, and we realize how strikingly different the fungi are. Indians used these ripe puffball spores to treat headaches and nosebleeds and to dust on wounds as styptics and antiseptics. Yet puffballs are among the more primal, mysterious fungi to many folks, as they seem to spring up suddenly, often after heavy dew or rain. They have long been eagerly sought by Native Peoples as fine foods and still are. From the size of pearls to golfballs to softballs to soccer balls, and much larger, and from summer through late fall, in urban lawns, across prairies, and in open woods, puffballs are emerging everywhere in August. White to creamy to tan, these puffballs are choice edibles when young and underripe.

Their interior spore mass (gleba) should be solid to powdery white, without any other markings or colorations. All puffballs, if wanted for food, should be torn or cut open to reveal their center for positive identification.

Sagebrush Giant Puffball, Calvatia booniana, *is often huge and white, warted or cracked, in semi-arid sagebrush regions in the Southwest. The Giant Puffball,* Calvatia gigantea, *is huge, white, and smooth, often found singly or in arcs or fairy rings in pastures and meadows and lawns. Skull-shaped Puffball,* Calvatia craniformis, *is also widely found, often near oaks or in open woods, much like the little Gem-studded Puffballs,* Lycoperdon perlatum, *which are usually clustered on wood or on the ground.*

# HOPI SNAKE DANCE CEREMONY AND FLUTE CEREMONY

Late August coincides the great needs for rain to feed the ripening fields with ancient, sacred rituals designed to draw down the rain. These two traditional, deeply respected events alternate years in this time-honored service. In the Southwest, neighboring Indians and great throngs of tourists draw together at Hopi to watch the culmination of the sacred Snake Dance or Flute Ceremony rituals, which never fail to bring welcomed rain. Hopi Snake Priests clamp their serpent messengers in their teeth and are shadowed by the Huggers, who soothe and distract the snakes with feathered wands. Together they dance around the village plaza, while other priests chant prayers of support. Hopi reverence for life embraces the belief that all members of the snake clans are their descendants and that sacred rites of the underworld were given to Tiyo, the Hopi Snake Youth in ancient time. The awesome Snake Dance is the climax of a sixteen-day ceremony at the end of which the snakes are cast into the plaza as symbols of watery lightning and are sprinkled with cornmeal by Hopi women before runners carry them off to the four directions, releasing the snakes unharmed to carry their "elder brothers'" pleas for sustenance to the rain gods.

The nine-day Flute Ceremony, performed every other year, begins in sacred Hopi kivas and culminates its rainmaking rituals at a sacred spring, where clans gather to strengthen these time-honored rituals, most of which are not open to the public. Fascination and respect draw returning visitors to the portion of Hopi ceremonial life that can be shared with them.

# HOPI BAKED YUCCA FRUIT

*About forty species of native yucca inhabit the warm southern regions of North America, and all plant parts were traditionally useful to Native People in constellations of imaginative ways. The Joshua Tree,* Yucca brevifolia, *the Banana Yucca,* Yucca baccata, *and the Spanish Bayonet,* Yucca alnifolia, *and* Yucca arizonica, *are a few whose ripe edible fruits were knocked off these tall plants with sticks in August. Only the ripe fruits come off easily, and the Hopi still bake these large, fleshy fruits in earth ovens. This recipe is adapted from Juanita Tiger Kavena's lovely book* Hopi Cookery. *Her instructions imitate the Hopi method of baking.*

**2 tablespoons sunflower seed oil**

**12 fully ripe yucca fruits, washed but not peeled**

**2 tablespoons honey**

**pinch of salt to taste (optional)**

Preheat oven to 300°. Oil a large, flat baking dish. Rub each yucca fruit with oil. Place the fruits side by side in the baking dish. Drizzle the honey over them. Add a pinch of salt, if desired. Bake for 2 $^1/_2$ hours until the fruits are tender. They should have the consistency of applesauce.

**Serves 4 to 6**

# PERUVIAN POTATO FEASTS

Following the Cordillero Blanco, which is the curving mountainous spine of North and South America, far south into the Andean highlands of Peru, we encounter the ancient roots of potato.

An entire constellation of varieties, colors, tastes, textures, and hardiness types of potatoes evolved through prehistoric Native American horticultural achievements. The earliest evidence in central Peru dates the potato back to about 8000 B.C. The Quechua (Inca) word *papas* is the ancestor of our word potato, and about a thousand different varieties can still be found in various Peruvian villages and Andean markets today. For countless centuries potatoes have been the "bread" of the Andes. Ancestors of the Incas developed the methods for freeze-dried potatoes, which they called *chuno,* more than two thousand years ago. This valuable process leached out bitter, possibly poisonous alkaloids and yielded sun-dried nuggets that were easily preserved for years.

Descendants of the Incas, the Quechua Indians perform a first plowing ceremony each year, as has long been done, offering flowers and fermented corn beer (chicha) to the spirit of the earth, the Pacha Mama. These ancient agricultural ceremonies were once performed with digging sticks of gold.

Energies and resources from ancient Peruvian potato feasts continue to be shared with us in countless essential ways especially in this following recipe, which is served, along with popular Andean music and performances, at many of our Native American festivals and street fairs today.

# Papas à la Huancaina

*This delicious national dish of Peru is particularly enjoyed at festival time. This especially popular version is named for the Huancayo region in Peru. Two versatile nightshades complement each other in this preparation, and another ancient pre-Columbian Andean original, the peanut, gives this dish a fine nutritional boost.*

6 red potatoes

6 eggs

1 tablespoon corn oil

3 cloves garlic, finely chopped

6 green onions, finely chopped

4 tablespoons chunky peanut butter

about 1/4 cup warm water to develop the sauce

1/4 teaspoon ground cumin

1 teaspoon lemon juice

salt and pepper to taste

1/2 cup cheddar cheese or Monterey Jack, cubed

1/2 cup cottage cheese, fine curd

3 mild red chili peppers, roasted and peeled and cut into strips

6 large lettuce leaves, washed and chilled

1/2 cup roasted peanuts, chopped (for garnish)

Boil potatoes until barely tender, keeping the skins on. Set aside (keep hot). Hard-boil the eggs and refrigerate to chill.

Heat the oil in a medium saucepan over medium heat, and sauté the garlic for 3 minutes, then add the green onions and sauté for about 3 additional minutes. Add the peanut butter and warm water, stirring well, and cook until the peanut butter melts. Add the cumin, lemon juice, and salt and pepper to taste, along with the cheddar or Monterey Jack cheese, stirring thoroughly. Lower the heat as necessary; this sauce can burn easily. When the cheese melts, add the cottage cheese and the chili peppers; balance the seasonings to your taste.

Place a fresh lettuce leaf on each of 6 plates and place a steaming potato in the center; slice in crisscross fashion the top of the potato, and gently squeeze it open. Arrange a quartered hard-boiled egg around each potato, and spoon the hot sauce generously over each potato. Sprinkle the tops with chopped peanuts. Serve and enjoy! A complete meal in itself, each of these garnished treats is often wrapped up in its crisp green blanket to be held and eaten like a steaming sandwich.

Experiment with various potato varieties and different sauce ingredients to create numerous variations on this nutritious theme.

**Serves 6**

## *A  Potato  for  Every  Purpose*

*W*hether baked, boiled, hashed, or mashed, french fried, julienned, scalloped, stuffed, or used in chowder, chips, or salads, potatoes are international treasures. Ancient Andean peoples fashioned potato pots for the potato gods; today we remain fixed on potatoes, esteemed as mineral-rich foods of distinction. But which one do we choose?

*Firm, waxy, meaty potatoes are best for chow-ders, chips, and fries, and moist, mealy potatoes make the best mashed potatoes and potato pancakes. Favorite boiled varieties of potatoes include the buttery Yukon Gold, Peruvian Blue and Purple varieties, Red Bliss and Red Pontiac, and the traditional Beltsville. Some of my baking favorites are the substantial Kennebec, Idaho, Frontier, Improved Butte, Norgold Russet, and Red Norland. Among my frying favorites are the firm Red La Soda, Jumbo Viking, and Irish Cobbler.*

# CHOCTAW POTATO PATTIES

*With special respect for the suffering of the Irish People, the Oklahoma Choctaw and their Irish friends have published a marvelous book called* Choctaw and Irish Foods, Facts, Friendships. *Compiled by Charleen Samuels in McAlester, Oklahoma, it reflects upon the historic similarities and shared experiences of the Choctaw Removal "Trail of Tears" in 1831–1832 and the Irish Potato Famine of 1845–1849. Both events were marked by many lost lives and permanent changes in living standards and ways of life. This little book is filled with bright promise and enthusiasm for enduring traditions. The following recipe is just one of the many fine dishes that celebrates many friendships.*

**2 cups mashed potatoes, slightly salted**

**1 medium egg, beaten**

**1 small onion or 2 green onions, finely chopped**

**1/3 cup self-rising flour or fine cornmeal**

**corn oil**

In a medium bowl, combine all ingredients except oil, blending well. Shape, as for croquettes, into generous patties, and sauté in medium-hot skillet in small amount of hot corn oil. Be careful not to make oil too hot. Brown patties briefly on one side, then gently turn over and brown on the other side (about 4 to 6 minutes on each side). Remove potato patties with spatula and set them on brown absorbent paper. Serve hot as a side vegetable on a nest of chopped green onions along with spring poke salad greens and "leather britches," which are dried green beans that have been rehydrated, cooked, and seasoned.

**Serves 6 to 8**

# Gallup Inter-Tribal Indian Ceremonial

Red Rock State Park in Gallup, New Mexico, welcomes thousands of folks for an intense week in the middle of August, drawing on almost three quarters of a century of celebrations of outstanding talents in Native America. The extensive ceremonial program includes fine competition powwow dancing, Indian ceremonial dances, a ceremonial parade and Indian Queen Contest, a half marathon, an All-Indian Rodeo and Rodeo Slack, indoor and outdoor marketplaces and exhibits, and an annual barbecue. All this is set against the backdrop of the Indian pueblos and reservations, numerous ancient ruins, and this unique region's scenic wonders and landmarks.

New Mexico is also famous for being the unofficial chili pepper capital of the world. The heat of the Southwestern August coaxes chili peppers and sweet peppers to ripened fullness. As you drive through the Southwest, you encounter generous wreaths and ristras of chilies beckoning from roadside stands and pickup trucks, chic central plazas, and open air markets, especially throughout New Mexico.

308

The following recipe celebrates two members of the nightshade family, peppers and tomatoes, which have been cultivated in the Americas for thousands of years. This dish is also likely to be enjoyed at the Gallup Inter-Tribal Indian Ceremonial and many other Native American events.

# Quinoa and Tomato Stuffed Peppers

*Known commonly as the Supergrain, quinoa has the "highest protein of all the world's grains." Part of the ancient harvests of the Incas, quinoa is highly valued for its seeds, which are the staple cereal food of the Andean highlands. The Quinoa Corporation (P.O. Box 1039, Torrance, CA 90505) is the conscientious distributor of this delicious high-protein (and high-altitude) supergrain, which the Incas called the Mother Grain. So popular now, quinoa can be found in most specialty and chain supermarkets. It is served like rice, with a wide versatility and appeal. This tasty modern dish is a celebration of ancient horticultural prowess in a fine festival presentation.*

6 medium green bell peppers

4 cups water or vegetable stock

1 cup quinoa, rinsed

2 tablespoons corn or sunflower seed oil

2 cups fresh mushrooms, sliced in bite-size pieces

1 medium onion, coarsely chopped

3 cloves garlic, finely chopped

3 medium ripe tomatoes, coarsely chopped

2 medium mild chili peppers, coarsely chopped

1/4 cup fresh cilantro, finely chopped

1/4 cup fresh epazote leaves, finely chopped

hot sauce (optional)

salt and pepper to taste (optional)

1/2 cup white cheese (favorite variety for topping)

Carefully remove the tops of the peppers and trim their bottoms, if necessary—without cutting into pepper cavity—so each one stands up well for stuffing. Scrape out seeds and some membrane; save for later use, if you wish. A few seeds and diced membrane added to the cooking enhance taste and pungency. Bring the water or stock to low boil in a medium pot. Lightly salt the water. Plunge the peppers into the boiling water for 2 minutes, then lift out carefully. Briefly rinse in cold water. Stand rinsed peppers in a flat baking dish. Reserve the cooking water for further use. Put 2 cups of this cooled liquid in a medium saucepan with the 1 cup of rinsed quinoa and bring to a boil. Reduce heat to simmer and cover pot, slow-cooking about 10 to 15 minutes, until most of the water is absorbed and the tiny bead-like grains appear almost translucent.

Heat the oil in a large skillet and sauté the mushrooms, onion, and garlic, stirring thoroughly, for 2 to 3 minutes. Next add the tomatoes and peppers, and a small amount of the reserved cooking liquid as needed. Simmer, stirring occasionally, for 10 minutes or longer, until vegetables are just barely softened and blended. Add the cilantro and epazote, and perhaps a dash of hot pepper sauce. Balance the seasonings to taste. Stir and simmer for another 2 minutes. Add cooked quinoa to this, blending.

Spoon this steaming mixture into the standing peppers, gently stuffing them generously. Spoon any remaining quinoa mixture into the dish around the peppers. Balance the quinoa with additional pot liquid as required. Top each stuffed pepper with a generous dusting of your favorite white cheese. Chopped hazelnuts, peanuts, or pine nuts can be added to or substituted for the cheese. Bake this creation in a preheated oven at 325° for about 30 minutes. Serve hot or cool on a plate of wild greens or lettuce leaves with additional homemade salsa.

**6 servings**

## In Praise of Peppers

*Domesticated in various regions of the Americas from different wild species, the Capsicums are grown as perennials in the tropics and as annuals in temperate zones. Cultivated into many varieties before the Spanish arrived 500 years ago, peppers have been used in Mexico since 7000 B.C.*

*Both the hybrid sweet and chili peppers, in their diverse colors, sizes, shapes, and tastes, are valuable foods, flavorings, and medicines.*

*Peppers appear in a remarkable range of color— deep shiny green, fire-engine red, banana yellow, orange, gold, lilac, deep purple, and waxy, vibrant shades in between. Their colors seem secondary, however, to their strengths in seasoning.*

Capsicum chinense *originated in tropical South America. Commonly known as the Habañero, or Scotch Bonnet, this "crushed hat-looking" chili pepper is considered to be fifty times hotter than the Jalapeño. These small, pale green, wrinkled peppers are extremely pungent and popular. The* Capsicum frutescens, *also of tropical South America, is primarily responsible for the tiny, pungent Tabasco peppers of Tabasco sauce fame. The majority of our commercial chilies and bell peppers come from* Capsicum annuum, *which originated in Mexico, and whose wild seeds in archaeological sites date to 7200 B.C. Chili peppers seem to be fiestas in and of themselves, and it is a stretch to think of a festival in Native America without a chili pepper present in one form or many.*

311

## Cookbooks

Coe, Sophie D. *America's First Cuisines. Austin,* Tex.:
University of Texas Press, 1994.

Cox, Beverly, and Martin Jacobs. *Spirit of the Harvest: North
American Indian Cooking.* New York: Stewart, Tabori & Chang, 1991.

Kavasch, E. Barrie. *Native Harvests: Recipes and Botanicals
of the American Indian.* New York: Random House, 1979.

Kavena, Juanita Tiger. *Hopi Cookery.* Tucson:
University of Arizona Press, 1992.

Keegan, Marcia. *Southwest Indian Cookbook: Pueblo and Navajo
Quotes and Recipes.* Santa Fe, N.M.: Clear Light Publishers, 1987.

Kimball, Yeffe, and Jean Anderson. *The Art of American Indian
Cooking.* New York: Doubleday, 1965.

McGee, Harold. *On Food and Cooking: The Science and Lore
of the Kitchen.* New York: Charles Scribner's Sons, 1984.

Niethammer, Carolyn. *American Indian Food and Lore.* New York:
Collier/Macmillan, 1974.

313

ENDURING
HARVESTS

Samuels, Charleen. *Choctaw and Irish Foods, Facts, Friendships*. McAlester, Okla.: Walter's Cookbooks, 1982.

Yturbide, Teresa Castello. *Presencia de la Comida Prehispanica*. Mexico City, Mexico: Banamex Fomento Cultural, R.C., 1986.

## Native American Culture

Davis, Mary B., ed. *Native America in the Twentieth Century: An Encyclopedia*. New York: Garland Publishing, 1994.

Kavasch, E. Barrie, ed. *Earthmaker's Lodge: Native American Folklore, Activities, and Foods*. Peterborough, N.H.: Cobblestone Publishing, 1994.

Weinstein, Laurie, ed. *Enduring Traditions: The Native Peoples of New England*. Westport, Conn.: Greenwood Press, 1994.

Woodhead, Henry, ed. *The American Indians* (series of books). Alexandria, Va.: Time-Life Books, 1993.

## Field Guides and Travel Guides

Campbell, Liz, ed. *Powwow 1995 Calendar: U.S.A. and Canada: Guide to North American Powwows and Gatherings.* Sumertown, Tenn.: The Book Publishing Co., 1994.

Eagle/Walking Turtle. *Indian America: A Traveler's Companion,* 3rd Edition. Santa Fe, N.M.: John Muir Publications, 1993.

Gattuso, John, ed. *Insight Guides: Native America.* Boston: Houghton Mifflin, 1993.

Kavasch, E. Barrie. *Guide to Eastern Mushrooms.* Blaine, Wash.: Big Country Books, 1982.

Kavasch, E. Barrie. *Guide to Northeastern Wild Edibles.* Blaine, Wash.: Big Country Books, 1982.

Lincoff, Gary H. *The Audubon Society Field Guide to North American Mushrooms.* New York: Knopf/Borzoi, 1981.

Tiller, Veronica E., ed. *Discover Indian Reservations: U.S.A.: A Visitor's Welcome Guide.* Denver, Colo.: Council Publications, 1992.

**Manitok Wild Rice** (Chippewa Indians)
Box 97
Callaway, MN 56521
(800) 726–1863

**The National Buffalo Association**
P.O. Box 580
Fort Pierre, SD 57532
(605) 223–2829

**Polarica—The Game Exchange**
105 Quint Street
P.O. Box 880204
San Francisco, CA 94124
(415) 657–1300
(800) GAME–USA
*Diverse fresh and dried berries, mushrooms, and game (alligator, crawfish, buffalo, caribou, antelope, elk, plus smoked and cured game, and more)*

**The Game Exchange**
73 Hudson Street
P.O. Box 1164
New York, NY 10013–1164
FAX: (415) 647–6826
*Call for extensive product list.*

**SeaBear Specialty Seafoods**
605 30th Street
P.O. Box 591
Anacortes, WA 98221

**Gatorland Zoo**
14501 South Orange Blossom Trail
Orlando, FL 32821
(407) 855–5496
*Alligator meats and products*

**Starfish Enterprises**
233 Ninth Avenue
New York, NY 10020
(212) 807–8106
*Alligator and other meats*

**The Quinoa Corporation**
P.O. Box 1039
Torrance, CA 90505
(310) 530–8666
*Quinoa grain and products*

316

**Los Chileros de Nuevo Mexico**
P.O. Box 6215
Santa Fe, NM 87502
(505) 471–6967
*Chili and sweet peppers*

**The Chili Shop, Inc.**
109 East Water St.
Santa Fe, NM 87501
(505) 983–6080
*Chili peppers*

**World Variety Produce, Inc.**
P.O. Box 21127
Los Angeles, CA 90021
*Sunchokes, jicama, and
other exotic produce*
(800) 468–7111, (800) 588–0151

**A Cook's Wares**
211 37th St.
Beaver Falls, PA 15010–2103
(412) 846–9490
*Chilies, berries, oils, vinegars,
wild mushrooms, and more*

**Native Seeds/Search**
2509 North Campbell Ave.
Tucson, AZ 85719
(520) 327–9123
*Native seeds and many other native items*

*In addition, the produce, meat, and deli
managers of local markets and major foods
stores and chains are usually very willing to
help customers locate specialty foods, and
often they will try to get them for you on
request.*

**Alaskan Harvest**
329 Katlian St.
Sitka, Alaska 99835
(800) 824–6389
*Pure, natural seafood; overnight
delivery; great selection*

317

# Acknowledgments

*T*he circle continues with much respect and love for all of the wonderful, talented people who have made this book possible. Very special gratitude to Betsy Amster, longtime friend, associate, and my first editor, who has guided me through some unique literary enterpri:es with vision, diligence, and patience. Great appreciation and regard also for Laura Strom and the entire Globe Pequot family for visionary tenacity and sensitivity to this book. Special thanks to Doe Boyle, Lisc Miceli Feliciano, and Saralyn D'Amato for their gifted guidance and thoughtfulness in handling our book project. What a great team! Much appreciation to Mitzi Rawls for her special talents and gifts.

Great respect and appreciation to Alberto Meloni and Trudie Lamb Richmond and our valuable staff, trustees, and friends of the Institute for American Indian Studies in Washington, Connecticut, for their generous encouragement and support. My gratitude also to my dear friends Margaret Cooper, in New York, and Myra Alexander and the good folks in Native Americans in the Biological Sciences Program at Oklahoma State University in Stillwater, Oklahoma. My appreciation to Monetta Trepp, Mary O'Brien, Lelani Stone, June Lee, Hattie Daniels, Rayna Green, Ruth Obenstein, Mikka Barkman Kelley, Reine Kohlmeyer, Drew Lewis, David and Lance Richmond, Gladys Tantaquidgeon, Katsi Cook, Jason and Erin Lamb and Wunneanatsu, Randy Whitehead, Ron and Cherrie Welburn, Sherman Paul and Mike Aganstata, Faith and Debbie Raney, Nancy and Wendell Deer with Horns, Dale Carson and family, Ella Thomas Sekatau, June Hamilton and family, Joan Avant Tavares, Marguerite Smith, Charleen Samuels

Enduring
Harvests

*Roddy and Josephine Smith and family, Chief Wise Owl, Henry Moneson, Barry Dana and family, Dancingfire, Acee Blue Eagle, and Juanita Tiger Kavena for all they have contributed to this work.*

*I am very grateful to my friends Jim and Peggy Duke, Shirley and Renee Siana, Pat Dowling and family, Peter Dubos, Peter Meng, and Ruth and Skitch Henderson at the Silo in New Milford; also to Adelma Simmons and Delia Griffin and all at Caprilands in Coventry, Connecticut, and to good friends at Mohonk Mountain House in New Paltz, New York, and to Carolyn Yoder and the entire Cobblestone family in Peterborough, New Hampshire, and to the Lenni Lanape Historical Society in Allentown, Pennsylvania.*

*This work has also been enriched by the vision and support of the Institute for American Indian Studies, the Elders Council of the Mashantucket Pequot Indian Nation in Ledyard, Connecticut, and the good folks in the American Indian College Fund in New York City. So many, many others have also contributed their valuable energies and inspirations to this work. My love and gratitude to my dear mother and our special family and relatives, especially my daughter Kim, son Chris, and wife Fran, and my four grandchildren. I apologize for any omissions or errors.*

319

ENDURING
HARVESTS

# A

# B

321

323

327

330

331

### About the Author

E. Barrie Kavasch is an author, ethnobotanist, and food historian of some
Cherokee, Creek, and Powhatan descent, with Scotch-Irish, English, and German heritage as
well. Her first book Native Harvests: Recipes and Botanicals of the American Indians
(1979, Random House) was hailed by the New York Times as "the most intelligent and brilliantly
researched book on the foods of the American Indians." As author and illustrator/photographer
of numerous books and articles on Native American foods, health and healing, and wild mushrooms,
she continues to collect research in these fields and consult for numerous organizations,
nationally and internationally. As a frequent lecturer and distinguished authority on
Native cultures, cuisines, and ethnobotany, she shares a deep reverence for
all of the people with whom she shares a common heritage.